SWORDS
AGAINST THE
SENATE

ALSO BY ERIK HILDINGER

*Warriors of the Steppe: A Military History
of Central Asia, 500 B.C. to 1700 A.D.*

SWORDS
AGAINST THE
SENATE

The Rise of the Roman Army
and the Fall of the Republic

ERIK HILDINGER

DA CAPO PRESS
A Member of the Perseus Books Group

Designed by Brent Wilcox
Set in 10 point Palatino by Perseus Publishing Services

Cataloging-in-Publication data for this book is available from the Library of Con-
gress.

First Da Capo Press edition 2002
ISBN 0–306–81168–5

Published by Da Capo Press
A Member of the Perseus Books Group
http://www.dacapopress.com

Da Capo Press books are available at special discounts for bulk purchases in the U.S.
by corporations, institutions, and other organizations. For more information, please
contact the Special Markets Department at the Perseus Books Group, 11 Cambridge
Center, Cambridge, MA 02142, or call (800) 255-1514 or (617) 252-5298, or e-mail
j.mccrary@perseusbooks.com.

1 2 3 4 5 6 7 8 9—05 04 03 02

CONTENTS

ACKNOWLEDGMENTS

The author thanks the Harvard University Press for the use of their Latin texts in the Loeb Classical Library Editions, from which he translated numerous passages into English. He also thanks the Société D'Édition "Les Belles Lettres" for permission to use their Latin text as a basis for translation of Velleius Paterculus's *Historiae Romanae Ad M. Vinicium Cos* All translations from Latin to English that appear in this book were done by the author using the cited Latin sources.

Introduction

This book treats three distinct but interrelated aspects of Roman life and tells how they worked for the dissolution of the Roman Republic in the welter of civil war during the first century B.C. It does so by showing the personalities involved, by showing in action one of their most powerful tools, the army, and by showing the gradual chipping away of the constitution that led to the swingeing conflicts and collapse of the eighties. Because of this, the book deals in rather more detail with the Roman army than might be expected, both as an organization and as a fighting force; we will see it in the camp, in the field and in the forum. The constitution, though more cursorily dealt with, will be there too, receding into the background as events and personalities overtake it. And so, a little must be said here of constitutions in general, and the Roman in particular.

The Roman Republic had a constitution—an agreed set of principles and strictures that maintained the operation of the state and that worked much as keel and ribs support a boat's hull, or a skeleton a body—something essential but not in view. It is a sort of ground, and if a state lacks it, the best it can do is totter. The Roman constitution was not a clearly stated set of principles, as in a written constitution, but it was there all the same, a set of principles derived from the traditional, immemorial customs and habits[1] that guided the citizens in enacting their laws. Because it was unwritten, this constitution was a cast of mind and properly reflected in those Roman laws and plebiscites consonant with it; these laws were a sort of shadow by which the shape of the constitution might be made out.

In the simplest terms, power was divided, very unequally, between the nobility and commons, the latter having relatively little of it. The nobility was of two kinds: the *patricii*, or patricians, families that had been noble from the days even before the kings had ruled the city, and the *nobiles*, or those from wealthy plebeian families who had been raised to nobility because an ancestor had held the high office of consul. Wealth, intermarriage and common interest made these two sorts of nobles politically indistinguishable; we might casually refer to both of them as aristocrats. Opposed to them were the commons, the poorer plebeians and the *proletarii* or *capite censi*, men so poor the censors did not assess them taxes or let them serve in the army. Provision was made to let the plebeians vote, but the manner of voting was sufficiently skewed for centuries after Rome became a republic that all but the wealthier commoners had little voice. Though in form a republic, Rome was in fact an oligarchy: The aristocracy served in the senate for life, and held the major offices of the state. The most important of these were the consulship, in which two men served each year as heads of the state, and the censorship, a five-year office in which two men decided, among other things, who should be in the senate and who should be given government contracts.

The constitution slowly changed in steps over time in response to social and political pressures, and these changes helped the constitution to keep knitted both aristocrats and commoners into a state. Though the commons gradually gained more power over the years, the aristocracy was able to keep most of it, but we should hesitate to condemn this imbalance—times were different. The aristocracy, because of their leisure, were the only citizens in a position to educate themselves to be fit for governing, and because of their wealth they were the only ones who could afford to perform public service. The commons might clamor about the unfairness of things, but the aristocrat might retort that it was not only the way of the world, but the way it must be.

Constitutional perfection is unattainable, and its lack is beside the point; the constitution performed one of its main functions when it lent certainty and stability to Roman society and protected the different classes of aristocrat and plebeian from exercises of strength against each other. Without a constitution a society breaks down into mutually antagonistic factions, each suspicious of another's interests, each doubtful of the other's power, each jealous of the other's advantages. The only protection in such a society is strength, and the individual must declare himself for a faction if he's to be protected. Anarchy is commonly followed by dictatorship, as it was in Rome. In short, a constitution—if honored—can replace government of one group over another through sheer force with a government of mutual agreement, even if the terms of the constitution are imperfect, as they are bound to be in this world.

A constitution misinterpreted or defied will first, however, lead to a different and more subtle sort of anarchy, not true anarchy because there will still be laws, but instead to a society pervaded with laws severed from any meaningful tie to the constitution, thus no longer holding any moral force. Few if any corrupt or even illegal governments lack laws, and yet we don't doubt their illegality. And such laws may be maintained, but it is done through the main strength of the most powerful, for these laws and misrepresentations will have been promoted by the strong for their own benefit. Lip service will be paid to the constitution, of course—at least by those who profit from that misrepresentation—but a misrepresented constitution is nothing more than a political weapon, and a very attractive one to any faction that discovers rights or privileges for itself. It would be more honest to openly disregard a constitution when it is inconvenient, as the Romans of the late republic did. Yet there was a price for this disregard.

Nowadays, constitutions are amended often enough, but it is dangerous to do so lightly, or informally—by whim, even. It is dangerous to do so in the face of crisis; it may be necessary then, but a good deal of care is needed for constitutional change has long-lasting and unforeseen effects. Great amendment or great disregard (which comes to the same thing) exacts a price that cannot be set before the bargain is made. Now, a little history.

In 143 B.C., after a siege of three years, Rome extirpated Carthage, her most implacable enemy. She had reduced it to a second-rate power after the Second Punic War some forty years before, but she could not leave her old enemy alone. Many years later though, it seemed that Carthage's destruction had come with a hidden and terrible price. Gaius Sallustius, a historian of the mid-first century B.C., gave the common view of his time:

> For before Carthage was destroyed the people and senate of Rome governed themselves peacefully and equably, there was a struggle neither for glory nor domination among the citizens; fear of the enemy kept the city in good conduct. But when this fear was lifted from their minds, naturally they did as they wished, and pleasure and pride appeared. . . . For the nobles began to turn away from dignity and the people from their freedom to their own inclinations. So everything was broken in two and the state, which was in the middle, was torn in pieces.[2]

The explanation is orthodox, but only hints at the trouble; it wasn't the destruction of Carthage that was the cause of the problem. At the heart of the Roman Republic was a peculiar flaw: a permanent and ineradicable tension between the aristocracy and the plebeians who regarded themselves, in many ways, as two different people. The republic was thus divided between those who contended for an oligarchy of the rich and those who sought a democracy of the commons. At the top of the social scale was a charmed circle of patricians and senators whose ancient families often went back hundreds of years to the days of the kings, men who shared out the better political offices among themselves, in particular the highest office of all, that of the consul invested with *imperium*—the power, formerly reposing in the kings who had ruled the city before the republic. Opposed to them were the *plebs*, the commons, the great mass of the people: farmers, tradesmen, merchants and the unemployed, whose envy and distrust of the nobility had simmered for centuries, kept in check more than anything else by the constant threats to the city from Etruscans, Samnites, Gauls and Carthaginians.

There were, however, three institutions that bound these peoples together: the constitution, the army and clientship, a Roman institution of mutual duties between a rich and powerful man and his hereditary personal followers. When, half by accident, the small-time country nobleman Gaius Marius coupled patronage with the army, he was able to thrust his way into the highest levels of society and place himself repeatedly in the consulship. But he set the republic on the road to civil war and dissolution, for the common people had set aside the constitution to allow his rise, and the senators, who should have known better, did not or could not prevent it.

It might be expected that the army would play a great part in this revolution. In the sixth century B.C., King Servius Tullius substituted a city militia for the aristocratic band of horsemen that had made up the Roman army. The commoners—the basis of the militia—gained a handful of political rights, and for centuries they pressed toward a limited democracy, resisted each step of the way by the nobles.

The new army did well—very well indeed. Across the centuries Rome's sway extended throughout the Italian peninsula, across southern Gaul, into Spain and, by the end of the Third Punic War, as far as North Africa.[3] The wealth of conquest made its way to Rome on the backs of the legions (and of their Italian allies)—more often to enrich the nobles than the commoners who made up the great mass of the armies. Much of the booty, however, was in slaves, and in time slave-worked estates belonging to great men began to displace the small farmers who formed the basis of the army. As the number of peasants dwindled, so did the numbers of those subject to conscription. By the second century, conquest had undermined the basis of the army.

This book tells how, through these stresses, the republic came apart; how the smoldering anger of the common people over the deaths of a pair of reformers, a petty war against a treacherous North African prince, an invasion of German tribes and an Italian political uprising led Gaius Marius to despotic power and a patrician noble, Cornelius Sulla, to march against Rome herself. This is the story of how the republic was toppled by men with private armies.

CHAPTER 1

An Unlikely Revolutionary

IN THE SPRING OF 137 B.C. A MOST UNLIKELY REVOLUTIONARY passed north through Etruria and along the Italian coast on his way to a war in Spain: Tiberius Sempronius Gracchus, twenty-six, a nobleman of one of the best families in Rome, his father a successful general and statesman, both consul and censor. In four years Tiberius would hold the office of tribune of the people, and be one of the most influential men— probably the most influential—in the city. He would be remembered as one of the greatest reformers of Roman history, but the nobility—the men of his very class—would kill him as a danger to the state. His would be the first blood shed in the forum since the founding of the Roman Republic three hundred and seventy years before.

Tiberius, though not himself a patrician, could hardly have stood higher in Roman society, for he was of the very highest plebeian aristocracy and descended of patricians. His mother was Cornelia, the daughter of the great Publius Scipio Africanus, whose defeat of Hannibal at Zama in 202 B.C. near the coast of North Africa had ended the Second Punic War. It had been the most damaging that Rome had ever fought, a war that had turned the Carthaginian leader into a figure of legend, a bogey to scare children, an enemy so daring that he had—in folk tales—thrown a spear into one of the portals of Rome when he could not take her.

Young Tiberius had some of his grandfather's luster. Fifty years after the conclusion of the Second Punic War had come the Third, and with it the destruction of Carthage. He was about twenty and was one of the first two men upon the walls at the final destruction of the city. Tiberius was almost certainly a military tribune then, and almost certainly he was too young to hold the office legally. This wasn't unknown, though, for men of illustrious families. His early command was an emblem of his privilege as a noble and a ticket into the all-important world of politics, for which military service was a prerequisite. The great Roman families were few and closely intertwined by marriage, alliance and expediency, and this last fight against Carthage, as with so many important ventures, was something of an extended family affair: The commander himself was Publius Cornelius Scipio Aemilianus, son of Aemilius Paullus, the great general of the Third Macedonian War, and, by adoption, the grandson of Scipio Africanus. He was not only Tiberius Gracchus's cousin by adoption, he was also Tiberius's brother-in-law, for he had married the young man's sister.

The Spanish wars, by contrast, were a sort of military morass that an experienced soldier would look forward to uneasily. Following Hannibal's defeat, Rome had taken the Carthaginian territory of Spain, but had spent years subduing it. The Roman army, composed chiefly of heavy infantry, wasn't well suited to the fighting: Much of it went on in mountains or defiles, and several commanders had come off badly from their experiences there, particularly at the hands of the guerrilla commander Viriathus, a Lusitanian with a particularly fine talent for trapping Roman armies in impossible positions. This skill of his had resulted, in 141, in a peace negotiated by the Roman commander Fabius Maximus Servilianus by which the Lusitanians were to be recognized as a free people. Though the treaty was ratified by the senate and the people, the Roman consul in 140, Servilius Caepio, took a dim view of the business and decided to undo Servilianus's embarrassing work. He convinced the senate to repudiate its treaty and take up the war again. Seeing that Roman perseverance, discipline and manpower hadn't put an end to Viriathus, Caepio took a decidedly underhand approach and did in his enemy "more through fraud than strength" as one Roman author delicately put it.[1] He bought three of Viriathus's friends and had him murdered in his sleep. Caepio's stratagem, however, didn't yield the results he might have wanted. Though the Lusitanians submitted in 139, the city of Numantia in north central Spain revolted. The intractable Spanish problem lingered. So now, two years later, the consul Gaius Hostilius Mancinus was in Spain, saddled with the job of subduing the Numantines, and his young quaestor Tiberius Gracchus was on his way to join him as paymaster, comptroller and supply master to the army.

Tiberius advanced along the coast on the Via Aurelia, part of the net of highways thrown over Italy to promote trade, communication—and the efficient movement of armies. Because he did not take a ship, say, from

Ostia to Massilia or New Carthage, but followed instead the land route, we may assume that he was leading some large contingent of soldiers, perhaps a thousand, perhaps fifteen hundred. As quaestor, Tiberius was likely bringing money for the troops already in Spain and his men, while acting as guards, were probably meant to replace losses in the legions engaged against Numantia. These soldiers would have been Romans or Italian allies, the latter banded into administrative units of several hundred men called cohorts. And then there would be mules, one for every *contubernium* or squad of eight men. A hundred and forty mules and as many *calones* and *lixae:* camp servants and slaves to attend the soldiers, mind the animals, and pack and drive the baggage train. There might be a squadron or two of cavalry as well, young, well-to-do men, the sons of *equites* or "knights," men assessed as wealthy enough to serve on horseback; and they brought servants and baggage too. In friendly country this column might be allowed to stretch back more than a mile.

At or near its head Tiberius and his attendants would have ridden on the beaten-earth path alongside the road proper, as horses were unshod at this time. The infantry and wheeled vehicles travelled the paved roadbed. The quaestor's appearance might not have seemed very military: He likely wore a simple tunic, though of finer stuff than those of the soldiers around him, and the round, wide flat hat of a Roman traveller.

Tiberius must have travelled slowly—slowly because the infantry covered fifteen miles a day, maybe a little more since he was not passing through hostile country. At this rate he could take a leisurely look at the country he passed, and he didn't like what he saw in Etruria day after day: There were few free peasants working the soil. Instead he passed the vast estates of great landowners who employed slave labor—hundreds, sometimes thousands of slaves to do the farming.

Now Tiberius would hardly have objected to slavery itself—it was quite a natural estate into which many were born and more fell as the result of successful Roman wars. Victories against Gauls, Carthaginians, Greeks, Macedonians and others had flooded Italy with slaves by the thousands. In Tiberius's day a very high proportion of the Italian population were slaves, and this abundant and cheap labor was leading to or accelerating social change: Impoverished men headed for Rome and other cities in hope of work and cheaper food; their land lay fallow unless the larger landholders chose to buy or seize and loose slaves onto it.

Slave revolts were a source of concern too; two years later, in 135, there would be a massive uprising of slaves in Sicily—some seventy thousand of them, many of them freemen illegally kidnapped abroad and sold into slavery. They were led by the Sicilian Cleon and a Syrian, Eunus, who styled himself "King Antiochus," doubtless after Antiochus the Great, the last of the Selucid kings of Syria, a general who had led his army to the border of India, as Alexander the Great had done. Together they defeated a Roman army led by Lucius Calpurnius Piso in 133, only to be defeated in 132 by Publius Rupilius.

But Tiberius saw something more insidious in the influx of servile labor than the mere danger of revolt: the displacement of the free peasantry who were the backbone of the Roman army. Slaves could not serve Rome, not even freedmen could do so except in emergencies. Who would fight if the great landowners were permitted to destroy what remained of the recruiting grounds?

This question preoccupied Tiberius, who, like any Roman, was a military man. Civil honors and duties came first at Rome, but the army lay always in the background if only because Rome had been at war with someone throughout most of her history. And so her army was very good—the best in the ancient world—but the slave-booty from recent conquests was a subtle plague. It must have seemed to Tiberius that Rome's very successes were cutting the ground from beneath her. He passed the large plantations for days on his progress through Italy.

Tiberius had more immediate problems when he reached Spain. His general, the consul Gaius Mancinus, was regarded later as one of the more unlucky of Rome's generals, and Julius Obsequens[2] in his list of prodigies says:

> The consul Gaius Hostilius Mancinus was in the Port of Hercules when, as he was getting on board the ship bound for Numantia, a voice was unexpectedly heard: "Stay, Mancinus." And when later he got off and boarded a later ship in Genoa, a snake was found in the ship and escaped capture. The consul himself was defeated soon and handed over to the Numantines.[3]

These prodigies, or omens, were certainly recorded after the fact, but they must reflect some half-articulated view that Mancinus's troubles weren't all of his own making. Whether this was the case, Mancinus did badly and was surrounded during an attempted night withdrawal and forced into negotiations. The Numantines, based on earlier experience with Roman commanders such as Servilius Caepio, distrusted Mancinus, but were willing to negotiate with Tiberius Gracchus out of regard for his father, who had campaigned years before in Spain. Through good treatment of the natives, the elder Gracchus had earned a favorable reputation that persisted even yet. He had managed, in fact, to make many Spanish clients and so, odd as it might seem, Mancinus's young quaestor alone had the prestige to negotiate a pact. Terms were agreed for the withdrawal of the army, Tiberius gave his promise that they would be honored, and the army was allowed to pull out. The situation was extremely humiliating, of course: There were something less than ten thousand Numantines under arms whereas a consular army was commonly of two legions and an equal number of auxiliaries, about twenty thousand soldiers in all, with a goodly number of *calones* and *lixae* who guarded the camp and could, in a pinch, fight as well. Tiberius's negotiations had saved them.

Did Tiberius feel uneasy about the business? The year before the Numantines had gotten the better of the consul Quintus Pompeius and besieged him in his camp. He had gotten good terms from them and had even extracted some tribute, which he kept for himself. As for the senate, it repudiated the treaty as it had done that negotiated by Servilianus with Viriathus in 140. Tiberius must have worried that the same thing might happen again, which would be very damaging to him and to the Spanish clients he had inherited from his father. In other words, politics at Rome was perverse enough that saving an army might cost him something. It is probably in this light that we should understand his concern during the retreat that his account books were missing; the Numantines had taken them while plundering the Roman camp.

Lost ledgers might seem a small thing when an entire army is at stake, but Tiberius's concern over them and the risk he took to recover them show this wasn't the case. These accounts would have contained every transaction of significance to the army: pay for the soldiers, money spent on provisions, purchases of draft animals, perhaps even bribes to spies and locals. These ledgers would literally have accounted for thousands of transactions and huge sums. Tiberius decided, after travelling several days with the defeated army, that he had to return to Numantia for them "lest his enemies should have it in their power to reproach him with not being able to give an account of the moneys entrusted to him."[4] And so he and a handful of companions rode back to the enemy, who treated him well. Plutarch reports that:

> The Numantines joyfully embraced this opportunity of obliging him, and invited him into the city; as he stood hesitating, they came up and took him by the hands, and begged that he would no longer look upon

them as enemies, but believe them to be his friends and treat them as such. Tiberius thought it well to consent, desirous as he was to have his books returned, and was afraid lest he should disoblige them by showing any distrust. As soon as he entered into the city, they first offered him food, and made every kind of entreaty that he would sit down and eat something in their company. Afterwards they returned his books, and gave him the liberty to take whatever he wished for in the remaining spoils. He, on the other hand, would accept of nothing but some frankincense, which he used in his public sacrifices, and bidding them farewell with every expression of kindness, departed.[5]

Tiberius had been wise to get his ledgers back, for though when he returned he found that the common people—relatives of the soldiers who had benefited from his actions—held him in some esteem, the aristocracy didn't share the commoners' views. The senate deplored the treaty, the retreat and the negotiations that had led to them, and it repudiated this treaty as it had those of Servilianus and Pompeius. This consistent treaty-breaking—or refusal to ratify—must have seemed expedient to the senators. After all, though Spain was a nagging problem, they could hardly doubt that Rome would ultimately dominate the peninsula in its entirety, but to accomplish this would require more dogged effort on the part of the army, and service had grown less and less popular. Resistance to service in the Spanish wars had reached a head twice: in 158 and in 138 when the commons appealed to their tribunes for protection against the levy. On both occasions the tribunes imprisoned the consuls. Such ugly scenes might be avoided through the abrogation of the Numantine treaty and a humiliating punishment for those involved in the debacle. Such actions might be of no real military benefit, but they could be politically useful by providing a sop to the pride of the Roman mob. It was easy enough to dishonor the treaty: As a purely legal matter only the senate could decide a peace, and so Tiberius's Numantine pact was not binding without its ratification.

Leaving the ultimate decision in the hands of the senate was a wise policy from one standpoint: Rome could hardly have her senators and generals autocratically conducting freelance diplomacy. On the other hand, the common ratification of tentative agreements strengthened the hands of generals (themselves invariably senators), who were often obliged to hammer out treaties to end hostilities in far-off places. Whenever the senate failed to ratify such a pact—except perhaps in cases where the terms were grossly improper—it undermined its officers' authority. It was, in fact, the senate's repudiation of the terms of the treaty he had made that had almost forced his successor Mancinus to fight from a hopeless trap. Only the Numantines' trust in Tiberius Gracchus as a private citizen had allowed the retreat; that he was a quaestor was unimportant to them—they trusted his honor and not his office, nor that of the consul who represented the senate.

Rome was a city of laws—the result of centuries of struggle between patricians and plebeians. The state was known as the "republic," the *res publica*—the common property—and though power never had been divided fairly, it was divided among people of various stations in accordance with law, and the rights of the people were exercised in strict accordance with legal procedure. The certainty this established was as important to the stability of the state as the notion of fairness, perhaps more so. Despots rule by whim, by decrees backed with force; republics, even oligarchical ones like Rome, need laws, and so the law was—and it had to be—held in esteem. The law was the glue that held together the different levels of Roman society: the aristocrats, the knights and the plebeians, even the poorest of them, the *capite censi*—men so poor that the censors took only a head count of them for they hadn't enough wealth to record.

The *capite censi* were legally barred from serving in the army. This would change, however, through the actions of a younger contemporary of Tiberius Gracchus: Gaius Marius. He was a country noble who would serve in Spain as a cavalry commander under Tiberius's brother-in-law Scipio Aemilianus, when in 133 he destroyed Numantia as methodically as he had Carthage.

But if the substance of the law was the glue that held the Roman state together, its forms were often the grease that allowed a certain slippage—legalistic rather than fair decisions, decisions that favored one party over another as in the matter of the Numantine treaty. A repudiation of it, the senate thought, would maintain the dignity of Rome. And Roman dignity was of course theirs and not, perhaps, a dignity of much interest to the commons, so many of whom would have to serve in the unpopular Spanish war.

But from the senatorial standpoint, here was an expedient way to use the law: Abrogate the treaty to save the nobility's face, and then try Mancinus and Tiberius Gracchus for negotiating the treaty. Their convictions should satisfy current anti-senatorial feeling among the commons who were tired of military service in Spain under doubtful aristocratic commanders; after all, the proposed victims were both aristocrats themselves: Mancinus a senator and consul, and Tiberius, like any prominent noble, on the way to becoming one as a matter of course.

Mancinus was tried and convicted by a jury of his peers (quite literally), for senators alone made up the courts in those days. This judicial monopoly went back centuries to the start of the republic and probably before, back to the days when senators were counsellors to the kings of Rome. It was a very useful arrangement in this case. Reviving an old military custom, the senate sent Mancinus back to Spain and delivered him, naked and with his hands tied behind his back, to the Numantines. They saw through the gesture; Velleius Paterculus, writing a hundred and sixty years after Tiberius Gracchus's death, writes, "They refused to accept him, just as the Caudini had once done, saying that an open violation of faith could not be cleared away with the blood of a single man."[6] The people rioted over Mancinus's treatment; apparently the senate had misjudged their temper. The commons preferred the rescue of the army to the senate's view of Roman dignity. The popular assembly took the measures necessary to restore Mancinus to his position in the city. The people's actions on behalf of the disgraced consul may have protected Tiberius against prosecution because the senate did not try the young quaestor. Instead, he was forced to abjure the treaty himself, under threat of the same prosecution. Perhaps his account books served him in good stead as well; aside from the support of the commons he seems to have had little support among the aristocracy.

The effect of all this on his later policies as tribune of the people cannot be known, but he surely came to the realization that, if he were to help the commons (and thereby the state), he would have to rely on their support above any other. This was the background against which Tiberius Gracchus was elected a tribune of the people in 133, and against which he began a series of radical social reforms including the distribution of land to the poor.

Though his policies were perhaps better understood by, and less distasteful to, the upper classes than might seem to have been the case, his naked reliance on the commons and his use of unconstitutional methods to push through his legislation were not provocations they could forgive. Velleius Paterculus states the aristocratic opinion:

> . . . he was elected tribune of the people during the consulships of Publius Mucius Scaevola and Lucius Calpurnius . . . a man who before had led the most blameless life, bursting with brilliance, obviously pure, so much showered with virtues, possessing the most perfect talents which nature and human talent can confer, he turned away from the good

people and promised citizenship to all of Italy and at the same time promulgated agrarian laws and to those who desired stability, he turned everything topsy-turvy and dragged the republic into extreme and twofold danger.[7]

The aristocracy saw him as one of their own who had thrown in his lot with Rome's lowest elements, and who had flouted centuries of settled law to help them. But why was this possible, and why was it so terrible to the Romans? Because Rome was not really a single city, and to understand the story of Tiberius Gracchus we must recognize this.

*   *   *

Rome had always been a two-headed city, a single city in which two distinct people lived: the *patricii*[8] and the *plebs*, the hereditary nobility and the masses, people not only distinct economically, but distinct by custom, social institutions and attitudes toward each other. This town of two populations had begun on the hilltops over the Tiber River, establishing herself as a largish settlement by the eighth century B.C. The largest social groupings were the clans who met in meetings called *curiae* to hammer out solutions, probably to such things as adoptions, inheritances, land disputes—things of concern to simple and simply organized people. The early Romans had kings, though they were not hereditary; instead they were chosen by the senate and people.

As time passed Rome fell under the influence of her more sophisticated neighbors, the Etruscans. These people were of uncertain origin; what is left of their lost language on monuments shows that it is not European. The Romans themselves accepted the Etruscan view that they had come from somewhere in the east of the Mediterranean and this may be so; perhaps they were Anatolian immigrants of some sort. These people, widely spread throughout the middle and north of the Italian peninsula, have left their name behind in the word "Tuscany," and they adopted a good deal of culture from the Greek cities in the south of the Italian peninsula, towns like Neapolis and Tarentum. Their sculpture and architecture reveal Greek influence and they adopted Greek military ideas as well.

The Etruscans, much like the Greeks, did not establish a single, large state, but remained a people of many cities, such as Vulcii, Vei, Tarquinii and Clusium, formed in loose leagues. They had a number of their own peculiar practices though, such as augury—predicting the future from the flight of birds or the entrails of sacrificed animals—and gladiatorial-ism. The latter began as combat to the death between a pair of slaves at the funeral of a great man. The Romans took up augury, and later gladi-atorialism too, which became a grotesque entertainment without even the thin support that it was a religious, if macabre, event.

Under the influence of their more cultured neighbors Rome adopted or was made to accept for the most part Etruscan kings and she was firmly under the sway of these powerful neighbors for about two hundred years. At this time the Roman people, who had been organized into their various clans, were broken into three official tribes bearing the Etruscan names of Tities, Ramnes and Luceres. The degree of Etruscan influence was signifi-cant: Rome took her name from an Etruscan family, the Ruma.

The army was important during the regal period, as it was in all city-states. It was led by the king, who was followed by his nobles and his per-sonal retinue of horsemen, called *celeres,* or "swift men." There was other-wise a loose general levy of the plebeians who fought as well as they might in support of the horsemen. In this regard the early Roman army was much like later medieval European armies: knights and undisci-plined footsoldiers. Some think the patricians began as the mounted guard of the king, because of the preeminence of horsemen in this archaic warfare.[9] Other historians disagree, but patricians must have fought on horseback like the king and the *celeres:* The patricians dressed in a horsey way that distinguished them from the plebs. They wore a gold ring, a pur-ple stripe on the tunic, a riding cloak and high shoes tied with straps, rem-iniscent of the boots that the early cavalry must have worn,[10] and certainly the *celeres* must have developed into the later *equites,* or "knights." For that matter, the costume of the knights during the republic resembled that of the patricians: Their rings were silver and the purple stripe narrower, but this, along with their very title, bespoke their origins in the cavalry.

The most important of the civil institutions began under the kings: the senate. Its name implies that it was a council of elders, and the first sena-tors were known as *patres,* or fathers.[11] As *patres* they must have been the heads of the patrician clans. The senate advised the king and, when he died, chose an *interrex* who conducted the election of the new king. In this sense power rested ultimately with the senate: Its vote legitimated the king and his power, or *imperium,* reverted to it after his death. It did not have any legislative power, nor did it ever acquire any—the senate's authority, whether in the regal or republican period, was purely moral.

Where did these *patres*—in short, the patricians—come from? The his-torian Géza Alfödy suggests they were the noble companions of the king, in distinction to his personal retinue of *celeres*. A more common view is that they predated the kings and were landowners who had gradually come to dominate their poorer neighbors, the plebeians. They had been able to maintain estates of some size while the plebeians slipped into poverty, perhaps through subdividing their land successively as inheritances for their sons. With straightened circumstances came a division in power and social standing between the two groups. This may have been one of the reasons for the patricians' cavalry clothes: They were a visible signal that here was a man who could afford to equip and ride a horse to war—a very expensive proposition—a man valued by the king and hence socially powerful. Others argue that the patricians were the original and earliest Romans who afterward absorbed into their community other people who had filtered in. The patricians kept these newcomers subservient by denying them any rights.[12] If this view is true, then there may be an echo of this in Livy's account of Rome's mythical first king, Romulus, who took in wanderers and criminals to populate his new city and pretended that they were merely locals. However this division arose between patrician and the plebeian, it remained and was a constant source of friction throughout the history of the Roman Republic.

But there was something to ameliorate the expected discord in a society divided sharply not only economically, but socially: clientship. This institution was perhaps not purely Roman. Apparently the Sabines and Samnites had something much like it, and the Etruscans may have had only two social orders, nobles and slaves. The Roman institution may owe something to its Etruscan counterpart particularly if, as seems to have been the case during the regal period, every plebeian was a client.

A client was a man who owed duties to his patron and whose patron owed him protection and support. For example, neither clients nor patrons were allowed by law to testify against each other in court. This reciprocal arrangement did not mean that the client was a slave, nor that, like a medieval peasant, he was essentially unfree, say, bound to a piece of land or the estate of a great man. He was bound, however, to do his patron favors and to support him politically. Some references to clients suggest that in the days of the kings they were even obliged to help patrons with gifts of money and pay the dowries of their patrons' daughters if this were needed. This certainly implies that not all clients were poor, though that must have been true of many of them.

So, in the days of the kings the power centered in the king himself and in the patricians who advised him and who, with clients at their call, could put pressure on him. Possibly in response to the power of these nobles with their clientele, the sixth-century king Servius Tullius[13] may have seen a chance to use the army to strengthen his hand against them. Rome's horsemen and rabble of clients were becoming more and more inadequate to deal with her enemies, and meanwhile the Greek cities to the south, like their sisters throughout the Greek world, were undergoing a military revolution. During the archaic period many of them, like Rome, had depended on wealthy horsemen as the main strength of their armies, but a new and more effective approach had been discovered: a trained militia of properly equipped footsoldiers, or hoplites. Armed with helmet, cuirass and large round shield, they fought with spears in a phalanx generally eight ranks deep. Advancing under discipline with the spears of the first two or three ranks levelled, and with adequate armor, they had little to fear from primitive cavalry, which they could push off the field. The Etruscans took up this method of warfare from the Greeks, and their protegés the Romans did so too, perhaps starting under the reign of King Servius Tullius. Later Romans certainly related it back to him along with certain political changes discussed below.

Thus, by the sixth and fifth centuries B.C. the Roman army was no longer a mob following a handful of young noblemen on horseback—it had become a hoplite army, a force of armored footsoldiers fighting in a simple formation and supported by the wealthy on horseback and by the poor as light infantry. This transformation shows that Rome now had the wealth for such a force: The infantry had to be men of some means because they supplied their own equipment.

There were a number of advantages to this arrangement. On most terrain trained infantry is better at fighting than cavalry, especially ancient cavalry, which rode without stirrups.[14] Infantry is much cheaper too: Two or three footsoldiers can be had for the cost of a cavalryman, and ancient cavalry in Europe generally depended on javelins, which minimized their value as shock troops. From the standpoint of a king, however, this new army would weaken the power of the horse-riding nobles as the defense of the city fell more and more on those of the middle class who could afford to serve in armor.

The last of the semi-legendary kings of Rome, Tarquinius Superbus, whose men had murdered Servius, was driven out by the nobility led by Lucius Junius Brutus, and a republic was established in 509. The power or *imperium* that had reposed in the kings was invested in two annually elected officers, at first called *praetores* and then soon afterward *consules*. These officers were a sort of replacement for the king; they acted as the executives of the *res publica* and led the troops in time of war, just as the king had done. They were, of course, patricians.

And yet, as in the Greek city-states that had taken to hoplite warfare, the arming of the middle class, and its importance to the defense of the state, gave the plebeians—the commoners—some political power. Not much at first, but these men could no longer be completely ignored and the wealthy among the plebeians still less. Offices were eventually opened to them—even the senate admitted wealthy plebeians, though at first they could not vote; that was reserved for the *patres,* the patrician senators. These new senators were called *conscripti,* the enlisted, to distinguish them from patricians. The senators were now addressed as *patres et conscripti,* a style later reduced to *patres conscripti.*

During the fifth century the formal Servian Constitution with all its details came into full existence. Though traditionally credited to King Servius Tullius, it was probably introduced much later, about 443 B.C., when tradition states that the office of censor was created; censors would have been needed to keep this constitution working because a man's place, both politically and militarily, was determined by his means and it was the censors' job to assess them. In this system the Roman people—all those who were not patricians—had their wealth determined and were broken into classes for both voting and military purposes. Those who had by tradition been horsemen and those who could afford cavalry service were classed as *equites,* or "knights." The class just below was made up of the next wealthiest men, the "first class"; the class below was the "second" and so on until the fifth class and finally the *proletarii.* Set aside were craftsmen and *cornicenes* (trumpeters) for the army.

This constitution was military in that a man's place in the army was determined by law: the wealthiest to the cavalry, the middle class to the heavy infantry, the poor to the light infantry or to the ranks of attendants and workers. It was also a political instrument because it established the relative political weights of the different economic classes—which were not equal. Instead of voting man by man, each class voted by century (*centuria*), and each century cast a single vote. The number of centuries into which a class was divided was not based on the number of men in the class. Instead, the number of centuries was carefully skewed to favor the wealthier men. The *equites,* or knights, were divided into eighteen centuries, and the first class into eighty—thus the two wealthiest groups had ninety-eight votes between them. By contrast the *proletarii,* the poorest men of all, were grouped into a single century with a single vote. All of the classes between them were variously divided into a total of ninety-five centuries and therefore ninety-five votes. This meant that if the knights and the first class voted together, the voting was finished because they had outvoted the rest of the electorate. A dispute among the knights and the first class might bring into play the votes of the second class, but those of the lower classes would very seldom mean anything.

The system was extremely unfair, but it had the virtue of keeping the power in the hands of those who had the greatest investment in the state, and the adoption of this constitution probably allowed clients to become citizens for the first time.[15] Although this citizenship may not, as a practical matter, have resulted in a meaningful franchise, at the least it gave them certain protections at law, even though the patricians kept the law as their own province. Furthermore the wealthiest men, the knights and the first class, were those plebeians who were most likely to share some common political interests with the senate. Still, under the Servian Constitution the patricians had, for the first time, to cooperate with the knights and plebeians of the first class.

But even though the patricians had conceded some political power to the more well-to-do plebeians, they could also influence the vote through patronage. Their clients needed patrons to protect them, particularly at law, especially if they were in trade and needed to enforce contracts because the laws were kept a secret by the patricians and were not published until 451 or 450 under the pressure of public sentiment. Even so, legal procedure was kept secret for a number of years thereafter, which was a great handicap for the plebeians; knowing what the law was could be helpful, but there was no practical way to use that knowledge before the courts because a single mistake in the form of pleading was fatal to the action. Therefore, the sanctity of the plebeians' contracts was actually in the hands of a sort of legal priesthood, and this monopoly on laws and procedure helped guarantee patrician power. They also held all the major priesthoods and took the auguries that helped shore up their position.

And patrician power was significant: In one instance the noble clan of the Fabii even took their clients to a private war. In 479 B.C., about thirty years after the expulsion of the last king, Rome was in conflict with the neighboring Etruscan city of Veii as she would be on and off for about a hundred years. As a public service Fabius Caeso, the head of the Fabian clan and a consul as well, went before the senate and offered to fight the Veientines with his resources alone: the young patricians of the clan, their clients and friends. The senate accepted the offer, and three hundred and six men of the clan, joined by clients swelling their numbers to four thousand, marched off toward the River Cremera, near Veii. The force was probably composed of horsemen and light infantry as in the older days, but in any case the war was really meant as a series of raids with lightly armed client-solders guarding the camp they had established on the Cremera. After annoying Veii for two years, the Fabii were defeated badly; according to the historian Livy only one Fabius survived to continue the line.

Whatever truth there is at the bottom of this dramatic legend, it does show that the clans, or *gentes,* were extremely powerful and could marshal huge numbers of clients, even for dangerous duty. It is a testament to the clans, in fact, that they didn't practice private war among themselves, as continental nobles would do in the Middle Ages. Although well supplied with clients, the patricians may have abstained from private war—it would have been civil war, in fact—out of a sense of their apartness from the great mass of the people. They were exclusive; they must not turn against each other. And they were right: In later centuries wealthy men turned the proletariat against each other and the result was incessant civil war.

In 493 the plebeians felt themselves so separate from their aristocratic masters that they established a temple of their own to Ceres on the Aventine Hill to correspond to the patricians' Temple of Jupiter on the Capitoline Hill, and they kept their own treasury there. As the fifth century wore on, the strain grew between the different social orders, between the plebeians of the common sort and the patricians and those plebeians who had reached the senate and whose interests and habits were aligned with those of their patrician comrades. *Nexum* accentuated the strain. This was a form of debt bondage by which a debtor unable to repay was made an indentured servant to his creditor until the sum was recovered. It was not quite slavery, but its effects must have been rather similar, and it was understandably hated by the common people; most of the creditors would have been aristocratic—the men with the money to lend.

Between *nexum,* few political rights, limited legal redress, exclusion from the magistracies and priesthoods, and repeated service in the army (Rome's enemies gave her little peace), the lot of the poor plebeians was harsh. Their solution was secession, or a strike. The first of these, in 494 B.C., was to the Mons Sacer outside the city, or to the Aventine Hill.

According to Livy the secession was provoked when the commons could get no debt relief after the Sabine Wars. He says of the debtors:

> They demanded much more menacingly than humbly that they convene the senate and they themselves stood around the senate house to be witnesses and directors of the public business.[16]

The commons got no relief, and at the suggestion of a certain Sicinius, in support the Roman army marched out of the city and across the Anio, a small river beyond the walls, and built a military camp on the Sacred Mount where they waited for several days. The predictable result was great disquiet in the city; the plebeians were uneasy, it is said, because so many of the fit were in the army and in the strike camp and this put them at the mercy of the senate and its minions. If so, they were wrong to fear—it was the senators who had the most at stake. With plebeians now forming most of the army and hence the real strength of it, their absence directly threatened the city; Rome had many enemies, the Sabines for instance, and such internal discord was an open invitation to them. Both parties were learning something that the Greeks were also finding out: that a middle-class militia army undermined aristocratic power. The arrival of hoplite warfare in Greece was followed in many places by democracy.

The senate recognized this new power in the people, and to mollify them acknowledged a new office among plebeians, that of *tribunus plebis,* or tribune of the people. Gaius Licinius and Lucius Albinus were the first two to be given the unusual tribunician powers. They chose three more to join them, and some time later the number of tribunes was raised to ten. At the time of their creation, the chief duty of the tribunes was to prevent oppression by the patricians and their representatives, the consuls and lesser magistrates. This they carried out in a shockingly simple way: They literally obstructed magistrates from carrying out their duties by standing in the way. Thus a tribune had the right of *intercessio,* or "getting in-between." A tribune's body was sacrosanct—he could not be touched in any way, and if he were called to a man's assistance he could simply put himself between the magistrate and the unfortunate man. Because he could not be touched, there was no way for the magistrate to carry out his errand. This office, which grew in importance over the centuries, was significant both in itself and as a symbol of the mass's new and growing power.

Debt bondage continued to be a burden on the populace, particularly after the terrible defeat on the Allia in 386. The Roman army, though already redoubtable, had been swept away by an army of wandering Gauls, who proceeded to sack Rome. When the disaster was over and the city rebuilt, *nexum* was more of a problem than ever, as those who had lost their property returned to rebuild. In response to pressure from the commons, *nexum* was eventually abolished, though one of the effects of this legislation would have been to make the borrowing of money more difficult. Who would lend without security? And what had the poorer plebeians as security but their labor?

And yet there were wealthy plebeians. Some of them, artisans and clever landowners, had money, enough to imagine themselves in the higher offices that had always been the domain of the patricians. These wealthy plebeians must have had an influence on their poorer cousins, and as they climbed socially they would have done so with their support; in turn, the now moneyed plebians supported and protected the poor commoners as they slowly rose. And there were results: The *Leges Liciniae Sextiae* in 367 opened the highest offices of the state to plebeians, and the *Lex Canuleia* dissolved the ban on marriage between patricians and plebeians. At least some of the patrician clans were willing to allow intermarriage with plebeians. Some needed money, no doubt, and another problem was that the old patrician clans were dying out, and there was a need for new men at the top. There were in fact many renowned plebeian clans whose names would appear over and over again in Roman history, and though many were noble because one of the clan had reached the consulship, they were never patrician—a patrician was descended from a patrician male.

There were two more secessions, or strikes, the last in 287 B.C., resulting in an extremely important change: the *Lex Hortensia*, by which the patricians agreed to be bound by any laws that the plebeians passed in their assemblies, and to recognize a new sort of popular assembly that voted not by century, but by the tribes into which the city was divided. As the population of Rome had increased, the number of tribes had risen from the original three to twenty-five and eventually, by the time of Tiberius Gracchus, to thirty-two. Because the population was distributed more or less equally among the tribes, the votes of the citizens were now fairly equal. Yet these changes, though important, did not shift the balance of power from the aristocracy to the plebeians, for the patron–client relationship remained extremely powerful and the aristocracy was able, in practice, to control much of the voting.

Therefore, these political gains didn't mean that the plebeians were now on an equal footing with the patricians—far from it. Only the wealthy plebeians had the leisure to agitate for rights, and only they had the money needed to hold the high magistracies. Service to the state was done at the magistrate's own expense; there was no pay. It did mean, however, that for the very wealthiest there was the prospect of holding the higher offices from which the senate was selected, marriage into the ancient families and a chance for the consulship, however slender. Indeed the plebeians were eventually able to wrest the concession from the senate that at least one of the consuls every year must be a plebeian; but it is interesting that the people, when they voted for the consuls, often ignored the law and elected a pair of patricians. This suggests that those plebeians who had lobbied for the rule were no longer sufficiently close to their poorer fellows to benefit from it very much. To the poor these men probably didn't seem very different from the patricians—and they weren't. As wealthy plebeian clans rose socially and began to share power with the old nobility, their interests and way of life became indistinguishable.

If a plebeian clan had had a consul to boast of, it became noble. This was the situation of Tiberius Sempronius Gracchus. His father had been consul and had held the even more prestigious position of censor. Tiberius was descended from the patrician clan of the Scipiones and was married to a daughter of another patrician clan, the Claudii. He was a plebeian, but he was wealthy and noble and at the very highest level of Roman society. And his politics ought to have been extremely patrician. But they were not.

CHAPTER 2

The Army

WHEN TIBERIUS GRACCHUS STOOD ON THE WALL AT CARTHAGE in 143 B.C., the army he served was essentially that which had come out of the great war with Hannibal decades before. The Greek historian Polybius had described it in some detail around 160 B.C., and the Roman historian Livy more than a hundred years after that. This army, with its solid organization and workmanlike, even plodding character, had bested every one of its opponents in the end, despite its militia origins. Losing battles now and then, even great ones like Cannae in which Hannibal had destroyed an entire army, the Romans had doggedly beaten every opponent, subjugated their neighbors, planted colonies and, by 133, the year of Tiberius Gracchus's tribunate, controlled most of the northern Mediterranean seaboard. The Roman army's successes—and its defeats equally—contributed as much as the natural division of the Roman people did to the dissolution of the republic.

What was this army like? It was efficient as no other would be until the modern period, but it was not purely a military institution: It was a microcosm of Roman society. The common footsoldiers were at the bottom of the system, and in by far the greatest numbers. High above them were the military tribunes—men of the senatorial and patrician aristocracy—and at the summit the consul or proconsul, a man of the highest social station whose family might trace itself back to the days of the kings. The cavalry or *equites* were chosen by the censors on the basis of wealth, a determination that applied to the rank of *eques* in private life. The army, like the centuriate assembly, was divided into centuries—the army was a reflection of civil life and a Roman's place within it was not far different. These centuries, though, were of uniform size, probably of about eighty men.[1]

For young men seeking political office, ten years of military service was obligatory. Military service was required of the common run of the population too, so long as they were not too poor to meet the property qualification, which in recent years had dropped. For those men unlucky enough to be conscripted, service was longer and more oppressive than it was for young aristocrats—it was an interruption from their usual occupations and not, as it was for the nobles, the first step in their careers. The wars in Spain, where there was danger and little chance for booty, had made army life disagreeable for many of the common people.

The army of the second century B.C. was divided into legions and had been for about three centuries. The number of soldiers in a republican legion varied from time to time as the senate might decree.[2] And so, though Polybius says that in his day four thousand two hundred footsoldiers made up a legion or, in an emergency, five thousand, his figures should be taken as averages that might be increased in emergencies or reduced by the usual causes of attrition: combat deaths, injuries, sickness, desertion. Attached to a legion were a small number of cavalry, usually about 300.[3] In short, Rome relied on her footsoldiers.

Nonetheless, the cavalry kept some of the prestige it had had in former days: The censors determined who would serve on horseback on the basis of a high property qualification, which meant the sons of the well-to-do. The cavalry was liable for ten years of service, the infantry for sixteen: another indication of their higher status. The terms sound high, though in practice this must have meant that the soldiers, cavalry or infantry, could be called up to serve for a maximum of ten or sixteen years. Very lucky soldiers might be mustered out after a campaign or two; unfortunate footsoldiers might be kept in the ranks for years on end. One historian suggests that it was usual for an infantryman to be made to serve six years and then remain liable as an *evocatus*, a soldier who could be called back, until the balance of the sixteen years had passed.[4] This sort of military duty commonly ruined small farmers whose property ran down during their years away, and this worked in tandem with the importation of large numbers of slaves to diminish the number of small farmers liable for military service. This too would spur Tiberius Gracchus to act.

Men were liable for service between the ages of sixteen and forty-six, except those poor whose capital fell below 400 drachmas. These did their service in the navy, most of them probably as oarsmen in the galleys where hundreds were needed on the larger ships. The poorest of all, the *capite censi* or *proletarii*—men with no property—were not liable at all:

The state trusted only those men with property to defend it. This had the result, curious perhaps to modern eyes, that poverty freed men from conscription. As matters developed later it might be argued that there was some sense in trying to limit service to those who weren't desperate, and besides the soldiers were expected to pay for their own equipment. It is true that after the disaster at Cannae two legions were raised from freed slaves who must have been fitted out by the state, but it was an expedient taken in the face of unprecedented disaster.

Although she might have many legions in the field in time of need, the core of Rome's army were four legions identified, in a matter-of-fact way, as one, two, three and four. These were mustered at the city from Roman citizens and distributed two to each consul. Ideally, to raise this force the consuls would announce the mustering day for the legions at a meeting of the popular assembly, and men liable for service would meet then on the Capitoline Hill. The censors would choose the cavalry, roughly twelve hundred men, to be distributed among the four legions, and then came the selection of the infantry, the most important business of the day.

The Romans, as always, proceeded in an orderly manner. Twenty-four military tribunes were chosen, ten of them with ten years experience and fourteen with five. These were men of the aristocracy who would serve as the highest officers beneath the consuls themselves. They were distributed among the four legions: two senior tribunes assigned to Legions I and III, and three senior tribunes to Legions II and IV. The junior tribunes were then assigned so that each legion had six tribunes: four juniors to Legions I and III, and three juniors to Legions II and IV. Next came the selection, the *dilectus,* of the common soldiers.

From each voting tribe four men of the same age and physical condition were called out and the tribunes from each legion took turns selecting one of them: The tribunes of the first legion took the first choice, and then those of the second, third and fourth. With the next four men the tribunes of the second legion chose first, and then those of the third, fourth and finally the first, and the rotation continued until the legions had been filled. Though this process would ensure that each legion had a fair distribution of fit men, it was a long process. The tribunes must have done it at several stations simultaneously if it were to be at all efficient, and the levy cannot have been handled this way in the press of wartime or for legions raised outside of Latium.

The military oath was then administered, though rather oddly: One man was chosen from the entire mass of soldiers and he took the oath alone, after which the other soldiers swore to do as he had done. The men were then dismissed and told when to appear, without weapons, for service.

To raise allied troops, the consuls simply sent word to the allied cities with the numbers they wished and the day and place for the men to appear. Local magistrates would raise the soldiers and send them off with an officer and a paymaster. When on campaign, allied troops were commanded by officers known as *praefecti sociorum,* and because there were customarily the same number of allied footsoldiers as Roman legionaries, there were twelve of these prefects in a consular army. These allied soldiers were armed and trained to fight in the Roman manner, but were organized into cohorts instead of legions.[5] On campaign these cohorts were grouped together into legion-sized units and fought beside the Roman legions. The allies were obliged, however, to supply three times as many cavalrymen as the Romans themselves did. From these allies were chosen the *extraordinarii,* the picked men who attended the consul and the quaestor, the army's financial officer, as special troops: from the infantry, a fifth of the men, and from the cavalry a third.

The cavalry were organized into *turmae,* or troops of thirty, each squadron under three officers called *decuriones;* under these were three *optiones,* or lesser officers. The senior *decurion* was in general command. The cavalry were equipped with helmet, round shield,[6] cuirass, sword, lance and javelins.[7]

The infantrymen were divided into four categories: *velites, hastati, principes* and *triarii.* The first category, the *velites,* were the youngest or poorest of the troops, and served as skirmishers—light infantry, whose job it was to open a battle by masking the heavy infantry as it maneuvered into position, and to disorder the enemy. They bore the least equipment and the lightest armament: a plain helmet, a round shield about a yard in diameter, a sword and some light javelins called *gaesa.*[8] These had wooden shafts about three feet long and soft iron heads that bent on impact so they couldn't be cast back. The *velites* often wore wolf skins over their helmets so that they could be identified by their fellows at a distance. According to Polybius there were 1,200 of these light soldiers to a legion, though in fact the number would vary with the size of the legion. The figure is probably not far off, but they might be estimated as making slightly over a quarter of the legion.

The rest of the footsoldiers were heavy infantry divided into three remaining classes that determined their place in the typical Roman formation of three distinct battle lines. The *hastati* formed the first line of battle. Their name is a holdover from earlier times when they must have been armed with the *hasta,* or spear. By this time, however, they were armed with the Roman javelin, the *pilum,* about six feet long. There were heavy and light versions of it for different purposes,[9] and it consisted of a wooden shaft about three or four feet long to which was fixed an iron shank projecting another two or three feet and ending in a small head. Its weight and small point were meant to pierce an opponent's shield. Like the *velis,* the *hastatus* carried a sword, the *gladius* or *ensis hispanicus*—the "Spanish sword," adopted from Spanish mercenaries more than two hundred years before. It was short and broad: the blade about two inches wide, the entire sword only about two feet long. It had a long point and, unlike longer weapons, was particularly fit for close combat.

An equal number of men made up the next class, the *principes.* These stood in the second line, so their name too belied their function: At some point they must have been in the first, as this is what their name implies. They were armed like the *hastati* with *pila* and swords. The *triarii* were the third class of soldier. Their name is accurate; they formed the third line of the Roman battle order and they differed in two ways from their fellows. They carried the sword of course, but because their job differed they were armed with a spear—the *hasta* instead of the *pilum.* They were only half as numerous, conventionally numbering only six hundred, even if the legion were enlarged. The *triarii* were a last-ditch reserve should things go badly. Polybius tells us that all the soldiers were also divided by age as well as position: the *velites* the youngest, the *hastati* next in age, followed by the *principes* and the *triarii.* While this may have been the case in earlier times, it was unlikely that this was still true in his day.

The armor of these three classes was heavier than that of the *velites.* They carried long oval shields called *scuta,* convex and made of plywood faced with leather and canvas and finally fitted with an iron binding on the top and bottom. The top binding prevented the shield from splitting when hit by the Gallic long sword, and the bottom binding protected it when the shield was set on the ground, as it must have been quite often. The round Greek hoplite shield was fitted with a strap for the forearm as well as a grip for the hand since it was meant to be carried throughout a battle, heavy though it was. By contrast the Roman *scutum* had only a single, horizontal hand grip in the center, protected by a large metal boss. This shield was about four feet tall and two and a half wide, enough to practically hide a Roman legionary, who probably seldom exceeded five and a half feet. Given the single handgrip and bottom binding, the shield must have been set down when not actually fighting.

Finally, Polybius informs us, the richer soldiers wore a chain-mail coat; chain mail had probably been adopted from Gallic enemies. He says the poorer soldiers wore a pectoral across the chest, "a span square,"[10] but this pectoral cannot have been the legionaries' only chest protection. The Latin for a cuirass or corselet is *lorica,* which meant, originally, one made of leather as opposed to one of metal.[11] The word *lorica* was later applied to other armors: *lorica hamata* being chain mail and *lorica squamata* scale armor, but there must once have been a clear referent to which the word applied—a leather cuirass. The pectoral that Polybius describes must have been an additional small defense used with this leather armor; the combination would have been much less expensive than mail and an adequate defense as well. The importance of armor to men who fight with bladed weapons can hardly be overemphasized. Apart from the actual protection it gives, it lends confidence to the wearer, and the confidence of soldiers is always extremely important. As Colonel Ardant du Picq noted more than a hundred and fifty years ago: "Armor, in diminishing the material effect that can be suffered, diminishes the dominating moral effect of fear."[12] We can be certain that the common Roman legionary had sufficient armor to protect himself.[13]

The Roman helmet of the period, which all of the common soldiers wore regardless of class, was of bronze or iron and usually of the simple type nowadays called "Montefortino" from the area where a number of them have been found. These helmets consist of a dome or pot with a short neckguard jutting straight out from the back, and they were fitted with a pair of large cheek pieces to cover the sides of the face. The helmets had knobs on top to which crests of feathers could be fixed.

Polybius tells us that in this period the soldiers themselves selected ten centurions, the officers who commanded the smallest administrative unit of the army, the century. These ten centurions themselves chose ten more, he says, and each of them selected a subordinate called an *optio* to assist him. However, a legion had sixty centurions and so the selection must have been somewhat different; perhaps the first ten chose more than ten. The centurions were selected, it is said, for coolness rather than for impetuosity, certainly the case given their duties on the battlefield: to know their positions, to maneuver as directed and to keep their men in line during the stress of battle. The centurions were marked out from the rest of the soldiers by their kit. They wore greaves, and the crests of their helmets went from side to side rather than front to back. Most important from the standpoint of day-to-day discipline, however, was the centurion's staff or rod, with which he beat recalcitrant soldiers. The staff became such a mark of office that it was sculpted onto centurions' tombstones to indicate their rank.

These centurions also directed the drills upon which the Roman army depended, because Romans maneuvered in the field more than other ancient armies. The Latin word for "army" is *exercitus,* and it meant originally an exercise—in effect a drill. That the term came to mean army tells a good deal about the Roman approach to war.

The Romans gave as much thought to their battle order as to the other aspects of their military. The Hellenistic armies of the east, which derived their tactics from the Macedonian armies of Philip II and Alexander the Great, arrayed their footsoldiers in massive, deep phalanxes, the soldiers wielding pikes of sixteen feet or even longer. Several ranks would lower their weapons and the whole mass advanced, five pikes extending out for each man in the front rank. These bristly fronts a thousand men wide seemed invulnerable as they advanced, though in fact they tended to suffer gaps if the ground were uneven—and even if it weren't as the Romans learned in fighting such formations. Opposition to a phalanx—and opposition was bound to be uneven across its long front—often caused gaps to open as different sections were able to advance at different paces. Roman swordsmen exploited this while fighting Macedonian phalanxes at Pydna and Cenoscephalae in the 160s B.C. At first driven back, the legionaries were later able to enter the breaches their retreat had caused and destroy the formation as they attacked with swords; the Macedonian pikemen were unable to use or even maneuver their clumsy weapons at close quarters.

Barbarians presented different problems. The Gauls, historically among Rome's most feared enemies, fought in an undisciplined mob, rushing and swinging long swords. The Romans had traditionally found the wild, tall Gauls terrifying, and Sallust wrote: "From that day to this the Romans took it that everything was subject to their bravery, but with the Gauls they fought for life and not for glory."[14] However uneasy the Romans may have been about the Gauls, they did not emulate them in war any more than they did the Hellenes.

Instead they adopted an articulated battle formation of three lines, each line made up of blocks of swordsmen in a loose enough order to use their weapons. These blocks, called *manipuli* or "handfuls," were each made up of two centuries—those small administrative units each under a centurion and an *optio.* The maniple was the smallest element in the Roman battle order and was under the command of the *centurio prior,* the senior of two centurions, unless something should happen to him, in which case the junior, or *centurio posterior,* took command. The two centuries in a maniple were probably positioned side by side. Some suggest that one century was placed behind another to form a maniple because of the terms *centurio prior* and *centurio posterior,* but Polybius states that the centurion first elected commanded the right century while the other commanded the left. It seems that *prior* and *posterior* really refer to the order in which the centurions were chosen or appointed. The German military historian Hans Delbrück asserts too that the centuries in a maniple were in fact arrayed side by side.[15] Those who differ claim that before closing with the enemy, the rear century moved out from behind the front century and came alongside it, probably to the left. Whether such a maneuver could even be done on the battlefield in face of the enemy seems very unlikely. Since a century on the advance probably had only ten men across the front and a depth of eight men, it seems at best an unnecessarily clumsy arrangement to put another such small unit behind it and then have it move alongside as the two closed with the enemy.

Surely a maniple with its two centuries side by side, a formation twenty men wide and eight men deep, could advance easily enough over rough ground and would not invite disorder by unnecessary maneuvering. This suggested shuffling of maniples on the battlefield just before meeting the enemy seems no more than a way of straining to find support for the theory that the prior and posterior centurions marched their centuries one behind the other even though Polybius tells us otherwise, and to place on the battlefield a description by Livy (discussed below) of what may be a parade ground drill.

All three lines were made up of these maniples, ten in each, the maniples of the *triarii* only half as large as the others, as there were only half as many *triarii* to distribute between them. The trick, though, was this: The maniples were not placed to form continuous battle lines; instead, small gaps were left between them. Many suggest that the maniples were placed so far apart that the gaps between them were as wide as the maniples themselves. Livy, however, states that the maniples were "a small distance apart."[16] Further, the maniples in the second or *principes* line were placed behind the gaps in the *hastati* line, and finally the *triarii* maniples covered the gaps in the *principes* line. The lines themselves were kept some distance apart, and as the army marched toward the enemy, the maniples, because they were much smaller units than a single phalanx, could keep better order. If one maniple drifted and crowded another, the problem wasn't communicated all down the line as was the case with a phalanx, and if an extremely large gap formed, it could be filled by a century or even an entire maniple from the line behind. This ensured that the entire battle line would complete its approach march in good order. The *velites*, who had been skirmishing, would then retreat through the maniples, or around the end of the line.

It is at this point that those scholars who believe the cohorts in a maniple marched one behind the other think the gaps between the maniples were closed when the rear centuries stepped to one side and then advanced until they were alongside their corresponding front centuries. Frankly, Delbrück's view, which differs sharply from this, seems the better interpretation. He was both a scholar and a military officer, and his opinion, based not only on reading the classics but on his experience in the army, shouldn't be discounted. In his opinion the centuries making up the maniples advanced side by side as Polybius's text suggests, and the spaces between them were small, as Livy says. As the *hastati* met the enemy, these small gaps between the maniples were filled up by those men in the rear ranks coming forward. This approach is altogether simpler and would not require the strict alignment and positioning of the maniples if they were really to have their gaps filled by their rear centuries.

Before closing with the enemy the soldiers of the front rank or two of the *hastati* threw their javelins, probably from sixty feet or so, to disorder the enemy, and then drew their swords and prepared to close. Each soldier would have about a yard within which to fight, about twice as much room as a phalangite of the Macedonian school, who, armed with a spear, depended on the density of his formation to roll over an opponent. The men in the second rank stood in the intervals between the men in the first, ready to protect their fellows' flanks and step up to replace them when they tired or fell.

Meanwhile the *principes* maniples waited at a sufficient distance behind them, far enough away that the men didn't become psychologically exhausted by their proximity to the fighting. The importance of this cannot be underestimated. Writing of ancient combat, du Picq stated with his characteristic clarity:

> During this engagement of the first two ranks, the one fighting, the other watching close at hand, the men of the rear ranks waited inactive at two paces distance for their turn in the combat, which would come only when their predecessors were killed, wounded or exhausted. They were impressed by the violent fluctuations of the struggle of the first rank. They heard the clashes of the blows and distinguished, perhaps,

those that sank into the flesh. They saw the wounded, the exhausted crawl through the intervals to go to the rear. Passive spectators of danger, they were forced to await its terrible approach. These men were subjected to the poignant emotions of combat without being supported by the animation of the struggle. They were thus placed under the moral pressure of the greatest of anxieties. Often they could not stand it until their turn came; they gave way.[17]

As du Picq notes, the great value of the Roman system was that it kept only those units that were necessary at the point of combat and the rest "outside the immediate sphere of moral tension."[18] As the *hastati* fought, the *principes* and *triarii* waited farther back. If things went badly for the *hastati,* if they had become exhausted or desperate or the ranks thinned, the *principes* would advance to their support.

Conventional accounts drawn from Livy, who seems to have been describing a sort of parade ground maneuver, have led most scholars to assume a maneuver altogether more elaborate. In this view the *hastati* would pull back from the enemy and pass through the gaps in the *principes* maniples behind them. The *principes* maniples would then close their gaps, either by widening themselves or by bringing their rear centuries out from behind and then forward. This seems to ignore the virtual certainty that exhausted or frightened soldiers fighting hand to hand could not be led backward in the face of a close enemy without falling into disorder or panic—if such men could even be commanded at all, once they were engaged. As they pulled back, or more likely fled, they would have disordered the *principes* and perhaps swept them away in flight. To allow for a large number of troops to pull back through them, the *principes* gaps would have to have been very large, and they would have been difficult if not impossible to close as the enemy followed the *hastati* up to the gaps. Livy's account of these maneuverings—possible perhaps on a drill field with no distractions—can hardly describe Roman practice during an actual battle.

Instead, the *principes* must have advanced up to the *hastati* and supported them by working to the front. This kept the front of the battle line stable, and a line of tired *hastati* could keep their attention on the enemy only yards, or even feet away, until they found themselves supported by the second line. In this way the *hastati* would be supported without even having to think of maneuver.

In the worst of circumstances, when even the reinforcement of the *principes* was not enough, the *triarii* would come forward. Though they were not many, with their spears they would help turn the formation into a sort of defensive phalanx. In fact their small numbers, which were kept the same even in large legions, is a proof that they were not intended to meet the enemy alone as a sort of thin rear guard while their fellows fled back between the *triarii* maniples, as is often suggested. The *triarii* must have been meant to advance and pass to the front rank of the first line where these fresh men with their spears, it was hoped, would provide enough strength to help stand the enemy off. At this point the Romans might try to fight their way off the field to their fortified camp. This organization, allowing as it did a steady approach, the methodical replacement of tired or defeated troops, and the hope of a safe retreat, made the Romans very hard to defeat.

Besides the *velites* and the Roman and allied cavalry, the republic hired contingents of mercenary specialists as auxiliary troops: Archers from Crete and slingers from the Balearic Islands were always popular. As at Numantia, Numidians might furnish horsemen, and as time went on Gauls, Thracians and Germans provided much of the cavalry. Many of the light troops skirmished before battle was seriously joined and then helped protect the flanks along with the cavalry. Cavalry, of course, tried to menace the enemy's flanks and rear and prevent opposing horsemen from doing the same. In short, Roman generals typically marshalled fairly well balanced armies of excellent footsoldiers supported by competent specialized troops.

The fortified camp, which the army might retreat to in emergencies, and from which they operated in any case, is an equal if not greater proof of the Roman genius for the practical. The Romans, who were builders and civil engineers by inclination, did not go to war without building fortified camps in which they spent every night of the campaign. They realized that these camps gave the soldiers peace of mind in the field, because they would have a place to retreat if needed, and the camps provided a safe place to sleep—passing the night behind guarded ramparts kept the army from any more mental or physical fatigue than necessary. The Late Roman military writer Flavius Vegetius said of the early Roman camps:

> The new recruit should also learn the building of camps; nothing is better or more necessary in war; especially if the camps are built properly, for the soldiers spend both days and nights safe within the walls, even if the enemy should attack. It is as though they carried a walled town with them everywhere.[19]

These camps could also serve a strategic purpose: dominating the countryside, or at least hindering the movement of an enemy who found the legions dogging him and camping in his neighborhood, as Fabius Maximus had done to Hannibal during the Second Punic War. Fabius scrupulously avoided pitched battles with Hannibal, whom he judged too clever for him on the battlefield. He refused to be drawn into a decisive battle; he operated out of camps behind or along Hannibal's march and effectively limited depredation of the countryside and wore down his enemy. Many generals had won and were to win nicknames for their victories over different peoples and lands: Africanus, Numidicus, Germanicus. By contrast, Fabius Maximus's wise policy earned him the cognomen *Cunctator,* or "Delayer." His strategy shows how Roman camps were as important to the success of a campaign as were Roman tactics on the battlefield.

A consular army of two legions and their allies could be accommodated in a single camp. These camps were always built as far as possible according to the same plan, and the soldiers were assigned their position by maniple and century in exactly the same place in every camp. This not only prevented disorder generally, but allowed the orderly mustering of the army within the camp; units could come and go without blocking each other. There was a further advantage: Even when caught by surprise each soldier knew where he was and where to go. The streets and gates had the same names and were always in the same places.

The camps were placed carefully. Scouts ranged ahead of an army on the march and found a suitable place. Surveyors then went ahead and marked with a white flag the site where the commander's tent, the *praetorium,* would be. Measurements were taken from this point. The camp was rectangular, about 2,000 feet on a side.[20] Two hundred feet were allowed between the ramparts and the first line of tents, adequate room for troops to form up without getting into jams, and cattle and booty could be kept there. The distance also protected the soldiers from missiles or fire, which could not be tossed effectually over the wall onto the tents.

When the army came up at noon or shortly after from a march of about fifteen miles, they would find the camp marked out with flags. The legionaries set to work to raise the two ramparts behind which they would set their tents, and the allies did the same. Areas were divided for each maniple to work on, and the centurions bossed the soldiers while two of the military tribunes supervised each rampart as it was put up. If the practice was like that of the later army, the digging was probably done only by the heavy infantry, or a portion of it, while the rest of it and the cavalry and light infantry mounted a guard against attack.

The soldiers dug a ditch, usually about three feet deep for a marching camp, and tossed the earth inward to form a rampart of about the same height. This could, of course, be varied at need. Each soldier carried a pair of sharpened pales, or stakes, and when the work was done they were placed along the top of the rampart. Four gates were set in the walls: the *porta praetoria, porta decumana, porta principalis sinistra* and *porta principalis dextra. Sinistra* and *dextra,* left and right, were determined from the standpoint of the general's tent as he looked down the central street to the *porta decumana* at the other side of the camp. A street, the *Via Principalis,* ran from one side of the camp to the other connecting the *porta principalis sinistra* and *porta principalis dextra,* passing the *praetorium* as it did so.

The area around the *praetorium,* the heart of the camp, was slightly off-center—equidistant from the right and left ramparts, but closer to the *porta practoria.* On the left of the *praetorium* was a forum—a marketplace and place of assembly. On the right was the *quaestorium,* the tent of the quaestor, who handled the army's money and accounts. The tents of the twelve tribunes were set along the *Via Principalis* in front of the *praetorium,* forum and *quaestorium.*

Five other streets ran at a right angle off the *Via Principalis* toward the rear wall of the camp and the troops' tents were pitched along these streets. The first maniple of each legion was placed at the head of the street at its intersection with the *Via Principalis,* the second maniple was next down the street and so on to the tenth maniple camped at the end of the street by the rear rampart. The centurions camped at each end of their maniples.

The Roman cavalry was put on either side of the center street, and the allied cohorts and cavalry were camped along the outer streets nearest the side ramparts. Another street, the *Via Quintana,* ran across the camp parallel to the *Via Principalis,* but between the tents of the fifth and sixth cohorts. The *extraordinarii,* both infantry and cavalry, pitched their tents apart from the rest of the allied troops and were placed in various positions behind and around the *praetorium,* forum and *quaestorium.* Any auxiliaries, such as mercenary slingers or archers, were put in this area too. At times, two consuls might camp together; in that case their camp was essentially two of these camps joined where the wall with the *porta praetoria* would have been.

The supervision of the camp was left to the tribunes, who handled the task in pairs, each pair doing it for two months at a time, while the allied prefects handled their duties in the same way. Each maniple of the *hastati* and *principes* took a turn at guarding the consul's tent while two maniples were given the duty of maintaining the area around the tribunes' tents. The remaining eighteen maniples were divided among the six tribunes and took turns attending them, putting up their tents and guarding them. The *velites* and *triarii* were exempt from this duty, though the *triarii*, who camped next to the Roman cavalry, guarded the horses and made sure they didn't get into trouble and range about the camp.

Thus, in a Roman camp every man had his place and knew where it was. All of this is in sharp contrast to the Greeks, who, though they had a long military tradition, did not make such orderly camps. They encamped themselves in those places that offered natural protection if they could find them, but didn't get the advantages of method and routine.

The Roman camp was protected not only by its ramparts, but by the watch kept at night. This was as organized and regular as the rest of Roman military life. In the evening one soldier each from the tenth maniples of the *hastati, principes* and *triarii* (and cavalrymen from the corresponding *turmae*) went to the tribune's tent where they were each given a wooden tablet with the night's watchword written on it. These tenth-maniple men took them back to their maniples and their centurions noted it and passed it on to a centurion of the ninth maniple who in turn passed it up the line. Upon receipt, centurions of the first maniples then handed the tablets back to the tribune, who could be sure that the watchword had been distributed. If a tablet failed to appear it wasn't difficult to hunt it down and correct the problem.

The night guards were then set. The *velites* guarded the outer wall and ditch. Some therefore patrolled beyond the rampart; ten of them guarded each gate. The other men who would do night guard duty were taken by their *optiones* to the tribune, who gave each one a tile with a sign marked on it, and the men went off to their posts. It was left to the cavalry to check the watch; this may reflect the higher social status of the cavalry, or it may have been thought that the cavalry would be more vigilant in watching the infantry than would the infantry itself.

The *optiones* of the cavalry drew lots to decide which watch they would take, and then they would go to the tribune, who would tell them which posts to check and at what time. Drawing lots was of course fair, but it also made it uncertain which watch an *optio* would have, a useful expedient to prevent bribery. The *optiones* stayed near the first maniple of the *triarii* and waited for the trumpet to sound the watches. As each was sounded, the chosen *optio*, with four witnesses, went out to check the guards. As he made his rounds he collected the tiles from those men he found awake and at their posts. He took none from any he found asleep. Instead he called the witnesses to observe the fact and went on to the next station.

At daybreak the tiles were returned to the tribune. If a guard had failed to turn his in, the centurion of his maniple brought him forward. The tribunes held an immediate court-martial and, if the soldier was found guilty, the tribune touched him with a staff. At once the soldier was cudgelled and stoned by his fellows, usually, Polybius tells us, right to death. If he managed to get out of the camp alive he was then a marked man and could never return home. Polybius adds:

> The same punishment is inflicted on the optio and praefect of the squadron, if they do not give the proper orders at the right time to the patrols and the praefect of the next squadron. Thus, owing to the extreme severity and inevitableness of the penalty, the night watches of the Roman army are most scrupulously kept.[21]

Punishment was severe, it is true, but with the safety of twenty thousand men at stake, the Romans felt these measures justified. And the Romans were used to harsh discipline—one of their most famous punishments was decimation. This measure was taken when entire units were judged guilty of cowardice. The unit to be punished drew lots and every tenth man was executed.

> The tribune assembles the legion, and brings up those guilty of leaving the ranks, reproaches them sharply, and finally chooses by lot sometimes five, sometimes eight, sometimes twenty of the offenders, so adjusting the number thus chosen that they form as near as possible the tenth part of those guilty of cowardice. Those on whom the lot falls are bastinadoed mercilessly in the manner above described; the rest receive rations of barley instead of wheat and are ordered to encamp outside the camp on an unprotected spot. As therefore the danger and dread of drawing the fatal lot affects all equally, as it is uncertain on whom it will fall; and as the public disgrace of receiving barley rations falls on all alike, this practice is that best calculated both to inspire fear and to correct the mischief.[22]

Most of Roman military life was less dramatic and harsh than its punishments; it couldn't have been otherwise. The army took care to feed the soldiers, who were given a grain allowance, mostly of wheat and probably on the kalends, or first, of every month. This the soldiers ground in stone hand-mills. The flour could be baked into bread, but was often cooked in a pot and stirred while it boiled and hardened into a dense loaf like a modern Italian polenta. The diet included oil, wine and some meat as well, and the soldiers scavenged and hunted for whatever else they could find. Sutlers often followed the army and sold to the troops.

The men were clothed with the short tunic peculiar to soldiers and, oddly, to slaves. They might wear a woolen cloak, either the rectangular *sagum* or the poncholike *paenula,* and they wore heavy, hobnailed sandals. Their pay, modest as it was, suffered deductions to pay for these things and for any necessary arms and armor the soldier might need.

Each *contubernium,* or squad of tent mates, often numbering eight, shared a single large, leather tent, and often had a servant as well. The tent, the hand-mill and their baggage were loaded onto the *contubernium's* mule when on the march. The baggage train of a consular army was therefore significant, including as it did a mule for each *contubernium,* the horses of the cavalry and ox-drawn wagons with more general materiel. A consular army might have 2,000 mules and 3,600 horses for the cavalry, both Roman and allied. In many instances the head of the army on the march must have arrived at the site where they would build the new marching camp as the tail of the army was leaving the old.

This was the army that had spread from Latium, bested sometimes in battle, but only seldom. It was an army that had not lost a war since the Gauls had swept down from the Alps three hundred years before. All the same, there was a problem as the second century came to a close: It was an excellent army, but would there continue to be enough of the right men to fill it?

CHAPTER 3

Fissures Show

TIBERIUS GRACCHUS WAS ELECTED ONE OF THE TEN TRIBUNES of the people for the year 133 B.C. and was in a position to address the issue that so concerned him: fostering the class of small farmers that was so necessary to the army. In doing so he became, briefly, one of the most powerful men in Rome, and for a number of the senators, the most alarming. His brother-in-law Scipio was already in Spain putting an end to the revolt there; he was reducing Numantia with massive siegeworks and his impending success promised to relieve the military burdens of the poor, who were so often forced to serve in the unpopular province.

The sixty-thousand-strong Sicilian slave revolt continued. Cleon and his ally "King Antiochus" had defeated a Roman consular army in the year of Tiberius's election. Even though they would be defeated the following year by more tested soldiers from the Numantine campaign, it was another proof that, for the safety of the state, there must be change—and quickly. The constant increase in the slave population was a clear social problem, and the massive slave revolt in Sicily was a symptom of it. As for the fighting in Spain, Tiberius would not have been so concerned from a purely military perspective. While it had been costly and at times humiliating, Scipio would bring the war to an end. It was just another conquest that Rome would effect through her customary diligence, discipline, training, equipment, supplies and sturdy men. Still, she needed those men.

Tiberius seems to have felt genuine pity for the Roman proletariat. His mother Cornelia had had him tutored in Greek by a certain Diophanes, and he had a friend and teacher in the philosopher Blossius of Cumae; he may have absorbed Greek democratic ideas from them. Still, true democracy was hardly a choice for Rome at this point in her development. She was no longer a small city-state with problems that might be grasped by simple, good-willed people. Instead, she was an imperial power embracing most of the classical world and much else besides. The city proletariat was unfit to exercise political power and Tiberius knew it. This was, of course, the common view of the aristocracy, but all the same it was true: Most plebeians had little education and no property to speak of, many lived in dependence on patrons, few of the *proletarii* were regularly employed, and all envied the wealth of their betters. Alleviating their lot from a material standpoint, however, was a matter of simple compassion likely to appeal to Tiberius as a man of principle, and by giving the commons more hope he could help stabilize matters in the capital. For there had been relative quiet since the plebeians had won the right to legislate for the entire state, but ill will was rising against the aristocracy and its privileges now that Rome was no longer directly threatened by external enemies as she had been throughout most of her history. In the eyes of the commons, the senate was losing its luster.

Tiberius Gracchus's tribunate was during the consulate of Lucius Calpurnius and Publius Mucius Scaevola, the latter a respected jurist who would help him draft some of his most controversial legislation. Tiberius's disquieting legislation bore on the issue of land reform,[1] and he worked for the reallocation of the public lands that had come into the hands of the state through centuries of war. It was the Roman custom to seize territory from defeated enemies, usually a third of their lands, sometimes half. The land was scattered throughout the peninsula, called *ager publicus,* and it was the property of the state as a whole and was meant for distribution to the people, should they want it.

Some had been used to found colonies, a favorite Roman technique to control strategic areas, and some had been given to Romans (and perhaps sometimes to men who held only Latin citizenship). Much of it, however, had fallen into the hands of great men: patricians, nobles, the senatorial aristocracy and wealthy knights. No one was supposed to own more than five hundred *jugera* of the public land, the equivalent of about three hundred acres. The wealthy, however, had ignored this law for decades. Because the aristocracy controlled the state, it controlled the public lands and, in practice if not theory, regarded them largely as their own, should they choose to take them. This seizure of large tracts resulted in the huge slave-worked estates that had so alarmed Tiberius as he made his way to Spain. To be fair to the aristocracy, they were often in a better position to farm the land efficiently. A great deal of land had lain fallow since Hannibal's campaigns in Italy—the peasants had given it up in the face of Carthaginian ravaging, and the heavy conscription required to counter the Carthaginian army had ruined many small holders. The senate, quite apart from its own interests in the public lands, knew that it was better to have more land under cultivation than not—the Roman world was essentially agricultural—and if the knights and aristocracy squatted on abandoned lands and made good use of them, it was, if not fair, at least to the public good from the standpoint of agrarian production. In other words, the issue was not as simple as it must have seemed to the Roman commons.

Some landholders were accused of driving small neighbors from their property and joining it to their estates, and no doubt this happened from time to time. But most of the land that the great men wrongfully held had been simply arrogated from the public lands, or perhaps fenced off to allow grazing. This had not happened overnight—by Tiberius's day much of this public land had been in certain families for years, generations even, and they had improved it through building and agriculture; it seems that this land was regarded so clearly as theirs that it furnished collateral for loans. It was in the face of all this that Tiberius proposed to take back and distribute much of the land to the poor in small parcels, perhaps of up to thirty *jugera.*[2]

This reform was not, perhaps, quite as disturbing to the senate as might have been expected; there may have been mild support for it, at least among those senators who could see, as Tiberius did, that the base of rural small holders was in trouble, and that Italy was flooded with foreigners. The consul Mucius Scaevola and Publius Licinius Crassus, both prominent lawyers, drew up Tiberius's land-reform bill, and their support can be understood in this light. There was further support from Appius Claudius Pulcher, Tiberius's father-in-law and a very prominent patrician, and this meant, of course, support from the Claudian clan generally and its clients and dependents. Tiberius's bother-in-law Scipio Aemilianus gave some support as well, though it appears to have been moderate. Yet this was not a generally popular bill among the highest in Roman society, quite to the contrary, for there were too many who had an interest in maintaining the status quo. This had been evident when, a few years before Tiberius's tribunate, the tribune Gaius Laelius—a friend of Scipio Aemilianus—had proposed some sort of land-reform bill, but faced so much opposition and so feared public disorder that he abandoned it. He earned the nickname *Sapiens,* or "Wise."

Unlike Laelius, Tiberius was not dissuaded by the opposition of the aristocrats and the wealthy. Plutarch, in the manner of all ancient historians, puts a speech into Tiberius's mouth that, though of course not his actual words, must resemble in tone—and probably in substance too—what he told the commons in the forum during the debate on his measure:

> "The savage beasts," said he, "in Italy, have their particular dens, they have their places of repose and refuge; but the men who bear arms, and expose their lives for the safety of their country, enjoy in the meantime nothing more in it but the air and light; and, having no houses or set-tlements of their own, are constrained to wander from place to place with their wives and children." He told them that the commanders were guilty of a ridiculous error, when, at the head of their armies, they exhorted the common soldiers to fight for their sepulchres and altars; when not any amongst so many Romans is possessed of either altar or monument, neither have they any houses of their own, or hearths of their ancestors to defend. They fought indeed, and were slain, but it was to maintain the luxury and the wealth of other men. They were styled the masters of the world, but in the mean time had not one foot of ground which they could call their own.[3]

Tiberius's bill was grounded upon the old law that no one should hold more than five hundred *jugera* of public land, and this was clever of him. Though the old law had clearly fallen into abeyance, yet it must have given a moral force to his bill that would be hard to argue against and, besides, the proposed legislation was mild in view of the problems it ad-dressed. Tiberius's proposed law allowed landowners who already held land in excess of the legal limit to keep up to five hundred *jugera* of it and an additional two hundred and fifty for each son (or possibly only the el-dest). The rest of their land would revert to the state, but the landholders would be paid for what they forfeited. Tiberius's law, however unpalat-able, was not punitive. As Plutarch puts it: "Never did any law appear more moderate and gentle, especially being enacted against such great oppression and avarice."[4]

The senatorial opposition feared, quite rightly, that the legislation would pass into law. If the people with their animus against the aristoc-racy were of a mind to enact the land bill, then there was little that the sen-ate could do directly. Tiberius's bill, though it provided compensation to landholders holding tracts beyond the legal limit, was still troubling to the senate because the legislation set the plebeians directly against senatorial interests. It was disturbing that a tribune would take such an action.

The reason was this: Despite their revolutionary origins and their early duty to protect the powerless from the magistrates, the tribunes, because it was they who proposed bills and put them before the people for the vote, were seen by the senate as a sort of legislative officer. In that capacity they had become one of the senate's useful tools. After all, the senate, for all its prestige, was a deliberative and not a legislative body: It could not pass laws; it only gave advice, just as it had done in the days of the kings. Now the tribunes, though always plebeians, were sometimes senators themselves and generally aspired to high office. They were therefore subject to social and political pressures, and while their persons were sacrosanct during their one-year term of office, they could be prosecuted for any illegal actions afterward. In this way the senate could use them to propose legislation that it thought necessary or to block bills they thought unwise, and to generally keep them under some degree of control. For example, tribunes brought bills to the senate before they were debated in the assembly. The senate deliberated over these proposals and decided whether they merited their support. Bills must often have been modified in accordance with points the senators raised before they were put to the people. If things looked bleak, the senate might use its influence on one of the ten tribunes to interpose his veto against legislation. Each tribune had the right of veto and could, through its exercise, halt the vote on any measure. The senate's understanding with the tribunes, and the patronage that the senators themselves had, until now managed to keep things fairly stable and to the aristocrats' liking.

Tiberius made a serious mistake with his land-reform bill, though: He introduced his bill directly to the popular assembly without first taking it to the senate. There was some precedent because another tribune, Gaius Flaminius, had done so too, but that had been two hundred years before. Tiberius's action was not only a breach of an important custom and a slight to the dignity of the senate, it was only narrowly legal. What did he intend? It would be no surprise if he felt ambiguity toward the senate from whom he had narrowly escaped trial four years before; still it is hard to see what advantage he could gain by throwing away whatever senatorial goodwill he might have had. He was probably just a young man in a hurry.[5] Whatever his motivation, the senate must have viewed him as a difficult man, perhaps a hothead. They mistrusted him.

The senate acted in its accustomed way: It convinced one of Tiberius's fellow tribunes, Marcus Octavius, to oppose the bill. When the people met to vote in the Campus Martius, the traditional voting grounds to the west of the city, Octavius interposed his veto and the land measure failed. Octavius's unexpected action shocked Tiberius, all the more so if, as Plutarch says, they were friends.

Tiberius was now persuaded to take his bill before the senate, but he had injured its dignity, and he got nowhere with it. He bridled at the frustration and proposed another bill, quite similar in fact, but harsher, though exactly in what way is not clear.[6] Marcus Octavius was no more willing to allow the new law to pass than he was the old. The pair debated daily in support of their positions, and Tiberius pointed out that Octavius himself held land beyond the legal limit. He offered to buy the land, ostensibly to remove any personal bias Octavius may have had.

When he was unable to move his bill along, Tiberius may have used his tribunician power to delay official business. Tempers were rising, and he began to sense that his person might not be safe in spite of a tribune's traditional personal inviolability. He carried a sword-stick wherever he went.

Tiberius then took a step even more disturbing to the senate. At a meeting of the popular assembly he proposed to the people that they depose Octavius for obstructing the will of the people. This was unheard of. Though he advanced the attractive argument that a tribune who flouted the people's will was no tribune in fact, and shouldn't hold the office, it was a dangerous stance from the standpoint of constitutional balance. In a strict sense the argument was untrue: The tribunate had long since changed character. Tribunes might still protect the plebeians from the patricians, but they were for the most part legislators elected to one-year terms. More serious than the question of strict legality was the unbalancing effect of the proposal, if carried. If tribunes could be sent packing at the whim of the public, then the senate, the only consistently educated, experienced and mature branch of the government, would lose a good deal of control over the people. Tiberius's proposal was an assault on the constitution: It not only violated custom, but upset the balance of power between Rome's two populations.

Tiberius assembled the people to vote on Octavius's deposition, including large numbers of poor who came from the countryside. Octavius would not relent, and the voting went forward until seventeen of the thirty-five voting tribes had decided against him. Tiberius asked him to relinquish his office at this point, a gesture that would have saved Octavius from the humiliation of being the only tribune to have been shorn of his office.

Octavius would not step down, though, and the voting continued until he was deposed. A riot followed as the people tried to get at Octavius as his senatorial supporters hustled him away. In the aftermath, Tiberius had one of his own clients elected tribune in Octavius's place. The road was clear and the land bill passed. The senate now had real reason for disquiet. All questions about the bill's merits aside, Tiberius's cal-

lous method had succeeded and there was now precedent for the impeachment of tribunes. A valuable check on bills that might be passed in
the heat of the moment had been cast away.

A commission of three was set up to carry out the land law's provisions and to establish some colonies as well. Tiberius was a member and
saw to it that the other two were men he could trust: his father-in-law,
Appius Claudius Pulcher, and his brother, Gaius Sempronius Gracchus.
Gaius, ten years his junior, was not in Rome at the time, but was serving
in Spain at the siege of Numantia under Scipio Aemilianus.

The senate managed to stymie the Gracchan land commission at first
when it refused to pay more than a pittance toward the commission's expenses, which were significant as they had to stock the new farms. At this
moment a lucky thing happened for the Gracchans: Attalus, king of
Pergamum,[7] died, willing his kingdom to the Roman people; a great deal
of money was about to come into the treasury. But how to get it?

Attalus's legacy offered Tiberius an effective weapon against the sen
ate, but it led him to another misstep. He either passed a law through the
popular assembly, or threatened the senate that he would do so, by which
the commission would be funded with the Pergamene money. In face of
this threat the senate relented and the work of the commission went on.

Tiberius had been too forward again. It was bad enough that he had
affronted the senate by first taking his bill to the people, and then used an
unconstitutional method to bring it to a vote. Now he had threatened the
senate and interfered in both finance and foreign affairs in a single
sweep. There was real danger here: Tiberius, bolstered by the support of
the urban population, was impinging on the senate's exclusive
provinces. As a practical matter the commons, whether small holders
coming to Rome for elections or the mob in the city that generally dominated them, were unfit to make decisions in any of these spheres, and the
impeachment of Octavius showed there was little to prevent further en-
croachment on senatorial prerogative.

And so Tiberius now faced solid senatorial opposition, and perhaps
had expected it. His actions—both those that might be narrowly constitutional and those that were not—clearly compromised the senate, but he
may not have considered very carefully the consequences. He may have
viewed some of the senate with personal distaste over his treatment in
the Mancinus treaty reversal, and he clearly fell into the habit of rash action; but given his station, upbringing and earlier life, it is unlikely that
he really intended any revolutionary political or constitutional changes.
He wanted to help the state attack a fundamental problem, and do it fast.

His concern with the land issue demonstrates his interest in the state as a whole, and not in the lower classes alone, if only because of its military aspect. A Roman noble, whatever his sympathies with the poor, could hardly have seriously considered transferring all—or even most—political power to commoners unfit to use it. But if he didn't consider the rift he was creating to be important, the senate knew better.

Besides, Tiberius's reforms, though helpful to many, were not really enough to permanently reestablish the small Italian farmer as a class: They were already too few, and slave-labor would remain a problem so long as Rome conquered and cared to enslave prisoners. Some senators may have been doubtful about the effectiveness of the Gracchan land reform and asked themselves if it were worth such social and constitutional danger to the state.

But if Tiberius didn't see the constitutional implications of what he was doing, he apparently felt threatened by those senators who did. His office was only a year long and he might face prosecution by the senate, or he may have judged that his land reform would be their victim, rather than he. In any case he took one final—and to the senate—most menacing step. He sought reelection as a tribune for 132.

As with his earlier actions this was only dubiously constitutional, for while the law didn't expressly forbid it, tribunes did not seek reelection, and custom was as strong as law in Rome. The senators did not like the prospect of a tribune who got what he wanted by tramelling them. At this point Tiberius's motives were of less concern to the senate than his methods, but all the same the senate and the people now stood at the juncture between the procedure of the law and its substance. In other words, Tiberius had abused procedure to achieve his goals, and if his actions were allowed to stand the popular assembly would feel entitled to dispose of issues that had never really been within its purview.

The election for the tribunate of 132 was held around harvest time, and Tiberius could not count on floods of peasants to appear for the election as they had for the passage of the land bill. All the same, there was great concern in the senate that he would regain his office, and this fear would only have been sharpened by new laws Tiberius apparently proposed at this time for the benefit of others besides the peasants. It is uncertain exactly what these proposals were, but they may have included shortening the term of service for soldiers and granting a right of appeal, in certain cases, from the courts to the popular assembly. He had begun to dabble in the military and judicial spheres and was clearly trying to broaden his constituency. There may already have been a decision, at least on the part of some senators, that violence would have to be used. Tiberius's appeals to other interests came late in his tribunate, and they may have been hasty. He was perhaps just trying to stay alive.

By the time of the elections Tiberius was again concerned with his safety, and a number of his supporters put tents up around his house and guarded it the night before the elections. The morning of the elections he left the house, ignoring bad omens it is said—he struck his left foot badly on the threshold, crows dropped a piece of tile at his feet. At the assembly Tiberius was well received and his friends and supporters surrounded him as a protection. Before things had gotten too far along, however, a riot erupted—probably as a result of men of the senatorial faction trying to press their way into the assembly.

The senate itself, alarmed at the prospect of Tiberius's reelection, was meeting in the Temple of Fides on the Capitol just in front of the temple of Jupiter Optimus Maximus, overlooking the forum some five hundred yards below. As word of the rioting came to the session the senators grew extremely alarmed. A report arrived that Tiberius had touched his head to indicate he wished a crown—wished to make himself king. The signal was almost certainly something else; Plutarch says that during the altercation at the assembly he "lifted his hand to his head, wishing to intimate the great danger which he apprehended himself to be in." It seems, though, that this was sufficient to move part of the senate. Publius Scipio Nasica, the Pontifex Maximus, chief priest of the Roman state—and distant cousin of Tiberius Gracchus—demanded that the consul Mucius Scaevola punish Tiberius as a tyrant. Scaevola replied that he would not be the first to do violence and he would not allow a free man to be put to death before sentence; however, he would not allow a law to stand if Tiberius had provoked an unlawful vote.

To Nasica this was mere equivocation. He rushed from the Temple and called out to all who wished to save the republic to follow him.

> Then the best men, the senate, the larger and better part of the knights, and plebeians who had not been turned by dangerous counsels rushed upon Gracchus standing in that place with his followers and riling up a crowd from all over Italy.[8]

These senators and knights were the most powerful men in Rome, and commonly went about with large entourages as a matter of status. They might walk through the forum with scores of clients in attendance, sometimes more. We can imagine these clients milling about, waiting for their patrons to emerge from the senate session, ready to do as they asked. They formed constituencies obliged to act as they were told, and were prey to the excitement of the day. The knights, many of whom had substantially the same interests in this matter as the senators themselves, would have crowded the neighborhood as well, waiting to hear what the senate might decide, and they too would be well attended. When Scipio Nasica called for action, he had a large and willing audience. The men quickly armed themselves with truncheons and staves and pushed aside the common people as they approached the forum.

As they flooded into the assembly, the senatorial faction swept away the Gracchan supporters, clubbing many and killing some outright. Tiberius himself tried to flee; when caught by his toga, he flung it off and ran in his tunic. He did not get far. Running down the slope of the Capitol, the senators' men on his heels, he tumbled over a man who had been knocked down, and one of his fellow tribunes, Publius Satureius, struck him with part of a broken bench or stool. A certain Lucius Rufus claimed the second blow. Tiberius Sempronius Gracchus was dead along with some three hundred of his followers. Their bodies, including that of Tiberius, were not given over to their families—as an affront to the Gracchan party they were tossed into the Tiber by night.

This was the first political row to end in bloodshed since the expulsion of the kings three hundred and seventy years before. As Velleius Paterculus says: "This was the beginning in the city of Rome of civil bloodshed and unpunished swordsmen."[9] The senate had come away from the debacle maintaining power, but the cost would prove too high. The people would never forget what the senators had done; their anger would smoulder for years, waiting for a chance of revenge, a chance that might come if they could support new men for the magisterial offices, or even for the consulship.

The senate, meanwhile, pressed its advantage the next year under the consuls for 132, Publius Popilius Laenas and Publius Rupilius: A great number of Gracchan supporters were abused. Many were tried and put to death, like Tiberius's Greek friend Diophanes, and others were banished. Blossius of Cumae fled east across the Mediterranean to Pergamum, there to follow the adventurer Aristonicus, a bastard of the Pergamene royal house, who had seized the kingdom and talked about establishing a country where all men would be free and equal.

Back in Rome, the land-reform legislation was not repealed. The senate left it alone, though perhaps not supporting it with enthusiasm.

CHAPTER 4

The Breach Widens

THE SENATE THOUGHT IT POLITIC THAT TIBERIUS'S KILLER, Publius Cornelius Scipio Nasica, should leave town. He was sent as ambassador to Asia, where he died the following year. Unfortunately, the example of political murder would not be forgotten.[1]

The people kept Tiberius in their hearts and were unhappy even with their national hero Scipio Aemilianus when they learned that he had expressed rather mild disapproval of his brother-in-law when, still at Numantia, he learned of his death. When he returned to Rome he was haled to the rostrum by a tribune to account for his reaction to Tiberius's death; he replied:

> ... that if he had had it in mind to take over the state, then his death was lawful. And when everyone at the assembly shouted at him he said "How can I be frightened of you, when I have so often stood without fear at the sound of armed enemies?, you to whom Italy is a step-mother?"[2]

Scipio's slight was meant to remind the mob that many of them were not "true" Romans, many of them not even of Italian origin: They were now freedmen but before that slaves. It displayed Scipio's natural patrician bias—nothing surprising there—but more than that it expressed rather elegantly what most of his fellows felt for the lower elements of their society—that they were a different people, almost alien. The late republican aristocracy of patricians, nobles and senators viewed the lower plebeians just as the patricians of centuries before had viewed them. Nothing had really changed in that regard; some families rose to the aristocracy from common origins, but they joined and helped form a group as exclusive as that of the patricians of old.

With the death of Tiberius Gracchus the senate reasserted control over the republic, but the naked application of force wouldn't conduce to stability. Still, the mob was cowed, and there were any number of distractions abroad. In 133 the former kingdom of Pergamum, whose finances had helped to fund the Gracchan land settlement, had become the province of Asia. And then it had gone into revolt. Aristonicus, an illegitimate son of Eumenes, who had held the throne of Pergamum before Attalus, had set himself against Rome. Publius Licinius Crassus, a member of the Gracchan land commission—and Gaius Gracchus's father-in-law—went off to lead an army against him, and got himself killed. Aristonicus wouldn't be brought to heel for three years. The commission continued its work, however, and the plebeians continued to elect Gracchan partisans as its members.

Scipio Aemilianus wound matters up in Spain and returned home where he became involved in the business of the land commission, but as a supporter of allied Italian cities, which complained that the land commission was redistributing their land in violation of treaties they held with Rome. Scipio urged that disputes of this kind go to one of the consuls for settlement. The duties of the commission were given over to the consul, who then left for military operations in Illyricum, effectively halting the land distribution. Scipio died shortly after this at the age of fifty-six, the premier statesman and general of his time. There were some unfounded allegations that he had been murdered, but they would seem to be only reflections of the passions of the day. His moderation and experience would be missed.

The land commission was reinstated after Scipio's death, probably in 128 B.C., and continued its work. Meanwhile Gaius Gracchus was sent as quaestor on a campaign in Sicily, and then to Sardinia in the same capacity under one of the consuls in 126. There was difficulty in getting supplies to the army, but Gaius managed to get wheat from King Micipsa of Numidia, son of Scipio Africanus's ally Masinissa. The king also sent an embassy to Rome to tell what he had done. The envoys stated that they had cooperated out of regard for Gaius Gracchus; this caused bad feelings. Like his brother Tiberius, he found himself in difficulty for solving a problem that his superior could not.

His real problem, however, came when his commander's commission was extended another year. Gaius returned home and faced charges by the censors that he had breached his duty. In his defense,

He made it appear that he had served twelve years in the army, whereas others are obliged to serve only ten; that he had continued quaestor to the general three years, whereas he might by law have returned at the end of one year; and alone of all who went on the expedition, he had carried out a full and had brought home an empty purse, while others, after drinking up the wine they had carried out with them, brought back the wine-jars filled again with gold and silver from the war.[3]

Putting aside the merits of his argument, he was an eloquent speaker—perhaps the best in Rome—and he would use this talent to advance his brother's programs when he had the chance. The senate had silenced Tiberius, but they would find as great a threat in the equally principled Gaius.

And there were other men of principle. The consul of 125 was Marcus Fulvius Flaccus, also a member of the land commission. As a land commissioner he had to struggle with the large Italian landholders who, as before, claimed that redistributing the land infringed on their rights as citizens of allied states under various treaties with Rome. Flaccus had a solution to this, which, he must have thought, would alleviate another problem too. The allies commonly supplied at least half the soldiers in a Roman army and sometimes more, and while they paid for their alliance in blood, they didn't receive the financial benefits that Rome did from conquest. They saw Rome getting rich on their labor and sacrifice, and there was widespread grumbling.

Flaccus proposed this: In return for submitting to the redistribution of land, the Italian allies would be raised to Roman citizenship or, if they preferred, could retain their allied citizenship and take a right of appeal from the decisions of Roman magistrates.

The allies were quite pleased at the possibility, though the same could not be said of the senate, which opposed it. Rather conveniently for the senate, Massilia[4] in southern Gaul, a Greek city and ally of Rome, petitioned for help in fighting barbarian tribes. The senate promptly assigned Flaccus the province of Gaul and sent him off with an army to meet them. He successfully fought the Saluvii, the Ligurii and the Vocontii in 125 and 124. He returned home to celebrate a triumph. Gaius Sextius Calvinus, a consul of 124, then took the Saluvii's main town and established the colony of Aquae Sextiae (which he named for himself). It was essentially a military colony: He stocked it with veterans to hold down the countryside. Further campaigns brought this area, known as Transalpine Gaul, completely under Roman control by 121.

But in Italy, there was still unrest over the issue of citizenship. In 125, after Flaccus's proposal had been quashed and its author sent to fight in the provinces, the city of Fregellae rebelled—formerly a loyal colony of Rome. The revolt was brutally crushed by the grim Lucius Opimius, who would show his colors once more in 121 against his fellow Romans.

It was probably after the Fregellan rebellion that the senate decided to move a bit on the question of citizenship; it extended it to all Italians who held public office. This was a step in the right direction, but it was not enough. The issue would continue to simmer, unnoticed in Rome, for more than three decades and then it would explode.

Some Romans, though, were not short-sighted on the issue. Like Flaccus, Gaius Gracchus was concerned with it too and he would make a push for it, even though it was not a popular idea with the Roman public. But he could see much farther than they; he knew that the spread of citizenship would ease tension between Rome and her allies. It would ultimately be stabilizing. He was elected tribune for 123, ten years after his brother had held the office; he continued his brother's work. Velleius Paterculus gives his opinion:

> Ten years having passed, the same madness which had seized Tiberius Gracchus seized Gaius, his brother, who possessed all the same virtues and vices as he, though he excelled him in talent and oratory.[5]

And Gaius met the same end as his brother, and at the hands of the same kind of men.

Paterculus is right when he says that Gaius was the more astute. He had suffered the horror of his brother's murder, the humiliation of having no funeral for him and the strain of having to rub shoulders for years with the men who had done it. But in the course of this he had learned something that his brother had not realized, at least not until shortly before his end: that a social reformer needed a wider political base if he were to challenge the senate. The poor were useful, yes, but they were fickle and too unsophisticated to always recognize what was in their interests. Citizenship for the allies, for instance.

When he was elected one of the ten tribunes for 123, Gaius quickly became the most powerful man in the state. Tiberius's reputation among the people and their natural affection for his brother gave him tremendous support from the very start, and his oratory was remarkable. His way of speaking was a winning trait in Roman society, a society in which common people could seldom read and the spoken word could stir violent emotions in a way that is largely lost today. We can imagine him, a young man in his unbordered toga (a tribune could not wear the purple stripe of the aristocracy), speaking to a crowd, in their very presence, reading their faces, gauging their temper, asking questions, replying with elegant, prepared answers. A flamboyant orator could play such people like a fiddle, especially Gaius, who was active: He would stride about the rostrum and sometimes pull his toga down from his shoulder, "the first of all the Romans that used such gestures."[6] Gaius could, in an excess of feeling, also ruin a speech, and so, as a remedy, he

> made use of an ingenious servant of his, one Licinius, who stood constantly behind him with a sort of pitchpipe, or instrument to regulate the voice by, and whenever he perceived his master's tone alter and break with anger, he struck a soft note with his pipe, on hearing which Caius immediately checked the vehemence of his passion and his voice, grew quieter, and allowed himself to be recalled to temper.[7]

He also gave his speeches facing the people and not the senate house, implying that he addressed the people directly and not at the sufferance of the senate.

But while his unquestioned mastery of oratory was useful in handling the mob, the mob wasn't enough support. He needed another part of society whose interests could differ from the aristocracy, and he found that part in the knights.

The knights had always been a separate order between the poor plebeians and the senators. Many of them were very rich and their interests were often not far different from those of senators. In fact, the senate was kept up to strength by knights who had held the offices from which the senate enrolled its members: curule aedileships, praetorships and so on. But even so, their interests were not precisely the same. Many of the knights were businessmen, many were publicans—men who handled what the government might have done had there been a bureaucracy. They set up corporations to win contracts from the senators to build public works, supplied the army and lent money for wars. Yet in 167 the senate had prevented them from working the lucrative mines in Macedonia. Their economic power was growing, but their political power didn't seem to match it, and they may have been chafing under the social exclusiveness of much of the senate. These were the men whom Gaius Gracchus had in mind as allies when he began his consulship.

As tribune he legislated on many things, but the order of the legislation is not clear; historians have different views.[8] Much of it seems to have been enacted in 123, during his first tribunate. Among his measures was a land redistribution law that replaced that of his brother from 133. The historian Peter Brunt argues that it was not much different from Tiberius's law and probably reflected a few changes suggested by experience in administering it.

As always, the land commission needed money for its work. Gaius's brother had gotten that money from Pergamum, and Gaius himself would have it that way too, and all by way of helping the knights. He passed a law by which the taxes of Asia (Aristonicus had been put down and the province restored) would be collected by publicans, in other words by tax farmers. These publicans paid the republic the taxes up front and then collected the money for themselves. It was a useful arrangement for both parties: The state received a sum certain and received it immediately, while any economic risk fell on the tax farmer. In practice, the tax farmers were hard and made fortunes in their work. By subjecting Asia to publicans, Gaius increased the revenue from it, and increased his popularity with those knights involved.

Public works were not neglected either: Gaius was an enthusiastic road builder and personally determined their courses. He had them marked every mile and set up milestones giving the distances to various towns. Stone blocks were placed along the way to help riders mount horses.

He alleviated the lot of the urban poor and enacted a law for the distribution of grain to the city populace at a price below market cost. This measure may have been intended in part to detach some of the poor from their patrons, or to loosen the bond. This would have been useful to Gaius but, like his brother, he seems to have been genuinely concerned about the poor. In keeping with this, Gaius also lightened the lot of the common soldiers, something he must have judged to be too severe during his military service in Spain, Sicily and Sardinia. He legislated that the state provide soldiers their clothing at its expense. He also enacted a law forbidding the conscription of boys under eighteen. The practice must have been common enough that these young men needed protection; it was another sign that the traditional base of the Roman army was declining.

Gaius Gracchus proposed and founded some colonies, and at some point, either in 123 during his first tribunate or in 122 during his second, he founded, pursuant to the *Lex Rubria*, Rome's first overseas colony on the site of Carthage. It was called Junonia, and its size and the terms of its colonization were unusual. There were to be six thousand colonists—a large number—and some of them were to be allowed two hundred *jugera* of land, not the customary parcel of thirty. This may have been to attract and support men who were well enough off to manage affairs in a colony so far from the motherland.

The colonization was controversial; some opposed its foundation, probably on the ground that it was too far away to defend easily if it got into trouble. Rome had responsibilities enough to allies and client kingdoms far away without increasing her obligations by establishing citizens in North Africa. Nonetheless, the colony of Narbo, in Gallia Transalpina, followed Gaius's tribuneships in 121.

The senate watched the tribune and bided its time during his first tribunate. It must have been quite provoked when Gaius put through a law by which the senate would have to determine which two provinces it would assign to the new consuls months before the election. This didn't prevent the senate from choosing which provinces would go to the consuls, but it did help the electorate decide whom they wished to elect consuls. Important provinces—or those involved in war—might suggest to the people whom they should elect. From the standpoint of the electorate, it was helpful—votes could be cast more intelligently—but from the standpoint of the senate, the arrangement was clumsy. If conditions changed before the elections the best men might not, in fact, have been elected. More to the point, though, Gaius's law was an intrusion into a traditional realm of the senate, foreign affairs.

Gaius, unlike his brother, was elected to a second, consecutive tribuneship without any public disturbance. The senate had decided to oppose him, though not with violence. Instead it set another tribune of 122 against him, Marcus Livius Drusus. Drusus's tactic for undermining Gaius's support was direct: He promised the poor more than Gaius did. He proposed a dozen new colonies, each for three thousand men, and he proposed that no rent be collected from those who had received land allotments from the state since 133. Further, there was to be no scourging of Latin citizens, not even on military service.

These were attractive promises, but it's doubtful they were ever seriously intended by the senate as anything more than manipulative distractions. The colonies were never founded, and the law against scourging Latins wasn't passed.[9]

But Gaius had his friends among the knights as well as the people, and he took a step to solidify his relationship with them and at the same time clean up the courts that tried cases of extortion against provincial governors. These courts were manned exclusively by senators, and it was their duty to try their fellows when there were charges that they had extorted monies from the provincials. In some recent cases senators had been lenient to the senatorial defendants, and this did not endear Rome to the provincials.

Gaius's solution was simple: He transferred these courts of extortion from the senators to the knights, who would thenceforth try these cases. As provincial governors the defendants were senators, and this arrangement exposed them, to some degree, to the power of the knights. Publicans in a given province who felt that the senatorial provincial governor had not treated them fairly (perhaps he had not given them free enough rein to oppress the tax payers) were now in a position to threaten a senator when he returned from his province—sometimes even accusing the senator of extortion himself. It became obvious later that this shift in jurisdiction was a problem, but in the short term it may not have been evident to Gaius.

This measure accomplished two things: It gave the knights power over certain of the senators—which should have redounded to Gaius's benefit—and gave the knights more of a sense of identity. Having done this, Gaius probably felt he could count on their support and not only that of the urban populace, which Drusus was chipping away at.

After this he sailed for Junonia, where he spent two months supervising the establishment of the colony. During that time false stories were circulated in Rome by Gaius's enemies to the effect that things were going badly at the colony, and his popularity began to sink. It seems doubtful that such stories could really have been the cause of his declining popularity; it is more probable that his absence was the cause as much as anything. The urban mob was a source of power, but it was short-sighted. These men needed to be coddled and flattered and stirred, and Gaius wasn't there to do it. They listened favorably to his opponents. When he returned from Junonia he was unable to legislate his final reform: full Roman citizenship for the Latins and Latin citizenship for the allies.

Gaius Fannius, the consul of 122, got the mob heated up against extending citizenship. Perhaps he appealed to their pride as Romans. The mob may have had almost nothing else, but they had that honor at least, and they were unwilling to share it, even with countrymen who spoke the same language and fought for them. The allies were not permitted to come within five miles of Rome while the issue was being debated. It failed to pass; the tribune Drusus may have vetoed it.

Gaius Gracchus's run was over. He failed to be elected for a third tribuneship; his support among the urban population and the knights had largely dissolved. It was time now for the senate to act. The year was 121 and the new consuls were the brutal Lucius Opimius, destroyer of Fregellae, and Quintus Fabius Maximus. In Opimius the senate would find its destructive champion. His consulship was known both for the murder of Gaius Gracchus and for something altogether more innocent and trivial: An extremely good wine vinted in the year of his consulate became known as "Opimian."

Julius Obsequens, the collector of prodigies, tells us something interesting about this year: "A pack of wolves knocked over the markers which had been placed during the division of fields by Gaius Gracchus."[10] Perhaps Lucius Opimius was that wolf.

A tribune, Minucius Rufus, proposed to repeal the *Lex Rubria,* the law that authorized the colony of Junonia. He was doubtless a mouthpiece of the senate as Drusus had been the year before. The senators prepared, no doubt marshalling their clients among the voting tribes and urging them with promises and threats to vote as they were told. The consul Opimius took a rather more direct precaution. He brought troops into the city, something never done before: footsoldiers and mercenary archers from Crete.[11]

Neither Gaius Gracchus nor his supporter Marcus Fulvius Flaccus, a consul of 125, was prepared to accept the repeal of the law lying down, but they were private citizens now and without much direct political influence; from a legal standpoint there was little they could do if the senate was poised to push the repeal through the assembly. This is not to say that they weren't extremely popular with a large part of the population, though, and the senate must have been uneasy about Gaius and Fulvius; at least some of the senators, like Opimius, were waiting for some breach of the peace to allow them to reassert control without regard to the niceties of the law.

The day came to vote on the repeal of the *Lex Rubria,* and a large number of both factions, including Gaius and Fulvius themselves, met on the capitol that morning. When the consul Opimius took the auguries, one of his attendants, Quintus Antyllius, carried away the entrails of the sacrificial victim and taunted Fulvius and a band of his friends, telling them to move away and make room for good men. Tempers were hot and some of the Gracchans answered the provocation; they stabbed Antyllius to death with styluses. Here was the senate's pretext.

Gaius knew it—he bitterly upbraided his supporters for the action and pointed out how they had given the senate cause to take action against them. And the consul knew it too.

Opimius, immediately seizing the occasion thus offered, was in great delight, and urged the people to revenge; but there happening a great shower of rain on a sudden, it put an end to the business of that day.[12]

The next day, Opimius called the senate together, and while he was speaking the body of Antyllius was brought into the forum and set down in front of the senate house—just as he had arranged it. There was loud mourning and feigned surprise and ignorance of what was happening. The senate came out of the house and viewed the body. As Opimius had wished, they expressed horror and disgust over what had happened— they were now in the right mood to act. Withdrawing to the house, the senators passed a decree of a new sort, later known as the *senatus consultum ultimum,* which presented the opinion of the senate that the republic itself was in danger. It didn't enlarge the power of the magistrates, but it suggested to them that their acts in defense of the state would have the backing of the senate.

Opimius then ordered the senators and knights to arm themselves and to be ready early the next morning. Everyone was to bring armed servants with them. The Cretan archers would be there too.

Fulvius gathered the Gracchan supporters around Gaius and himself. The crowd posted themselves as guards around the two men's houses throughout the night. Banded together as the Gracchans were, they gave color to the senate's claim that they constituted a menace that must be met by force. In the morning those who had guarded Fulvius's house were issued weapons that he had taken from the Gauls during his campaigns in Gallia Transalpina several years before, and the Gracchans then seized the Aventine Hill. Perhaps this was for tactical reasons, perhaps it was symbolic; it was on the Aventine that the plebeians had built their temple to Ceres centuries before.

Gracchus and Fulvius tried to negotiate—Fulvius sent his seventeen-year-old son down to the forum with a herald's staff in his hand to put terms to the senate.

The greatest part of the assembly were inclinable to accept of the proposals; but Opimius said that it did not become them to send messengers and capitulate with the senate, but to surrender at discretion to the laws, like loyal citizens, and endeavour to merit their pardon by submission. He commanded the youth not to return, unless they would comply with these conditions.[13]

Plutarch reports that Gaius was willing to go before the senate himself, but was dissuaded by his friends. Fulvius sent his son before the senate a second time, but Opimius seized him and kept him prisoner. It was then that Opimius sent his troops against the Aventine, where the archers—professional soldiers—were particularly effective against the civilian crowd. They killed and wounded many of them, and the rest fled. Fulvius and his eldest son fled to a bathhouse, but were discovered and killed. Gaius got to the Temple of Diana, where he was prevented from suicide by two close friends, Licinius and a knight named Pomponius. Instead they urged him to escape.

His followers were melting away—there was a promise of pardons. Gaius and his two friends ran down to the Tiber, Opimius's men on their heels, until they reached a narrow bridge, apparently the Pons Sublicius, where, centuries before, the legendary Horatius Cocles and his companions had held off the Etruscan army. There his friends Pomponius and Licinius[14] turned about and held off Gaius's enemies at sword point, just as Horatius had done.

Gaius continued to run, his only companion a slave named either Euporus or Philocrates. The people along his route

> encouraged him, and wished him success, as standers-by may do to those who are engaged in a race, but nobody either lent him any assistance, or would furnish him with a horse, though he asked for one; for his enemies had gained ground, and got very near him.[15]

His end was near; he must have sensed it. He stopped in a wood dedicated to the Furies and there asked his slave to behead him. The slave, after killing him, then killed himself—or in an even more affecting version of the story he hugged Gaius so tightly that their pursuers had to kill him first before they could kill his master.

The aftermath was grisly. Opimius, to encourage his followers, demanded the heads of Gaius and Fulvius—he promised to pay for them with their weight in gold. A further macabre detail is probably untrue: that a friend of Opimius, one Septimuleius, snatched the head from another and poured lead into the skull to increase its weight. As for Gaius's companion, "There were others who brought the head of Fulvius too, but, being mean, inconsiderable persons, were turned away without the promised reward."[16]

During the rioting and the treason trials that followed—under the control of Opimius and the senators—three thousand Gracchan supporters are said to have been killed or executed. The number must be exaggerated, but the exaggeration shows how deeply the massacre and trials affected the people, and what impression it left on their minds. The senatorial view of Opimius was milder. As Velleius Paterculus stated it: "The only vile crime attributed to Opimius is that he put a price on the head, I would not say of Gracchus, but of a Roman citizen, to be given and paid for in gold."[17] The commons did not see Opimius in quite this light. They knew of people, friends perhaps, who had suffered at Opimius's hands during and after the rioting. Fulvius's youngest son, for instance, who had gone with a herald's staff to parley with the senate and been arrested. As he was led to prison he was seen by a friend of his, an Etruscan augur who could see what was in store for the boy. He asked him how he would like to handle the matter. The boy understood the oblique question: He rammed his head into the doorpost of the prison, killing himself.

The Gracchi and their deaths impressed the people immensely. Even though the senatorial party had tossed Gaius's body, and Flaccus's too—and those of all their slain followers—into the Tiber as they had done with those of Tiberius and his supporters a decade before, the people, though intimidated, could not forget them. They left offerings at the places of their deaths and said prayers there. The people put up statues of them, even a statue to their mother Cornelia. If the people were kept in mind of what could happen to those who opposed the senate, the senate in turn was reminded of the reformers who had opposed it so effectively, and of the people who had given them the power to do so. Both sides were now openly at odds, though the senate, for the time being, held the whip hand.

The Gracchi were true reformers, whatever unintended consequences followed their actions. Tiberius had served his city loyally, showing remarkable bravery in two campaigns and extricating an entire army from an impossible situation in Spain. The centerpiece of his tribunate was his land law to help the poor. Yet he showed no signs of trying to foment any kind of revolution. His reforms were radical in the true sense of the word—they went to the root of the problems that concerned him. But they were not revolutionary—there is no good evidence that he intended to upset the basic order of the state. He wanted to save its underpinnings, not destroy its head.

Gaius's concerns were much the same. He tried to help the poor as his brother had done: He continued with land reform, introduced a grain dole, paid for soldiers' clothing and protected boys from military service.

That he fought unsuccessfully to extend citizenship—a measure he knew would be unpopular at Rome itself—suggests that he would undertake measures he thought worthy, even at the expense of putting off his supporters. Had the Romans listened to him, thirty years later they would have avoided a bloody war.

At the same time, some of Tiberius's political maneuverings had been unconstitutional, or very close to it. Gaius's actions, though apparently not so, were equally alarming to the senate, perhaps as an extension of his brother's programs and because, in a larger sense, his approach implied that political power rested entirely in the people. Between the two brothers the senatorial fields of foreign policy, finance and the judiciary had been invaded, and with the impeachment of Octavius in 133 the senate had lost an important check on the people's power to legislate. The senate was losing its grip on the government, and its response to this had twice been murderous. Although it may not have been entirely apparent at the time, the state was slowly coming apart. As a gesture to unity, however, the senate ordered Opimius to restore the Temple of Concord in the forum.

CHAPTER 5

The Jugurthine War

ONE OF SCIPIO'S LIEUTENANTS IN THE NUMANTINE CAMPAIGN was a young man named Gaius Marius, a Roman citizen and knight from the country. He was a born soldier, coarse and consumed by two desires: to fight and to hold high office. He led the Roman cavalry at Numantia, but over time would rise to become one of the most powerful men in Roman history and, in a haphazard way, dismantle the constitution on his way there. His first steps to real authority would be taken in Numidia a few years hence in a campaign against a North African prince, a certain Jugurtha. Oddly, Jugurtha was serving at the head of a Numidian contingent under Scipio, light horse mostly—the same who had done such useful service for Hannibal in Italy two generations before. The two cavalry commanders must have been well acquainted.

Marius was born near Arpinum about 155 B.C. To gain political advantage with the common people he later claimed to have risen from poverty, but actually his father had been some sort of local knight or noble and he held the Roman citizenship—it had been granted to Arpinum in 188. Far from being a mere son of the soil, as he'd later have the ignorant believe, Marius was a knight, and though his fortune must originally have been modest by the standards of the Roman aristocracy, it would not have been entirely negligible. Whatever the exact measure of his wealth, he would add immensely to it through war and politics.

Marius was a rough man; in this, at least, he did resemble the commoners, and he was able to communicate this. He had the common touch, which, combined with common sense, bravery and steadiness, made him the general of his age and the only man to hold seven consulships.

He didn't have much truck with Greek culture either, and this set him apart from the Roman aristocracy, which had taken to it without reservation, as had the Gracchi and the Scipiones. Plutarch recounts:

> He is said never to have either studied Greek, or to have use of that language in any matter of consequence; thinking it ridiculous to bestow time in that learning, the teachers of which were little better than slaves.[1]

He enjoyed war and command, and the simple tastes and habits he had acquired growing up in the country served him well in his military career. These attributes endeared him to soldiers, particularly to those who had served under aristocratic commanders who had shown themselves both effete and incompetent. After the disastrous campaigns in Spain, the soldiers were likely to have regarded overrefinement as a telltale of military incompetence. Like his men, Marius was certainly not effete—and unlike much of the nobility, he was not militarily incompetent. He must have been a comfort to them, even when he kept them under his customarily strict discipline.

His toughness must have been legendary. There is a story that his legs had tumors that marred their appearance; he decided to have them taken out surgically.

> . . . he determined to put himself into the hands of an operator; when, without being tied, he stretched out one of his legs, and silently, without changing countenance, endured most excessive torments in the cutting, never either flinching or complaining; but when the surgeon went to the other, he declined to have it done, saying, "I see the cure is not worth the pain."[2]

If it does nothing more, the story shows how people saw Marius: as a man of incredible inner strength.

Marius began his army career as a cavalry officer, probably in 132, under Scipio Aemilianus in Spain. He enhanced his reputation there when he killed one of the enemy in single combat—and in full view of Scipio. All of this led, we are told, to a telling incident at a subsequent social engagement: The question arose where another commander of Scipio's stature might be found.[3] It was obvious flattery, but the general replied all the same.

. . . Scipio, gently clapping Marius on the shoulder as he sat next him, replied, "Here, perhaps." So promising was his early youth of his future greatness, and so discerning was Scipio to detect the distant future in the present first beginnings.[4]

Marius was close, then, to Rome's leading general and, operating out of his headquarters, familiar with the Numidian prince Jugurtha. He was the commander of some Numidian troops—for the most part they must have been light cavalry, always the strength of that nation. Marius himself was a cavalry commander years later in Numidia—he was already in charge of Roman or allied Italian horse under Scipio. Perhaps they discussed things from time to time, the prince and the legate.

Marius was by nature a soldier—much in his later life would show it. But Rome, however warlike, still honored the civil over the military. There was an old Latin expression: *Gladius cedet togae* ("The sword gives place to the toga"). If a man would be great, he must be great in the civil sphere. Military service was an obligation—and one that could enhance a man's reputation and let him rise—but the capstone of a Roman's career was not merely to be a military legate. A Roman of the right station dreamed of being consul and thereby ennobling his family. For the very select few there was even the office of censor—a position held by former consuls who had the responsibility, among others, of deciding whom to expel from the senate as morally unfit.

Marius was ambitious, though not a patrician, not a noble, not even a senator. Still, as a young man he probably at least dreamed of a consulship—his later actions suggest that this might have been the case. But the consulship was a jewel carefully handed back and forth among a score of families; there was almost no hope for a *novus homo,* or "new man" to touch it. But if the consulship were out of reach, there was still a good deal of honor in reaching high office.

Marius's family were clients of the patrician Metelli, one of the most powerful—perhaps the most powerful—in Rome. With their help he was elected one of the tribunes for 119. His actions in that office show that he was independently minded, or at least that he didn't feel the need to truckle to his patrons. It became plain later that he wasn't an astute politician, and we may see some evidence of it even now.

During his tribuneship Marius managed at different times to favor and to alienate both the commons and the nobles. Roman politics was not party politics—there were in fact no established political parties with given aims. Roman politics held something of the moment in it; it addressed immediate problems, it was short-sighted (the Gracchi were an exception), it was sometimes a contest of personalities, sometimes a contest over a particular program and sometimes a naked struggle between the rich and the poor. Seen this way, Marius's actions as tribune were probably not as incoherent as they seem—they were probably legitimate responses to current, pressing problems. But he doesn't appear to have handled matters with much of a view of consolidating any base of support, either among the nobles or among the commons.

The nobles he offended with a voting reform. To vote in the *comitia,* a man mounted one of several bridges and walked along it to a stage or platform, where he dropped his vote in an urn. The voters were, of course, observed by everyone—in particular the wealthy—and Marius was concerned with their persuasion and bullying. He proposed a bill that, in some way, would keep the great men at a distance from the voters, where they presumably could exercise less influence on the actual voting. Marius was called to the senate to explain his action, but though the senators made their opposition plain, he refused to buckle under their pressure. He is reported to have even threatened to jail the two consuls, Lucius Aurelius Cotta and Lucius Caecilius Metellus— one of the leaders of the clan of which he was a client. Metellus appealed to the other tribunes, but they refused to support him. Seeing that they could expect no veto from any of them, the senate withdrew its objection.

In contrast, however, Marius opposed an extension of the grain dole, which had been established for the benefit of the poor. Predictably this made him unpopular with the commons.

Without the patronage of the Metelli, and with the commons looking askance, it's no surprise that Marius failed to win the next office he sought, the aedileship—an office concerned with the maintenance of public works. But of course he didn't give up on politics, for that was what Rome was all about.

He ran next to be one of the praetors of 115. He was elected last of all, and even then he was accused and tried on charges of bribery in winning the office. Whether this was a politically motivated prosecution, or one of merit, he prevailed at trial, but by the thinnest of margins: The numbers of votes for his guilt and innocence were equal, and he had to be acquitted.

His praetorship seems to have been of only middling success, but his office was extended to that of propraetor and he was sent to Further

Spain,[5] where he spent time clearing the country of brigands. Sometime after his return, perhaps in 111 B.C., he married into the patrician family of the Caesars: He took Julia Caesar as his wife. Her young nephew is more famous than his new uncle—he was Gaius Julius Caesar, then about eleven years old.

*   *   *

While Marius was advancing his political career, an unknown people had been advancing toward northern Italy. No one knew who these strangers were; the Romans guessed they were Gauls, their usual northern enemy. Gauls were always a terror to the Romans—they had even sacked Rome in 390, and Sallust wrote of them: "The Romans had it that from then until our own age that all others were defeated by their bravery, but with the Gauls they fought for life and not for glory."[6]

However, the Romans had mistaken these people; they were Germans—Cimbri and Teutones—the first they had ever encountered, the first of a people that would infiltrate and dismantle the Roman Empire in the west, though that lay some five and six hundred years in the future. They had left their homes near Jutland and had been migrating as an entire people, looking for a home elsewhere. This was the beginning of what German historians would later call the *Völkerwanderung* when they described the migrations of later German peoples such as the Goths, Franks and Vandals around and into the Roman Empire in the third, fourth and fifth centuries A.D.

The senate dispatched one of the consuls of 113, Cornelius Papirius Carbo, to keep them out of Italy. These Germans knew something of Roman power even if they were strangers to Rome, and they agreed to pull back from Italy. Carbo unwisely attacked them anyway, in hope of an easy victory over the barbarians. It didn't turn out that way. Julius Obsequens, recording his prodigies for that year (641 from the founding of the city, or *ab urbe condita* as the Romans would say), recounts that "The Cimbri and Teutones crossed the Alps and made an awful slaughter of the Romans and their allies."[7] This occurred at Noreia, near modern Ljubljana.

Undoubtedly the senate and people were aghast at what had happened, though not for the same reasons. To the commons the defeat must have seemed another example of senatorial military incompetence, which it was. To the nobility Carbo's incompetence was the sort of thing that made the people restive and hampered their control of the state. And beyond mere military considerations, here was a people who had beaten a consular army sitting on the frontier. Whether or not they could reach so far south as Rome, they could certainly threaten Roman colonies and Italian allies. An incursion would be devastating. The Teutones and Cimbri, though, were taken rather aback by their own victory and declined to follow it up with a descent into Italy. Instead they wandered in a circuit about the Alps and headed west toward Gaul, gathering to them Celtic tribes like the Tigurini. They were gone for years; Rome could concentrate on other things.

*   *   *

The opportunity of the commons to bridle the senate followed upon the actions of the murderous and arrogant Numidian prince Jugurtha, Gaius Marius's old comrade-in-arms from the Numantine War. With Jugurtha's actions came war, and with war Marius's chance to win the summit of Roman power. During the conflict the indifferent success and occasional incompetence of senatorial generals led the senate into allowing the commons to arrogate the choice of commander. This in turn increased the power of the generals and ultimately led to civil war. But this was not apparent at the time. What was evident to the senators and people was that a North African client kingdom was dissolving into civil war, and they wanted no part of it.

Toward the end of the Second Punic War, King Masinissa of Numidia had done Rome the signal service of deserting his ally Carthage and furnishing much needed cavalry to Cornelius Scipio Africanus at the battle of Zama. As a result the Romans faced Hannibal with more cavalry than he, cavalry that had often fought for Carthage. No doubt Masinissa had seen the main chance: He had gauged that the Romans, more tenacious than the Carthaginians, would prevail, and when this happened he was rewarded, as he'd doubtless hoped, with a good bit of Carthaginian territory—those cities and lands that he'd seized during the war.

Masinissa was succeeded upon his death in 148 by his son Micipsa, whose brothers Mastanbal and Gulussa had already died. Mastanbal, however, had had a son, Jugurtha, by a concubine, and Masinissa had kept the boy a commoner because of his mother's low status. Though he had common origins, Jugurtha seems to have grown up with all of the conventionally desired traits: strength, handsomeness, intelligence, skill at arms, athleticism. And he was popular with the people.

All of this presented Micipsa with some difficulty; he himself had two sons, Adherbal and Hiempsal, whom he naturally wished to see succeed him. He had, however, raised his dead brother's son Jugurtha in his palace with the two younger boys, making little distinction between their status. Sallust, writing years later, suggests that Jugurtha's qualities began to trouble Micipsa, who saw the young man as a threat to his own children, particularly in view of his popularity. It was this popularity, Sallust says, that protected him from his uncle, who feared rebellion if he murdered the young man. So, Sallust tells us, Micipsa hit upon the expedient of sending Jugurtha to the Numantine War in 134 as leader of the Numidian auxiliary cavalry to serve under Scipio Aemilianus; in Spain there would always be a chance that the impetuous young man would be killed in action.

Jugurtha served with distinction, undertook difficult tasks and grew popular with Scipio himself. As a friend of Scipio, Jugurtha would have known that other favorite of the general, Gaius Marius. But Jugurtha is said to have become involved with other and less savory Romans: Men who saw opportunities as cronies of Jugurtha when the old king died. These men, Sallust tells us, pointed out to Jugurtha that he was preeminent in Numidia, while at Rome anything could be bought. Now this assertion was probably largely anti-senatorial carping on the part of an historian who was himself opposed to the senate and engaged in the ever-popular Roman historical pose of denigrating the current age as one of lost virtue. Yet it is true that Jugurtha's later conduct was extremely egregious and successful beyond reason; he may well have had some assurance from the *equites* that he should act as ambition and opportunity prompted him.

Numantia was destroyed in 133 and Scipio mustered out his auxiliaries, including Jugurtha's Numidians. Jugurtha returned to his home with his reputation enhanced through successful military service; he'd operated as part of the Roman army itself and he had a pretty good knowledge of the Roman character—he had even learned Latin. He was altogether more fit to rule than his younger cousins and certainly more than willing to take the kingdom from them when the time came.

That time came in 118 at Micipsa's death. The king had adopted Jugurtha three years before, and it was the king's intention to give his kingdom to the three young men in common, an extremely bad idea in any case, particularly in a semibarbarous country with little if any legal tradition. At Micipsa's death it was done, however, and Adherbal and

Hiempsal soon found themselves at odds with their cousin. They would not survive his ambition.

The three princes met amid some acrimony to decide the fate of the kingdom. Hiempsal, the younger of the two brothers, held his cousin Jugurtha in some disdain because of his mother's origins, and seems to have gone out of his way to offend him. At the conference Jugurtha proposed rescinding the last five years of Micipsa's decrees on the ground that the old king had not quite been in his right mind. Hiempsal seconded this, jibing wickedly that Micipsa had, after all, only adopted Jugurtha three years before. Unable to reach any other agreement, the three princes decided to divide the treasury and the land, the money to be divided first.

Jugurtha, Adherbal and Hiempsal went off to the treasury in Thirmida by different routes, another example of their discord. Hiempsal stayed in a house in Thirmida that conveniently belonged to one of Jugurtha's lieutenants.[8] This functionary pretended to inspect the house on behalf of Hiempsal, but used this chance to have a second set of keys made for the door. At night Jugurtha's soldiers swept into the place, killing the household and searching until they found Hiempsal in a servant girl's hut, where, unfamiliar with the place, he'd hidden. Jugurtha's men struck off his head and brought it to their master. Jugurtha was on his way up.

Hiempsal's murder caused an uproar in Numidia and divided the country into two camps: supporters of Adherbal, the surviving brother, and supporters of Jugurtha. Jugurtha did not rest on this success; he mustered troops. Some towns came over to him and he took others. It was clear that he meant to seize the whole kingdom. Adherbal, hoping for Roman aid, had sent envoys to Rome upon Hiempsal's death, but he prepared to fight as well. He was bested, though, in the first battle and fled east to safety in the Roman province of Africa.[9] From there he went on to Rome to plead his case personally before the senate. It was there that he probably did say something quite like that which is attributed to him: "Your legacy has been snatched from me, Senators, and through my injury you are shamed."[10] The senators could not have been happy to hear this painful but accurate observation.

Meanwhile, back in Numidia, Jugurtha began to worry about the Romans. He too sent envoys to the city to plead his case. Conventionally he is said to have bribed many of the senators whom he judged to be useful in supporting his case in the senatorial debate that would follow, but the constant allegations of massive bribery suggest exaggeration and the anti-senatorial bias of a later time. A fair question would be to ask where a semibarbarian king could have gotten enough money to tempt the wealthy senators. Whatever the truth of the allegations, the commons had come to hate the senatorial nobility and were quite prepared to believe the worst of them.

Even so there might be something to the allegations of bribery, though not in quite the crude sense that the term commonly suggests. Senators were wealthy and by the same token had great expenses. Their privileged position depended, to a great extent, on the number, stature and success of their clients. All of this, coupled with the conventional and legal prohibition against senators engaging in trade, caused many of them to set up clients in business and to help and foster them. Senators were permitted to earn percentages from their interests in the businesses of their clients, and this was important to men who could not openly use business to maintain their position. In short, senators had a serious interest in the financial well-being of their clients.

After the destruction of Carthage, the Romans had done their best to develop Numidia economically, and there was an important colony of Roman and Italian traders in the town of Cirta. Jugurtha's agents might very easily have suggested to prominent Roman traders that, should the senate go hard on their master, trade concessions in his portion of Numidia, at least, might be granted to others. By the same token, support might be recompensed by further concessions should Jugurtha win the entire kingdom. Not bribes perhaps, but these understandings would be difficult to prove, and yet could be immensely valuable to the clients of patrons interested in their success and to senatorial patrons generally, who stood to lose face if their clients were slighted. Perhaps this is what Sallust meant when he wrote of the senators that "Part of them were led by hope and others by bribery."[11]

Whether cash actually changed hands, both the senate and the commons could see little more in Numidia's situation than a murderous and squalid succession struggle. They were unwilling to come to terms with it and, in effect, Jugurtha was able to get away with murder. From the standpoint of those senators who may have had a financial interest, the Numidian problem wasn't a matter of great national interest, and so they may have had little reason to suppress venal impulses. In any case the senate's failure to grasp the nettle only emboldened the Numidian, and led to much more trouble later. All in all, the incident showed that the senate, as an institution, was not well suited to conduct foreign policy. Roman territory and foreign relations had both expanded drastically during the last hundred years, and the senate was a deliberative body made up of scores of men from great, old families. These men regarded politics as a sort of game in which they all took turns in the higher offices but through which no man or family should be allowed to became too powerful. Senatorial politics was dominated by personal and familial clashes that must have gone on for decades because the senators held their office for life.

During the senatorial debate on the Numidian question, the patrician senator Marcus Aemilius Scaurus took Adherbal's side. Scaurus was a man of high standing and great ability, but in the end the senate's decision was a compromise: Numidia would be divided between Jugurtha and Adherbal; ten commissioners were appointed to decide the division. The commission's leader was the former consul Lucius Opimius, known for his part in achieving the murder of Gaius Gracchus, Marcus Fulvius Flaccus and their supporters pursuant to the *senatus consultum ultimum*. Opimius was at first opposed to Jugurtha, but he was later accused of having been won over by Jugurtha's bribery. The theme of the venality of the senators is constant over the history of the Roman Republic.

Numidia was duly divided and Jugurtha received that part bordering on Mauretania,[12] Adherbal that nearer the province of Africa, the part having more ports and towns. Jugurtha was emboldened by this. Murder hadn't led to punishment, but rather to advancement: Killing his cousin had had the pleasant result of increasing his share in the kingdom from a third to a half. Jugurtha wouldn't forget this happy lesson.

In fact, Jugurtha's experiences evoked in him a design on Adherbal's half of the kingdom even though he knew he'd have to cross the Romans to get it. In 112 he began raiding with cavalry into Adherbal's territory; the Numidians, famed for their light cavalry, were particularly apt at this sort of hit-and-run adventuring. He meant to provoke Adherbal into counterattacks, and hoped that, given the great distance to Rome and the primitive communications of the age, he could characterize any response by his cousin as an aggression. Armed with this flimsy excuse he could then engage in open war with Adherbal and keep the Romans out on a pretense of pursuing justice.

Adherbal would not be provoked. He put his trust in Roman power and sent envoys to Rome. He also sent envoys to remonstrate with Jugurtha too, but to no effect. In view of his earlier defeat, Adherbal refrained from a military response. Jugurtha took this passivity as an invitation and began war in earnest, taking towns. Adherbal raised forces himself and met Jugurtha near the sea, by the town of Cirta. The armies approached each other late in the day and did not fight. During the night, however, Jugurtha's men attacked Adherbal's camp and inflicted a solid defeat. Adherbal escaped in the confusion and fled to Cirta, where he was saved from capture by Roman civilians, part of the trading colony in that town. They obstructed the pursuit from the walls, probably with slingshot, javelins and arrows, or possibly with a threatened sally. At this point Jugurtha may have been unwilling to involve himself directly with Romans and his hesitation allowed Adherbal to make his escape into the city.

Jugurtha settled into a siege and attacked the city with mantlets, towers and other siege machinery. This approach showed that his army was more sophisticated than might have been expected from an out-of-the-way semibarbarian, and it also showed that he was a danger not only to the Numidians in Cirta, but to the Romans and Italians there as well. Jugurtha did not have much time to finish the operation; he knew of Adherbal's envoys and he wanted to take the town before they could reach Rome.

By this time the senate had learned of the war and dispatched three young men[13] to Numidia to inform the princes that they must lay down their arms and settle the matter according to law. The envoys came as quickly as they could because news had reached Italy of the battle at Cirta. The danger in which the Roman traders found themselves must have been of great concern in Rome to both the *equites* and merchants there, many of whom must have been in business with them, or even in some cases related to them.

Jugurtha replied to the envoys that he was only defending himself from an attempt by Adherbal to murder him. He told them that he too would send envoys to Rome. He would not, however, allow the senatorial envoys to speak to Adherbal. Jugurtha waited until he thought they had left and then resumed the siege with greater effort: He circumvallated the town, put up towers, attacked constantly and offered bribes to defenders. It became pretty apparent to Adherbal that he could expect little help in the present state of things, and so he convinced two of his most loyal followers to slip out through the enemy's camp by night and head for Rome with yet another letter for the senate.

Once again the senators had to listen to Adherbal's catalogue of Jugurtha's offenses, and must have felt humiliated when asked to recall how Jugurtha had flouted the senate's decree that the cousins share the kingdom. Furthermore, the siege of Cirta had now lasted five months, and it must have been clear the city might fall at any time; the Roman public was growing restive as the senate failed to resolve the conflict.

Even so the senate was divided: Some were for sending an army to relieve Adherbal and in the meantime take official recognition of Jugurtha's failure to obey the envoys. Other senators prevented such a decree and their indecision once again gave rise to rumors of bribery. Sallustius says, "So it happened that the public welfare, as in so many affairs, was defeated by personal interests."[14]

In fairness to the senators, though, Rome's legal right to intervene in Numidia was tenuous; the kingdom was at least nominally independent. Thus, though Jugurtha's conduct was an affront to the senate, it was insufficient cause to launch an expensive war. Besides, the senate had another, more pressing issue to deal with: the possibility of invasion from the north. The Cimbri and Teutones were on the move and there was good reason to think they intended to invade Italy. Following their defeat of Carbo at Noreia,[15] they had remained in the Alps and in the year 112 they hung like a sword over Italy. These people were mysterious—practically unknown to the Romans, who as stated before, thought they were Gauls. They must have reminded the Romans of the terrible invasion of 390 when Gauls swept down from beyond the Alps, crushed the Roman army on the banks of the Allia, and went on to seize and burn Rome itself, all save the Capitoline Hill. With the possible need for troops in Italy at an uncertain time, the prospect of sending an army to Numidia was particularly unattractive.

In the end a new commission was settled on: a number of men of the first rank, including the former consul Marcus Scaurus, leader of the senate, who had taken Adherbal's side in the earlier senatorial debate. In view of public opinion they took ship within three days of their appointment. These men soon landed at Utica, the provincial Roman capital, and dispatched a letter to Jugurtha. The news of the arrival of such powerful men prompted Jugurtha to make one last, great effort to take Cirta, which would have put Adherbal in his hands, something useful before any negotiations. But he was unable to capture the city and had to meet the envoys without this advantage; furthermore he feared Scaurus. Nonetheless the prince went to the Roman province of Africa in the company of a few horsemen.

The parley must have been quite unpleasant for Jugurtha, but he managed to avoid any compromise and returned to continue the siege. The failure of the conference caused the Italians defending Cirta's walls to fear for their safety; they decided that their best hope of being spared lay in the surrender of the town—after all, as Roman and Latin citizens they could expect to come off unscathed. They prevailed upon Adherbal to surrender Cirta on the terms that he would be spared and that the Roman senate would then sort the mess out. Adherbal was rightly dubious, but submitted to the Italians' pressure. Adherbal's assessment of the situation was more astute than that of the Romans: Upon the surrender, Jugurtha tortured Adherbal to death and killed all of the adult Numidians and traders who were found with arms. This meant a massacre of Roman citizens. Possibly Jugurtha's soldiers overstepped their master's wishes, at least with regard to the Romans. Possibly Jugurtha had grown confident in the success of a career based on murder, deceit and temporizing. But Romans were dead, and allied Latin citizens too, and now it would be war with Rome, plain and simple.

In Rome, Jugurtha's representatives tried to delay any senatorial action until popular feeling might abate, but the outcry was too great. In accordance with the Sempronian Law of Gaius Gracchus, Numidia and Italy were set aside as the provinces of the consuls for 111. Those elected were Publius Scipio Nasica, who was given Italy, and Lucius Calpurnius Bestia, who was to handle Numidia. Bestia had a good reputation as an intelligent, vigorous man, hardworking and careful and with a good deal of military experience. Bestia mustered his army and prepared to take it to Numidia. As a consular army of two legions and an equal number of allies, it probably numbered twenty or twenty-two thousand men.

From the writings of Julius Obsequens we learn the following for the year 111 B.C.:

> A great part of the city was burned, along with the temple of the Great Mother. It rained milk for three days, and the expiation was done with full-grown sacrificial victims. The Jugurthine War began.[16]

What meaning the Romans drew from these prodigies is unclear, but Bestia's campaign, though initially successful, came to nothing. But of course this would have been unknown as the army was being enrolled, and Jugurtha, leaving nothing to chance, sent a son and two friends to the Roman senate. Bestia, quite reasonably, put the question to the senate whether they should even receive these ambassadors within the walls of Rome. The senate decided no, and gave the envoys ten days within which to leave Italy, unless they wished to surrender the Kingdom of Numidia; only then would they be received. Jugurtha had not sent them to do any such thing, they were meant only to cause delay, and the consul had been quite right to see to it that they never reached the senate house.

Bestia enrolled his army, putting over it as officers a number of nobles, including Marcus Scaurus, the former consul. Thus the army had the usual aristocratic stamp. It marched to Rhegium and was ferried to Sicily and then to Africa, where the campaign began well. Bestia attacked hard, taking towns and prisoners.

After these initial successes, however, he entered into negotiations with Jugurtha and worked out an armistice. Again there are hints of bribery, but they are unlikely; Bestia was a consul of the Roman Republic, and his lieutenant Scaurus had held the same office and been leader of the senate. Their positions at Rome were assured; senators sat for life unless expelled by the censor for unbecoming conduct, of which the acceptance of bribes would have been a good example. In short, there was nothing that Jugurtha could really have offered them and no way that it could have been kept sufficiently secret among the circle of aristocratic officers, most of them from the city of Rome, and all of whom, as members of a closed society, must have known each other intimately.

The clue would seem to reside in Bestia's office: the consulship. Recall that he was not merely a general, and that in Rome "The sword gives way to the toga." In other words, the civil authority is superior to the military, or, more broadly, civil concerns are the most important. As one of the two most important officers of the Roman Republic, Bestia's duties were more than purely military; he had to consider the welfare of the Roman state as a whole. His colleague Scipio had Italy as his province, and it would be his duty to defend the home country from the Teutones and Cimbri if they passed the Alps. Bestia knew that troops operating in Numidia were not available to keep the Germans out of Cisalpine Gaul, and even a moderately dishonorable peace might be better than a long campaign. Bestia had already shown what Roman arms could do, and he might be able to fob off a shoddy peace as sufficiently honorable once he got back to Rome.

So, it was likely with good enough motives that Bestia's quaestor Sextius met Jugurtha at the town of Vago to receive supplies that had been promised to the Romans by the terms of the armistice. At that time Jugurtha met with a council of officers and asked them to receive his surrender. The terms of his surrender, though, he worked out in secret with Bestia and Scaurus. This was followed by some sort of informal vote among the Roman commanders, at which the surrender was accepted on easy terms; Jugurtha handed over thirty elephants, a good deal of cattle and horses, and some silver to the quaestor. Peace had been restored and Bestia returned to Rome to supervise the elections.

However the commons weren't happy with the peace and the senate too was in doubt whether to approve the surrender terms. A tribune of the people, Gaius Memmius, an inveterate hater of the nobility, saw in the recent developments his chance to turn the people against the aristocracy. Calling a popular assembly, he addressed the people, reminding them of the fifteen years that had passed since Gaius Gracchus and his followers had died at the hands of the senators. He played on the class envy natural in a society with gross distinctions between rich and poor, and he voiced their complaints:

> Years ago you were mutely angered as the treasury was looted, kings and free peoples paid tax to a few nobles and only these had glory and the greatest wealth. Yet it was too little that they commit these crimes unpunished, but in the end the laws, your dignity and everything divine and human are given to enemies. Nor are they who do these things ashamed or penitent, but they parade splendid priesthoods and consulships before your eyes, some of them displaying their triumphs just as if they were honors and not booty.[17]

The thrust of the speech was clear: Only the nobles would benefit from Jugurtha's surrender, at least on the terms that had been offered. The larger theme? That Jugurtha had obtained favorable terms through bribery. Memmius continued:

> Should someone ask "What then do you advise?" There must be a judgement against those who betray the republic to the enemy. Not by violence or force, which it would be more shameful for you to do than for them to suffer, but instead by trial and the evidence of Jugurtha himself. If he is a prisoner he will be actually obedient to your commands, if he defies them then naturally you will judge what sort of peace and surrender this is, by which Jugurtha has gained impunity for his crimes, a few powerful men great riches and the republic damage and dishonor.[18]

Memmius knew what the common people wanted to hear and he persuaded them to send the praetor Lucius Cassius Longinus to Jugurtha and bring him to Rome to testify in a bribery trial against Scaurus.

Meanwhile the Roman army, now at peace, fell into slack discipline. Jugurtha got his elephants back, though this may have been merely a gesture of conciliation. Those left in charge in Bestia's absence may have thought that giving the beasts back was a cheap method of buying the prince's cooperation. After all, elephants had never been much of a military threat to the Roman army, and the Romans themselves seldom used them. More troubling was the practice of selling Jugurtha's deserters back to him and of pillaging the friendly countryside. Without the active threat of an enemy and without the necessary activities of an actual campaign, the army was not able to maintain discipline.

Longinus the praetor was able to convince Jugurtha that it would be in his best interest to come to Rome, as the people demanded, and he gave the prince his personal assurance of safety. Longinus, who would become consul in 107, had such a reputation that Jugurtha relied on his word and agreed to make the journey. Although it was Scaurus who was to be tried and not Jugurtha, the prince took no chances and arranged for his protection. He could do this because the Romans had law and tried their best to honor it, or at least its forms.

The Romans were a people careful to build checks and balances into their government. With the establishment of the republic, the ancient kings had been replaced not by a single officer, but by a pair of annually elected consuls, co-equal in power and authority. Tyranny was avoided because one officer could block the other. In a like manner, when the commons had wrested from the nobles the right to officers, or tribunes for their own protection, they grew in number until there were ten, each of equal authority, any one of which could veto legislation or action proposed by another. The arrangement was clumsy and did in fact lead to deadlock, but these impasses were then worked out through compromise so that with sufficient civic goodwill the republic had continued to muddle along.

Jugurtha, of course, was aware of this peculiarity of Roman government and, upon his arrival, he cultivated and bribed one of the tribunes, Gaius Baebius. A tribune was a valuable man to have in one's pocket, as the people would learn.

A popular assembly was convened to hear Jugurtha's evidence. The crowd jeered and threatened, calling for punishment of the man who had slaughtered the Romans at Cirta. The tribune Memmius, who had called Jugurtha to Rome, calmed the crowd and recalled to them that Jugurtha was there under a pledge of personal protection. To their credit, a reminder to the Roman commons of the promise was enough to keep Jugurtha unharmed.

And then Memmius went on, detailing Jugurtha's crimes. He did say, however, that the prince could expect the forgiveness of the Roman people if he would give the particulars of who had helped him in his crimes, even though the people knew, in a general way, who had done what. Although Jugurtha himself was not on trial, to answer this request meant to betray any who had helped him during his rise, and this would destroy whatever support he had among the senators, support he would need now that he was in their power. To shield his supporters, or to claim there were none, would be dangerous to himself as he stood before a mob of thousands of angry citizens. It was an unenviable choice that he'd known he must face when he left Numidia. The tribune Baebius, however, got Jugurtha out of this tricky spot. Armed with his tribunician power, he ordered the prince not to speak, and he held to this position even in the face of threats from the crowd. The star witness in the bribery inquiry had been silenced. Again, there is the chance that Baebius had not actually been bribed—that instead he had been suborned by those senators who feared Jugurtha's testimony. From a practical standpoint, though, the effect was equally bad: Jugurtha came to Rome only with the assurance of a legal immunity for testifying, and the senate's moral position was lowered once again.

Meanwhile, other things were afoot in Rome. A cousin of Jugurtha named Massiva had fled there after the fall of Cirta and the murder of Adherbal. This Numidian had fallen in with Spurius Postumius Albinus, one of the consuls for 110, who had drawn Numidia as his province.[19] Albinus proposed that Massiva be made king of Numidia in place of Jugurtha. When he took office Albinus would replace Bestia in command of the Numidian army and if he could place Massiva on the throne, he would practically have a client running the country. It must have seemed a very sweet proposition.

Jugurtha was alarmed at the possibility so he turned to the usual Jugurthine solution: murder. He ordered a follower of his, Bomilcar, to hire out Massiva's murder. It was to be done secretly, if possible, but in any case it was to be done. This move was extremely audacious even for the unscrupulous prince; Jugurtha was essentially powerless in a foreign capital, known to be guilty of any number of crimes, he was planning yet another capital crime, and his safety was based on the honoring of a pledge given by people whom he had injured and whose laws he was about to flout.

Massiva was duly murdered, though the murder itself was bungled in that one of the assailants was caught and persuaded to confess. Unable to put Jugurtha on trial because their pledge gave him immunity, the Romans prepared to try Bomilcar for the murder. Fifty men stood as sureties for Bomilcar, but Jugurtha secretly sent him out of the city before there could be any conviction. Jugurtha understood that it was more expedient to betray fifty friends to a lesser penalty than to give up to justice a single close Numidian retainer. To have done otherwise would have undermined his support back home, and he would need that support in the coming struggle—Massiva's murder could only renew the conflict, this time against the consul Albinus. The senate then ordered Jugurtha to leave Italy. Once out of the city he is said to have turned back often and finally said, "A city for sale and ready to perish if it should find a buyer!"[20]

The Romans may appear naive to have let themselves be outmaneuvered by such a transparent scoundrel, but though the republic was showing the strains of faction, it was still a state that honored law above everything else. And they were right to honor it; it was the rule of law that had lent Rome stability between the commons and the aristocracy—order enough to overcome one peril after another and dominate the Mediterranean.

Upon attaining office, the consul Albinus hurried to the war—he meant to complete it before the next consular elections. Unless he were awarded proconsular power after the end of his term (and this was unlikely), a new consul would then arrive to prosecute the war; if Albinus were to get the prestige of victory, he would have to get it quickly. Jugurtha, for his part, dithered: He waged a half-hearted war and sued for peace as well. It was probably his plan to draw things out until Albinus, as consul, was forced to return to Italy to conduct the consular elections for 109. The delay tarnished Albinus's military reputation and eventually he was suspected not so much of incompetence as of connivance with Jugurtha. At Rome, Jugurtha's failure to testify against the senators on the bribery question must have put many Romans in an extremely suspicious frame of mind. Still, it is fair to ask whether Albinus, as consul, wasn't subject to the same concerns as Bestia had been. His plan was probably to get in a few victories, enhance his reputation and wind up the Numidian affair so that Rome could turn her attention to matters of real national interest, such as the Germans north of the Alps who were marching slowly west toward the Roman province of southern Gaul.

Albinus sailed back to Rome, probably in November of 110, to conduct the consular elections for 109, and he left his incompetent brother Aulus in command. At Rome there was more civil strife as two tribunes, Publius Lucullus and Lucius Annius, tried to extend their term of office, normally one year, by delaying the election of new tribunes. Tribunes in office were not subject to prosecution for their actions and these men were probably trying to extend this immunity by extending their office. The effect of their tactics was to delay the election of the new consuls too. Back in Numidia, Aulus saw this as a chance to improve his prospects. He took his soldiers out of winter quarters, perhaps in December of 110, and went out against Jugurtha.[21]

Aulus's immediate object was Suthul, the town where Jugurtha kept his treasury. This was a sound strategic move. The best of the Numidian army were essentially light horsemen armed with javelins, adept at raids and skirmishing, whereas Roman strength lay in their heavy infantry. However, in the open hilly country of Numidia, an army marching twelve or fifteen miles a day was unlikely to catch the enemy. If Aulus could take Suthul and deprive Jugurtha of monies necessary to conduct the war, he might severely curtail the Numidian's activities. Jugurtha himself would realize this, and to avoid being so severely compromised he might risk a fight. Either situation was to Aulus's advantage: the glory and loot of taking Suthul, or the glory of winning a large, set battle.

Romans were masters of siegecraft and Aulus might have expected to take the town as a matter of course, but he found the town on heights above a plain muddy from the winter rains. Nonetheless he set about reducing the place, either because he thought he could do it despite the problems he faced, or because he wished to alarm Jugurtha; he built an assault ramp and mantlets.

> But Jugurtha, knowing the worthlessness and inexperience of the commander, added cunningly to his madness by sending him suppliant envoys, he himself, as though fleeing, led his army through highlands and trails.[22]

Jugurtha had recourse to his most successful tool: trickery. Aulus let himself be drawn away from Suthul and he met with Jugurtha, who offered to cut some sort of deal with him, suggesting that they do it out in the field where there would be fewer prying eyes. Jugurtha, however, didn't limit his negotiations to the commander; he managed to suborn a number of the allied troops. He bribed a cohort of Ligurians, two troops of Thracian cavalry and a handful of common soldiers. His prize, however, was the chief centurion, the *primus pilus* of the Third Legion.

At night Jugurtha attacked the Roman camp. The chief centurion allowed the Numidians into that part of the camp over which he had responsibility. The Ligurians, Thracians and some of the common soldiers whom Jugurtha had paid came over to him, and there was complete disorder in the camp. Some soldiers fought, of course, but panic spread, as it does in such a situation and most of the soldiers fled to a nearby hill, leaving the Numidians to loot the camp. Pillage and darkness saved the Romans from suffering an utter defeat.

The following day Jugurtha conferred with the much-compromised Aulus and pointed out his difficulties. He offered the Roman commander an unpleasant choice: to pass under the yoke and leave Numidia in ten days or to chance starvation and further fighting. Perhaps the ten days offered to Aulus were an echo of the ten days the senate had given Jugurtha to leave Italy after Massiva's murder. Why Jugurtha didn't press his advantage isn't known; he may have seen it as a conciliatory gesture (in spite of the yoke), a gesture that might redound to his benefit. After all, though he'd had a good run so far, Jugurtha must have observed that while Romans lost battles from time to time, they never lost wars. He may also have recognized the uncertainty of battle even against Aulus's disordered men. These Romans may have been demoralized, but it was never an easy or cheap thing to defeat them.

Aulus chose the yoke: an ancient and humiliating Italian custom in which a defeated army marched beneath a yoke made of spears as a public admission of defeat. It must have been doubly galling that Jugurtha had chosen this gesture since he had borrowed it from the Romans themselves, and no Roman army had passed under the yoke since their defeat by the Samnites at the Battle of the Caudine Forks two hundred and fifty years before. The army passed under the yoke and marched back to the province of Africa; the two nations were now at peace according to the treaty worked out between Aulus and the Numidian.

The news caused great consternation at Rome and the consul Albinus was justly afraid to be implicated in his brother's disgrace. To clear himself as much as possible he put the question of the validity of the treaty between Aulus and Jugurtha before the senate and bustled about raising more troops from among the Latins and the allies. The senate meanwhile discussed the treaty and reached the expected decision: It was invalid. The senate, after all, was responsible for foreign policy and no agreement of this type could bind Rome without the senate's and the people's approval.

Albinus left for Africa, but the tribunes of the people prevented him from taking with him the newly raised troops. This shows the obloquy in

which the people held the consul, but more importantly it was a dangerous intrusion into the actual conduct of the war, something that should
constitutionally have been left to the senate and the consuls. The senate
and senatorial aristocracy in command of the army hadn't acquitted itself
well, but the war could hardly have been conducted by ten tribunes passing decrees in turbulent public meetings.

Upon his arrival in Africa, Albinus took the usual step after a Roman
defeat: improving the discipline of the common soldiers. He recognized
the disorder into which the troops had fallen through lax discipline and
the moral decline that followed his brother's defeat. To his credit he did
not rush into the field to recover his and his brother's honor.

While Albinus worked on the army, at Rome the politics of faction
continued as usual, commons against nobility. The tribune Gaius Mamilius Limetanus proposed a bill in the popular assembly to prosecute those
who had encouraged Jugurtha to disregard the orders of the senate, any
envoy or military commander who had taken his money, any who had
returned his elephants and deserters and any who had made treaties of
war or peace with him. The bill provided for a commission of three
quaestors to handle these matters. The nobility opposed the measure, but
had to do so behind the scenes lest their opposition be seen as an admission of guilt. The commons, however, passed the bill—Sallust says it was
done more to cause trouble for the nobility than because it was in the interest of the republic.

The nobility were frightened, but remarkably enough in the turmoil
following the passage of the law, one of their number, Marcus Scaurus,
who had been Bestia's lieutenant, got himself appointed as one of these
quaestors. The panel is supposed to have carried out its duties harshly
and according to the whims of the commons, but given Scaurus's position as a senator and former consul, it is hard to imagine that he didn't
moderate things for others of his station.

By this time it may have become apparent to observant Romans that
the conflict between the commons and the nobility was noxious to the
state, but there probably seemed little that could be done, even though,
as Sallust would write sixty years later, the state "was torn in pieces."[23]

But things had not yet gotten so far along; the nobility still had the
upper hand, and after the consular elections for 109, Numidia became the
province of Quintus Caecilius Metellus, a patrician of irreproachable reputation. He sized up the situation and took up his job in the grand old
Roman manner.

CHAPTER 6

The Jugurthine War Continues

THE ELECTIONS OF 109 B.C. HAD PUT GAIUS JULIANUS SILANUS and Quintus Caecilius Metellus in office. Silanus was defeated that year near the frontier of Gallia Transalpina by the Cimbri, Teutones and Tigurini. He was only one of a string of generals who did poorly against them.

The people rightly had confidence in the rectitude and ability of Metellus though. He came of a patrician family of particularly great prestige; the Metelli were the most prominent family in Rome at this time; they had risen past the Scipiones, who had held this position since the war with Hannibal. In a sense, Metellus's election was surprising: He had strong anti-popular sentiments, but no doubt his clients worked hard for his election and the prestige of his family was great enough to overcome any difficulty in this line. His uncle, Quintus Caecilius Metellus Macedonicus, had been the victor of the fourth and final Macedonian War in 148. Metellus's reputation was irreproachable and this could only have helped him in the current situation where the commons believed that many of his predecessors in Numidia had been corrupted. Simple incompetence goes a long way to explain these Roman military failures, but to the commons, from whom the soldiers were taken, and who could hardly have been expected to understand the strategic situation in Numidia, bribe-taking was a simple and satisfying answer.

Metellus arrived in Africa in the summer of 109. He had no faith in the army Albinus had left him, though the latter had tried to reform it after the embarrassing defeat of his brother. As Sallust says:

But when he came to Africa, the army given to him by Spurius Albinus, that lazy, unwarlike proconsul, was suited neither to danger nor to toil,

was faster with the tongue than the hand, a predator to its allies and itself the prey of its enemies, and accustomed to be without discipline or
self-control.[1]

The army had gone completely slack. Trusting to the relative safety of
Africa, the camp had no wall about it and no regular watch, and the soldiers plundered the locals with impunity.

The new general enrolled new soldiers and got himself new supplies,
horses and equipment to bolster the army. His lieutenant was Gaius Marius, who had set himself right with the Metelli in the years following his
provocative proposals as a tribune. Metellus's next step was the traditional Roman response to military defeat: to put the common soldiers
under stricter discipline, and in this case he was right to do it. He enforced the regulations, fortified the camp, checked the sentries himself
and then moved it from place to place, forcing the soldiers back into
army routine and hardening them. He forbade the soldiers to keep attendants or buy their own food and managed in these ways to reform the
army without punishments. This approach was extremely valuable; he
didn't want to trust in the obedience of sullen soldiers.

Jugurtha kept himself informed of developments in the province of
Africa and decided that Metellus would not be as easily handled as
Aulus had been. It was time to send envoys again. These men offered
peace on the condition that Jugurtha and his children's lives be spared.
The Roman knew who he was dealing with: He dealt with each of
Jugurtha's envoys one by one and offered each a reward if he would turn
Jugurtha over to him alive or—if need be—dead.

It might be said that this was hardly the Roman way of doing business, but it was extremely clever in several ways. For one, it might have
worked. What would be the harm in a bit of trickery if it brought the war
to an end? A second and rather more cunning point is that the envoys
were now tainted; if some spoke, then those who didn't stood to suffer
and Jugurtha might distrust other men close to him.

Officially, however, Metellus agreed to the king's request. He then advanced with the army into Numidia, where he found no obvious preparations for war; officers from Jugurtha even cooperated with Metellus to
supply him. All the same, the consul advanced cautiously. He expected a
trap from Jugurtha and so he reconnoitered and took the precaution of
advancing in careful formation: The legions and allied cohorts of heavy
infantry marched down the center of the column while Metellus himself
was at their head with light infantry, slingers and archers. Marius led the

cavalry in the rear, and the auxiliary cavalry, under the command of the
legionary tribunes and cohort prefects, marched on either side of the column, with light footsoldiers mingled with them. In this way the column
could form up for battle if unexpectedly attacked.

Near the march route lay the large town of Vaga, and Metellus left a
garrison there to protect a supply dump he established and to look after
Italians living in the town. The occupation of Vaga provoked Jugurtha
into sending more envoys to reiterate his earlier terms: peace, but his and
his children's' lives to be spared. Metellus again tried to suborn the envoys, but gave no answer to the king. It was now apparent to the king
that Metellus was using the sort of chicanery at which he himself was so
adept. And this meant that he would have to fight instead of talk. He assembled his forces, light cavalry as usual, infantry and elephants. The latter he put under his old friend Bomilcar, the murderer of Massiva. He got
his troops ahead of the Roman column and decided to fight among hills
near the Muthul River. Jugurtha placed his troops in a line along the top
of a hill overlooking the route the column would pass along. He hid his
men as best he could among the scrub trees on the hill, and concealed his
banners. He waited for the moment of ambush.

The Roman column was descending from a height and heading toward the Muthul when Metellus saw them.

At first he wondered what the unusual sight was, for the horses and the
Numidians stood among thickets; they were not hidden by the lowness
of the trees and yet it was uncertain what they were because they themselves and their military standards were obscured by both the nature of
the place and the ambush itself.[2]

Metellus halted and had his column turn to face the enemy, thus
putting his army into battle formation. He bolstered his right wing, that
closest to the enemy, with three more lines of maniples and distributed
slingers and archers between them. He then divided his cavalry and set
them on the wings. Jugurtha did not attack at once, and Metellus, concerned that his men might be worn down by thirst, sent one of his officers, a Rutilius, with a body of horse and some cohorts of light infantry
down into the plain to establish a camp near the Muthul. As the Roman
detachment passed below the Numidians, Bomilcar proceeded after it
with his elephants and infantry.

The Roman army then faced left, and became a column once more.
With Metellus and cavalry at the head, and Marius and more cavalry at

the rear, the army descended slowly into the plain. As the rear of the Roman column reached the plain, Jugurtha sent two thousand men to occupy the pass or route through which they had come, apparently to trap them on the plain.

Jugurtha then began to attack the Romans' right and left flanks with his cavalry, which dashed about casting javelins. When pursued they simply melted away, fleeing in all directions and trying to cut off any isolated Roman cavalrymen they could find. Sallust says that these attacks disordered all the ranks, and this, if true, suggests that they began before the Roman column had been quite able to face right and form a proper battle line. Yet this could just as easily be dramatic license on the part of Sallust. We can be sure that Metellus was able to get his army in proper order, for there was apparently a good deal of fighting, and a final successful charge by four cohorts toward some of the Numidian infantry that had pulled back upon high ground put an end to the battle in this quarter. Most of these Numidians slipped away through the countryside.

Rutilius and his men had found a suitable spot, had marked out a camp and begun to entrench when clouds of dust appeared before them. They guessed at first that it was merely dust that had been carried up by the wind—there were trees and bushes on the plain, and it was difficult to see that it was really a sign of approaching enemy soldiers. Dust clouds, however, were a common telltale of the advance of ancient armies in dry country, and the truth became apparent when the dust did not disperse, but instead approached them. They took up their arms and, meeting the enemy, defeated them. Sallust reports that the Numidian infantry had placed their confidence in the elephants, and that they broke when the Romans killed a number of them.[3] The cavalry of the divided Roman forces met in the dark and recognized each other; the army marched to its camp.

Sallust gives no figures for either side. Metellus was consul and his army was probably of the usual consular strength, about twenty thousand. It may have been smaller—he must have left a few cohorts to protect the province of Africa, but then he had brought some additional troops with him when he took command. Twenty thousand troops seems a fair guess. As for the Numidians, it is impossible to say. A great strength of the Roman army lay in the efficiency with which it supplied itself, and the result is that Rome could field and feed large armies. It may be that the Romans outnumbered the enemy in this engagement. It seems unlikely that the Numidians had the sophistication to field and feed more men than the Romans at any given place.

As with the reports of many ancient battles, too much seems to have happened too quickly: There are marches, perhaps hours of fighting ("And so, much of the day had passed . . . "[4]), an advance force has time to find a spot and measure out and set up camp, another fight follows, and only then is it night. At the heart of the problem is, of course, a certain exaggeration. Ancient historians valued drama; Sallust is rather unsparing in his account of the Jugurthine war. But beyond this it may be useful to recall that fighting in the ancient days quickly exhausted men. The Romans were burdened with armor, and did their fighting with the sword when they could. Actual combat could seldom have lasted very long. An hour or two, probably often less. Much of a battle would have consisted of the ordering and alignment of thousands of troops—doing it by messenger, the shifting of standards, and by shouting—of observing the enemy in order to change dispositions (the Romans could do this more easily than others because of their articulated battle-order), and of judging the correct moment for engagement.

When Metellus checked and put his army in order on the heights near Jugurtha's men, this took time. Jugurtha, observing that his ambush had been discovered, would have taken time in rethinking and perhaps reordering his army. Hours could pass. Rutilius advanced into the plain with his cavalry and light soldiers while the main body followed more slowly. Though Bomilcar pursued him, this tactic had to be decided upon, and the men had to be selected and given the order to advance. Furthermore, Bomilcar may have depended on stealth as much as anything; perhaps he determined to catch the Romans at work on the camp rather than alert them as the result of a visible pursuit. This independent phase of the battle may have taken several hours as well. In short, it may be useful to think of ancient battle as a slow, deliberate affair—hours of marshalling and preparation ended with an hour of fighting and followed, sometimes, by hours of pursuit.

Metellus kept his men in camp for the next four days, tending the wounded and awarding prizes to men who had distinguished themselves. Prizes were an important part of military ritual and there were a number of them, disks called *phalerae*, and the civic crown for instance, awarded to a soldier who had saved the life of a fellow citizen. Metellus was working on his men's morale. He was also working on bringing Jugurtha to bay: He sent deserters and spies to discover what Jugurtha was doing. He also dwelt on Numidian tactics—ambushes and skirmishes. Jugurtha's natural strength lay in light horse, which the Roman heavy infantry could not catch in the flat country of Numidia, and so

Metellus set upon viciously ravaging the enemy country. He seems to have intended to drive Jugurtha into a set battle, though this strategy could also estrange the common Numidians from a king who could not protect them.

Jugurtha, meanwhile, had fled to wooded country with his mounted guard. Most of his men had abandoned him after Muthul, and so the king's first order of business was to put together another army. In reply to Metellus's depredations, Jugurtha took to a policy of shadowing the Romans, attacking stragglers and hiding in hilly country. A guerrilla strategy suited the means left to him, and was in his best interest anyway. He had learned from experience that Romans might talk peace even if they were unhappy about it, and if he could draw the war out long enough they might do so again. At the least he could hope that by the turn of the year, when Metellus's consulship ended, the war might be put into the hands of another, less competent commander.

Jugurtha had suffered a good deal of desertion from the Muthul battle; Metellus's reputation rose very high at Rome. The senate decreed public prayers in honor of it, and the public, who had been quite uneasy about the war, held him in the highest regard.

Though Metellus had acquitted himself well enough at Muthul, he now became more wary of traps and was particularly careful to keep his men in order and alert while moving across country. In order to despoil more enemy territory, though, he divided the army, leading one division himself and leaving the other to Marius. The armies operated, however, closely enough for mutual support—they camped closely together and joined forces when the need arose. Jugurtha, for his part, continued the same guerrilla tactics:

> During this time Jugurtha followed through the hills seeking a time and place for battle, and where he heard the enemy was about to approach he spoiled fodder and springs of water, of which there were not many, and in this way he showed himself sometimes to Metellus [and sometimes] to Marius, attacked the rearmost men in the marching column and immediately retreated to the hills, attacked others and then threatened others, neither fighting a battle nor allowing rest, so in this way prevented the enemy from carrying out its plan.[5]

It became apparent to Metellus that his strategy was not as effective as he might have wished—or if effective, it wasn't fast enough. Metellus would have discussed this issue in the military council, which Roman

generals conventionally held. Such counsels included the military tribunes and often the *primi pili,* or first centurions of the legions under a
general's command. And this means, of course, that he would have
talked the problem over with his chief lieutenant, Gaius Marius. He had
forgiven Marius for his independence as a tribune of the people—quite
probably because of the man's proven military ability rather than from
any personal sense of friendship. Marius's military competence had been
demonstrated in Spain under Scipio Aemilianus and would be shown
soon enough in Numidia itself, and then later in Transalpine Gaul and
Italy. He would have seen as clearly as Metellus what lay behind the
Roman troubles: too small an army for a country of Numidia's size, too
few cavalry to chase Jugurtha's light horse, open flat land where cavalry
couldn't easily be trapped or ridden down, and hills and scrub for the
enemy to hide in. He must have agreed with Metellus's plan—take a
major town or two and try, at least, to force a set battle. But it is unlikely
that he wasn't already tackling in his mind a way to do a little better than
Metellus, a way that would enhance his chances to advance to the top of
Roman society despite his origin as a country knight. He had been a military tribune, an aedile and tribune of the people. He must already have
been aiming at higher things.

Metellus settled on taking the city of Zama. It was large, at least for
Numidia, and functioned as the fortress of that part of the country. While
he advanced on it he sent Marius foraging around Sicca, which had come
over to the Romans after Muthul, with a few cohorts of infantry. Jugurtha
had learned of Metellus's plans for Zama from deserters and so he
rushed ahead to the town and ordered them to stand fast. He strengthened the garrison at Zama with Roman deserters who dared not fail in
the town's defense; Rome punished her deserters with hard deaths. He
then told them he'd return and relieve the town with an army. He turned
his attention next to Sicca.

The Romans were at Sicca when Jugurtha appeared from Zama, and
he was driven away in a short engagement. Marius had probably collected the provisions he had been sent to get at Sicca for he soon led his
cohorts to Zama in support of Metellus, who was besieging the town.
Jugurtha headed to Zama too.

Metellus was carrying out the siege in his deliberate, Roman way: He
surrounded the town completely and fixed a time for an assault at several
points along the walls simultaneously. Jugurtha took his opportunity and
suddenly attacked the Romans' camp while they were busy at the walls.
Jugurtha, who had served among the Romans in Spain, could expect the

camp to be defended by *calones* and a handful of soldiers whom he might expect to overcome. A successful attack on the camp might not relieve Zama, but it would certainly add to the general difficulty of the siege; the town was well fortified and energetically defended.

The king's men managed to break through one of the camp gates and, while a small band of men fought them with determination and held some small area of it, the camp generally fell into the hands of the Numidians. Many men fled from the camp toward the siegeworks. Metellus could see this and, realizing what it must mean, he ordered Marius to the camp with a troop of cavalry. Marius's counterattack was effective enough: Many of the Numidians were trapped within the camp and unable to escape from his troops. There was no sustained pursuit of the fugitives because of oncoming night.

Although Sallust reports that in this engagement Jugurtha suffered considerable losses, this was probably not the case. He reports as well that the following day Metellus set all of his cavalry to patrol the area around the camp to prevent any more surprises. He must have considered the threat real enough, even after the skirmish in the camp, and this implies that Jugurtha hadn't suffered so very much. Cavalry is not useful in sieges; why it wasn't already performing this duty is unexplained, though it may in fact have been performing it, but perhaps not as competently as the commander might have wished. His army, though it had proportionately little cavalry, should still have had a good two thousand horse, enough to scout the country. The answer may be that the main informant of this war, Sallust, was simply inaccurate on this score—it is suspicious that he describes a very similar battle taking place almost the next day. In fact Metellus gave up on the siege of Zama, finding it too difficult to attack and too well defended, and the two battles are probably one single fight, doubled and embroidered in the telling.

The unsuccessful attack on Zama ended the campaign of 109. Metellus garrisoned those towns that had come over to him and that he gauged could be successfully defended because of either fortification or position, and then sent the rest of the army into winter quarters in the province of Africa, but near its border with Numidia. Although he had pursued the war with competence and some success, he hadn't ended it. This would tell against him eventually.

He did not pass that winter

the way others do and surrender to laziness and repose, but because the war was proceeding slowly by the sword he prepared to set traps for the king through his friends and use their treachery in place of weapons.[6]

Metellus managed to get Bomilcar to meet him in secret and told him that if Jugurtha were handed over—or convinced to surrender—the senate would restore the property that Bomilcar had pledged and forfeited through his flight after the murder of Massiva in Rome. At some point after this, Metellus received envoys from the king stating that Jugurtha was ready, yet again, to surrender.

Metellus was careful this time. He didn't want to repeat the mistakes of Bestia and Calpurnius by entering into private negotiations of the kind that had effectively destroyed their reputations. He would act openly: He sent for all men of senatorial rank who were serving with the army, and others whom he thought appropriate—perhaps some of the more influential knights—and met them in a council that set the terms of surrender. Jugurtha was to hand over all his elephants, a great number of horses and arms and, it is reported, two hundred thousand pounds of silver. The figure must be exaggerated, but whatever it was, it must have been large. One of the conditions may have been some Numidian horsemen to serve as Roman auxiliaries because they suddenly appear under Metellus's command after these negotiations.

Jugurtha met the conditions and, upon Metellus's orders, handed over those Roman deserters whom he had; those deserters with more forethought had headed farther west to Mauretania and King Bocchus.

At about this time Marius was told by a diviner in Utica that he was destined for great things and should, therefore, push his chances. The advice agreed with him; he was ambitious and the prediction conferred a certain license to press for the consulship, the office he desired and meant to have. And yet it might have seemed impossible that a man of Marius's standing—honorable, yes, but not of a great family—could attain that office. The consulship was practically a bauble passed about between a handful of the most powerful patrician and noble families, not something to be awarded to an outsider, whatever his accomplishments or qualifications.

Metellus's moderate successes were not enough to satisfy the public; by 108 the commons were growing unhappy with the war. They could hardly appreciate his difficulties, and upright though he was, he couldn't count on pubic opinion; he might rely on the senate, but the senate was already losing its influence.

Jugurtha, as he'd always done before, reneged on his agreement and returned to war. Had he gone through with the surrender, Metellus would have been the hero of the war, and the reputation of the aristocracy might have been shored up for a while. In the face of Jugurtha's accustomed behavior, the senate took the step of making Metellus proconsul—essentially extending his consular powers in that area so that he could continue the war. It was a reasonable step on the senate's part; Metellus had done much better than his predecessors, even if his progress was slower than the people had hoped for. He was familiar with the enemy and with his army, he hadn't shown the incompetence of a Bestia or Aulus, and he couldn't be attacked for venality. All in all he was the best choice to finish off the war and restore some of the old senatorial luster.

Marius had by now settled on a run for the consulship and asked Metellus for leave to return to Rome. Sallust suggests that Metellus was shocked that a man of Marius's background and social standing could even think of such a thing. The Roman historian is probably right enough about the general sentiments of the proud, traditional, patrician general, but whatever his exact view of the matter, he denied Marius's request. Though he is said to have told Marius that he'd give him leave when affairs were more settled, he wasn't given a chance to head back to Italy for some time. When Marius repeatedly pressed Metellus for leave, the exasperated general is said to have used sarcasm, telling him that he should seek the consulship when his own son sought it. Metellus's son, then about twenty, was serving on his father's staff. Marius, then forty-nine, could hardly have taken the jab with equanimity.

He began to work against Metellus in subtle ways. He slandered the general to the Roman merchants in Utica, suggesting that Metellus could not finish up the war. These merchants would not have been mere small-time traders, but men with the capital to set up businesses abroad or to supply the army. They were, in fact, knights. The protracted war in the nearby territories had caused them losses and no doubt slowed down the development of the area generally. As men of Marius's class they were sympathetic and generally hostile to the senate. Marius himself was in a rather good position. He could promise peace to those traders who wanted it, and favors to those who supplied the army.

These men had friends and business associates at Rome, men with influence, men with the time and money to trouble the senate and stir the mob to their advantage. These knights began to write disparaging letters about Metellus to their friends at Rome, and suggested that, if Marius were consul, he could bring the war to an end.

Marius had grown popular with the army during the course of the campaign; he was known to live more like a soldier than an aristocrat—he ate a common soldier's rough food, for example, and sometimes stood guard duty. He now loosened the discipline of those troops under his command to enhance his popularity.

Marius's timing was good too—the anti-corruption legislation proposed by the tribune Gaius Mamilius Limetanus had passed some time before, and there was still a good deal of popular sentiment against the senate. Still, Marius had to get away if he were to take advantage of his preparations and of the situation in Rome. He was delayed by Jugurtha's return to war; it gave Metellus the need, or the excuse, to keep Marius with the army.

The town of Vaga, which Metellus had garrisoned while passing through Numidia at the start of his campaign, had a change of heart. During a festival, the centurions, the military tribunes and the prefect Titus Turpilius Silanus were lured into the homes of the town leaders, where all but Turpilius were murdered. The common soldiers were wandering the streets unarmed, and a general massacre of them followed. Turpilius alone escaped. Sallust asks the question that must have been on a number of tongues, and expressed what was probably a common opinion:

> Whether this happened through the sympathy of his host or by agreement or chance, I can not determine; but because, in such a terrible situation, he preferred a disgraced life to a good reputation, he seems unfit and detestable.[7]

It seems to have been the opinion that Marius held of Turpilius.

Metellus was appalled and furious at the news. He left winter quarters at nightfall soon after with one of his legions and with some Numidian light horse. They marched through the night, through territory that Jugurtha had assigned to a certain Nabdalsa whose charge was to keep the Romans from devastating the country near their winter quarters. Nabdalsa missed the Romans; no warning was sent to Vaga. Metellus reached the outskirts of Vaga late the next morning. After some promises of booty to urge on the sullen and tired men, he put the horsemen in front of his column in loose order to screen the infantry behind, which followed in close ranks. They hid their standards.

The townspeople rightly took them to be Romans at first and closed the gates. They could see, however, that no one was despoiling the surrounding fields, and that the army was led by Numidian horse. They decided they had been mistaken, and that the army was in fact Numidian. Opening the gates, a number of townspeople went out to meet them. The troops attacked them and seized the town.

Even so, the matter of Vaga was not finished yet: There was the problem of Turpilius. The man was an old friend of Metellus, in fact he was probably one of his clients, and this put the general in a difficult situation. If Turpilius had been incompetent, then something must be done for the discipline of the army. As a friend or client, however, punishing the man would be difficult. Marius wasn't constrained by any such personal ties and he had developed an enmity toward Turpilius. "Marius, being one of the council of war, was not only violent against him himself, but also incensed most of the others, so that Metellus was forced, much against his will, to put him to death."[8] He was flogged and executed, "for he was a Latin citizen."[9]

This seemed to mark an open break between Metellus and his lieutenant. Plutarch tells us that Turpilius was later found to have been wrongly charged,

> and when others were comforting Metellus, who took heavily the loss of his friend, Marius, rather insulting and arrogating it to himself, boasted in all companies that he had involved Metellus in the guilt of putting his friend to death.[10]

Marius's motives were likely mixed. He was first and foremost a soldier. He would be consul seven times and he craved more than anything the social position of the aristocracy, but he would turn out to be a clumsy politician, as his tribunate had showed. It was by his soldiering that he had made his reputation, and by soldiering that he would enhance it. True, he had allied himself through marriage with the patrician house of the Caesars, but it was his military career that would make him. He took a great interest in war and command, and in his soldiers, and Turpilius's misfortune was just the sort of thing Marius could never have tolerated. The account shows something of Marius's character, for though Sallust does not record it, Plutarch's mention of the incident, even if exaggerated or untrue, illustrates the way in which Marius was perceived and foreshadows his willingness, toward the end of his life, to kill those who opposed him.

A second point is this: The mere fact of pushing Metellus into a position where he had to order the death of his client was a test of power—

Marius himself was not acting as Metellus's client, he was acting independently and undercutting Metellus. And furthermore, the estrange-
ment between the two men was useful. Metellus might now be inclined
to let Marius leave the staff, and the lieutenant, by distancing himself
from Metellus and therefore from the Metelli generally, was positioning
himself all the more effectively for the consular elections. He was less
likely, now, to be seen as attached to the aristocracy.

But if there was dissension in the Roman camp, something like it was
happening at Jugurtha's court. Bomilcar grew anxious about his relations
with Jugurtha because he had tried to persuade the king to surrender.
With Jugurtha's refusal he began to worry about his own safety, and it is
likely that Metellus's continued though moderate successes were disquieting to him too. If eventually the king were to lose the war, then what
safety was there in sticking with him? Wouldn't Bomilcar find himself in
a poor situation after a Roman victory? Murder and bail jumping would
give the Romans all they needed to put him out of the way, the Massiva
affair would not be forgotten. On the other hand, Metellus's offer of senatorial leniency and financial restitution in the event of Bomilcar's
treachery would have seemed doubly attractive if he were losing
Jugurtha's confidence.

Bomilcar's solution was to form a cabal of important Numidians including Nabdalsa, captain of the forces near the border with Africa.
Whatever their exact plan—apparently murder—it failed to come off
when Nabdalsa didn't appear at the rendezvous. Bomilcar took the dangerous expedient of sending Nabdalsa a letter about the matter, but the
man's secretary happened to read it and fled to the king. Nabdalsa did
the same and won the king's pardon—it must have been on an assurance
that he really had no truck with Bomilcar in the matter. He must have forfeited the king's trust, but Bomilcar and others were executed.

Metellus's constant intrigue with Jugurtha's envoys and lieutenants
had not succeeded in provoking a treacherous hand-over of the king, or
his murder. But as to the probable secondary purpose of eroding
Jugurtha's confidence in his associates, it was working. Jugurtha lost
faith in his fellows and began to live under great strain, taking precau-
tions. He slept in one place and then another. Metellus, meanwhile, prepared for the new campaign.

But as he prepared, he made a crucial political mistake: He allowed
Marius leave to visit Rome and seek the consulship at the end of 108. The
men were estranged and Metellus couldn't have placed much confidence
in his aggrieved lieutenant, but all the same he gave Marius leave so late

in the season that it must have seemed unlikely that he could reach the city in time for the election. He had about twelve days to get there from the province of Africa. Marius spent two days and a night racing from the camp to Utica, where he took a ship and with a fair wind reached Rome in four days.

He was received joyously by the commons, who had been worked up by the letters of Marius's friends in Africa.

> The general's nobility, which before had been an ornament, was now a source of discontent, but the other's humble origin added to his popularity. Still, on both sides the enthusiasm of the parties was more important than the candidates' good or bad qualities.[11]

Marius and his friends had done well: The knight from Arpinum was now a country bumpkin who'd made good. And the view was widely accepted. Plutarch, writing years later, repeated the propaganda that Marius had come off the farm: "He was born of parents altogether obscure and indigent, who supported themselves by their daily labor. . . ."[12]

The tribunes did their part, abusing Metellus at the *contiones*—public debates—and praising Marius. The commons were spoiling to teach the nobility a lesson, and elected Marius, the first *novus homo* in years. A "new man" was one who held the consulship for the first time in his family's history. This was not in itself a bad thing to the aristocracy—perhaps the senate would have found it useful as a way of dispelling anti-senatorial feeling—but Marius's election stunned it. His victory gave the mob a feeling of power and encouraged the tribune Titus Manlius Mancinus to propose a scheme: that Marius be given command of the war in Numidia. Although the senate had already given the Numidian war to Metellus as proconsul, it acquiesced in the people's unconstitutional demand. This was a fatal step; it was the senate that controlled foreign policy and military affairs, and the senate's action showed the commons what power it had. Despite its flaws, only the senate had the experience to handle these matters. By caving in to the commons the senators had begun to cede one of their greatest responsibilities to a section of society unfit to exercise it, and the Roman Republic—so finely balanced by tradition, law and social division—began to wobble. Among themselves the Romans had always been great compromisers. Perhaps this wobbling seemed tolerable.

*   *   *

Things were continuing apace in Numidia. Jugurtha executed a number of his associates in order to maintain the loyalty of others, but in fact he only became more isolated. A number of his friends ran off to the Romans, others to King Bocchus of Mauretania, Jugurtha's father-in-law. After losing another engagement, Jugurtha fled with some cavalry and fugitives to the town of Thala, where his children and most of his treasury were. When Metellus learned of this he was determined to take the town, though it was protected by fifty miles of empty desert. It was an ambitious undertaking for an army of the time. The old patrician must have gauged that working such a seeming impossibility would in itself be a stunning surprise. Jugurtha could not expect such a thing; he would likely be trapped in the town and captured. Whether he took the entire army or not is unclear, but he must have taken most of it.[13] Metellus was preparing to move, perhaps, fifteen thousand men, most of them marching, across the desert.

He ordered that the baggage animals carry nothing but water and ten days of grain and he requisitioned herd animals from the locals and loaded them with vessels too. He ordered the Numidians of the neighborhood to meet the army with water part way along his march to Thala. Metellus then marched off toward Jugurtha's stronghold. When he reached the rendezvous he'd arranged with the pacified Numidians, there came a heavy rain as the soldiers were pitching camp—enough, it is said, to supply the troops. The Numidians too had brought water, more than Metellus had expected; the solders preferred the rainwater, seeing it as heaven-sent. The next day the Romans appeared before Thala to the shock and horror of the townspeople. Jugurtha prudently fled in the night with his children and most of his treasury. He continued to move restlessly after that, not spending two days in the same place. "Besides he feared betrayal which he hoped to defeat by movement for such plans need leisure and opportunity."[14]

Metellus let him flee and concentrated on the town. He displayed the Roman penchant for engineering: He built a palisade around the town and circumvallated it. At two points he brought up mantlets and with their protection raised ramps against the wall on which he set siege towers. The town was taken in forty days, but there was little booty for the troops. Among the defenders were Roman deserters who, realizing the end had come, took the more valuable items to the palace and set fire to everything. Palace, treasure and deserters were destroyed.

Jugurtha's flight took him to a subject people of his, the Gaetulians, a rather barbaric tribe from whom he conscripted soldiers. He also contrived to maneuver his neighbor King Bocchus of Mauretania into the war. Jugurtha was married to one of Bocchus's daughters and he offered him a good deal of the territory of western Numidia if he would join him against Rome. Bocchus had already been unwisely rebuffed by the senate at the beginning of the war: He had sent an embassy seeking alliance and it had been discourteously refused. With Bocchus, Jugurtha could expect three things to operate in his favor: greed for territory, anger at the senate's slight and ignorance of Rome's real power.

Marius, meanwhile, was making plans and carrying them out. Metellus, fighting in the wastes of Numidia, had no idea that his command was at an end and that his former lieutenant would now try his hand at ending the war.

CHAPTER 7

Marius and Jugurtha

STRIKING THE ATTITUDE AS AN OUTSIDER HAD PLAYED WELL with the public, and the support of his friends in the knightly order had paid off—Marius had pulled off one of the most difficult coups for a plebeian in Roman politics: He had gotten himself elected consul for 107. Now it was time for business. After his election to the consulate and the delivery of the Numidian command to him, Marius called the people to an assembly and took the opportunity to enthuse the commons about his coming campaign. A reason for this was to roil them up against the nobility. Now that he'd reached the consulship and thus ennobled himself and his family, he lost no time in taunting the rest of the nobility—showing at the same time his terrific ambition, his hatred of the established aristocracy and his political ineptitude. Plutarch states that Marius claimed

> that he had carried off the consulship as a spoil from the effeminacy of the wealthy and high-born citizens, and telling the people that he gloried in wounds he had himself received for them, as much as others did in the monuments of dead men, and images of their ancestors.[1]

Marius provoked the nobility with speeches like this after his election knowing that the crowd loved such bold attacks on them. They wanted to hear them, he was willing to do it and he gained a good deal of political capital in return. The aristocracy had criticized Tiberius and Gaius Gracchus for appealing too much to the mob but they at least were tribunes. Marius was now one of their own order.

Marius had learned something during his lieutenancy to Metellus: There were too few soldiers in Numidia. In fact—and he knew this full well too—the Roman army was not well-suited to this sort of campaigning but, all the same, more troops wouldn't hurt. Another few thousand men might help tip the balance. But where to get them?

Marius strengthened his forces, asking the senate to countenance it. He called up veteran soldiers and auxiliaries—experienced and toughened men—and he induced them to join him through various promises. And he called on subject kings to send troops as well.

The senate happily allowed him to do this, judging that increased enrollment would dissipate his popularity. They were quite wrong. Marius had thumped hard during his campaign, and the people listened approvingly to their new common-man consul, veteran of Numantia and Numidia. And he gave many speeches, on the one hand taunting the aristocracy and on the other promising victory and spoils to divide among the troops. Consular generals were often stingy with spoils. He made it clear he would not be.

He was able to get veteran volunteers and perhaps the senate ought to have guessed that he would. The decades of war in Spain and other places had turned out thousands of trained soldiers and many of them would have found themselves strangers to civilian life after years of fighting in the provinces. Many were doubtless impoverished at home through their service abroad. The army had been their life and Marius was calling them back home. These men were professional soldiers with loyalty perhaps tilting from the state and toward the army—an institution that had looked after them more completely than the republic.

Marius enrolled another and more numerous kind of recruit. "He [Marius] himself meanwhile enrolled soldiers, not according to the old custom, nor according to the classes, but whoever wished to be was taken, mostly the *capite censi*."[2] These men, the men with nothing, were willing to join for any number of reasons. While not high, there was pay, and there was an ordered life, decent clothing and the chance of booty and perhaps even a land allotment at discharge. For a desperately poor man with no real future, living a precarious and empty life, the army would look good—especially an army led not by the usual senatorial incompetent, but by a proven commander.

These men, even more than the reenlisted veterans, had cause to take Marius as their patron. He equipped them with clothing, food, armor and weapons.[3] He set these men up and trained them, and he put them on the road to make something of themselves. They wouldn't forget—they were his clients.

Marius's action in taking the *capite censi* when there was no emergency was a revolutionary step in another sense: By taking volunteers instead of conscripting soldiers from among the people generally, he had shifted the Roman army toward becoming a professional organization, distinct from a well-ordered militia. And this held real menace for the state. A militia army should have felt its first duty to the state and to the senate at its head. Marius's half-professional army quite naturally had an interest in his happiness and success. He was a senator, he was a consul; but more than that, he was their patron.

Marius left his quaestor, Lucius Cornelius Sulla, behind with the duty of raising a number of cavalry in Latium and from allied cities. This man was singularly striking in appearance. He was blond and blue-eyed, and his face apparently wine-marked: white and splotched with vivid red marks. His future was to be as remarkable as his appearance—he would become Marius's bitterest enemy and, in time, would march upon Rome with his own army.

He was a patrician, not merely an aristocrat or noble. But his branch of the Cornelii clan, unlike, say, the Scipii, had fallen into obscurity and straitened circumstances. As a young man he had lived in a cheap apartment and had come into a moderate fortune through inheritance. His stepmother, who adored him, left him her entire estate, as did his mistress Nicopolis, a women several years older. He was intelligent and politic, and he enjoyed luxury. Velleius Paterculus would later say that he was a "man who, at the very point of victory, could not be praised enough, nor after victory reviled enough."[4] This would be the common opinion after his death.

Sulla was unlike Marius in several ways: He was well-educated in Greek and Roman letters, had a smooth personality, made friends easily, enjoyed actors and clowns and, in sharp contrast to the consul, had no military experience. He proved to be a quick learner, however, and not just of tactics and strategy. He made friends among his troops with gifts, loans and an easy manner. Marius had married into a patrician clan; perhaps he thought it would be good to have this patrician in his pocket.

Metellus, meanwhile, was still struggling to defeat Jugurtha and prevent Bocchus from allying with his son-in-law. He had learned already that Marius had won the consulship, but he then found out he had been stripped of the Numidian command, only to have it given to a man who had been his client. He is said to have become terribly distraught at the news, beside himself with frustration. He decided not to prosecute the war for Marius's benefit; he sent envoys to Bocchus and remonstrated with the Moorish king, telling him that he was unwise to choose war on behalf of Jugurtha when he could have peace with the Romans. Messages were sent back and forth, but though Bocchus may have equivocated, he did not abandon his ally. Metellus stalled the war until Marius was ready to prosecute it in his place.

Marius's legate, Aulus Manlius, appeared in the African province first, with supplies, arms and money. He was joined shortly by Marius with his new troops. The Roman army already in Africa—Metellus's troops—were turned over to Marius by Metellus's legate, Publius Rutilius, because Metellus could not bear to turn them over himself.

Metellus then returned to Rome and was quite surprised to find himself warmly greeted by the commons and the nobles alike—the hard feelings that the knights had whipped up against him in the mob were already forgotten. He acquired the cognomen, or nickname, Numidicus for his successes against Jugurtha. It was likely he had mixed feelings about his unsuspected rehabilitation—he had regained his standing, but it was among the mob. He couldn't have put much value in their opinion, for they were prey to demagogues, who used them to take him away from a campaign he was slowly winning. Their reversion to former opinion was cold comfort—they'd already been used against him. His natural allies the nobles had failed him when they allowed the mob to arrogate the senate's right of appointing generals. Their good opinion of him had not been enough of an inspiration to them to protect his interests.

While Metellus settled back into the life of the city, Marius began his campaign. Much of the army was now experienced; they'd been put back under discipline by Metellus, he had led them with constant, if moderate, success, and they were hardened to campaigning in the hot country. This was not the case with Marius's poor volunteers, and he knew to break them into the war slowly. Accordingly he exposed his troops to small fights until they were confident of themselves and the new and old soldiers grew easy with each other. He kept his promise about booty; he was liberal in giving it to them, and this increased their enthusiasm for campaigning.

Jugurtha and Bocchus decided not to meet Marius right away. The two separated and went into difficult country, inviting the Romans to divide themselves. Marius, for his part, carried out careful reconnaissance and kept his troops in hand. He engaged and defeated Jugurtha near Cirta, which suggests that Jugurtha may have continued to threaten the town as he had when Metellus was still in command. After this Marius occupied towns that were strategically important to Jugurtha because, like Metellus, he found that winning battles did not bring the war to a close. In short, for all of the criticism he had levelled at Metellus, he himself followed the same strategy. In Marius's case he was likely to be somewhat more successful if only because he had more troops at his disposal and could garrison more places. In other words, he could occupy a bit more ground than Metellus could have done. But still Jugurtha remained elusive. Bocchus, however, began to make overtures to Marius, though again nothing came of it.

Marius continued to take Jugurtha's towns by either force, fear or bribery, though Jugurtha could not be provoked to attack. Marius, who followed the very strategy he had criticized in Metellus, decided to emulate him in another way: As Metellus had taken Thala, he would take Capsa. Capsa, like Thala, was surrounded by desert, except that there were no springs at all outside of the walls. There was only one spring within them, and the townspeople had to supplement this with rainwater. If the capture of Thala was the product of foresight and daring, this attack, given Sallust's description of Capsa, would seem to have been foolhardy. Still, Marius was nothing if not the practical soldier; he doesn't seem to have been a commander to take unnecessary risks. Therefore, it may be that Sallust has magnified the danger of the march on Capsa in his account of the war.

Marius prepared carefully; he sent Aulus Manlius with some light-armed cohorts to the town of Laris, where he had left money and supplies, and let it out that he would join his legate there to forage. Instead, Marius marched for six days to the river Tanaïs, where the army camped until sunset. They put aside most of the baggage and loaded themselves and the animals only with water. In the evening the army headed out, marching only by night until it reached hilly ground close by Capsa at the end of the third night. Marius hid the army as well as he could, and waited for sunrise.

But when the day began and many Numidians came out of the town fearing nothing hostile, suddenly he ordered all the cavalry and with them the swiftest of the footsoldiers to race to Capsa and attack the gates.[5]

As at Vaga, which Metellus had tricked into opening its gates, the town was taken. The townspeople surrendered when they saw so many of their fellows outside the walls and the enemy literally at the gates. Yet Capsa's fate was much worse than Vaga's for Marius treated it with calculated cruelty. All the adult males were killed, the rest sold into slavery and the town burned. The money made by selling the people of Capsa into slavery was distributed among the troops. Sallust himself calls the treatment of Capsa a violation of the laws of war, but excuses it, rather ineffectively, as necessary since the place was useful to Jugurtha, hard for the Romans to reach, and the inhabitants, as Numidians, untrustworthy.

Marius apparently took the town without loss, and this increased his already high reputation. Booty—and no doubt the money from selling the inhabitants of Capsa—made him extremely popular with the soldiers: He was looking after them, just as he said he would.

And the destruction of Capsa was a key to future successes. A few towns resisted Marius, but many he found abandoned and burned; the inhabitants had fled in dread of him. In the course of this town-taking campaign, Marius decided to seize Jugurtha's treasure house, a fortress near the Muluccha River, situated on a plateau and difficult to reach. Again there was a precedent for this: It was what the incompetent Aulus Postumius Albinus had tried when he besieged Suthul.

Marius at first made little progress. The ground proved to be too steep to allow siege machinery, and the consul was stymied. Meanwhile, Marius's quaestor Sulla arrived from Italy with a large number of horsemen. Just as Marius had determined that more infantry were needed to finish the war, he had decided that he must field more cavalry as well, to meet the threat posed by the Numidian and Moorish horse.

Marius then was very lucky. A Ligurian soldier from an auxiliary cohort was going for water when he noticed snails in the rocks near the bottom of the hill on which the fortress sat. He set to work trying to gather them and found a way up the edge of the plateau. He was able to clamber onto it with the help of a large oak that grew near the edge. He went back down, careful to remember the path, and reported it to Marius.

The following day Marius sent a handful of men up the path, guided by the Ligurian: five trumpeters, four centurions and a number of common soldiers. Each man was lightly fitted out, only a Numidian shield and a sword slung over his back. When Marius heard from a messenger that they had made the plateau, he ordered the men besieging the walls to form the *testudo,* or "turtle" formation. They formed themselves into blocks, the men on the outside with their long shields held vertically edge-to-edge, the men in the center of the blocks holding their shields over their heads horizontally to form a roof. This was a popular Roman formation for approaching enemy walls since the men were protected on all sides, and above as well, against missiles. Archers, slingers and catapults supported them, and this attack, as intended, occupied the enemy's attention. It even drew some of them out of the walls and onto the plateau to meet the attackers.

As this was happening the trumpet squad, which had scaled the plateau on the side away from the general attack, sounded their horns, giving the impression of a second attack. The enemy, confused and panicked, lost heart, and the Romans were able to take the wall.

After the fall of Capsa, Bocchus wavered, and it may have been at this time, rather than earlier, that Jugurtha offered him Numidian territory in exchange for his help.[6] Bocchus held to his alliance, and the two decided to attack the Romans as they marched to winter quarters.[7] They attacked near the end of the day:

> . . . they thought that the night, which was already approaching, would be a protection for them if they were about to be defeated while, if they prevailed it would be no obstacle because they knew the country, while against the Romans either result would be more difficult in darkness.[8]

Sallust could only guess at the kings' intentions, but he was surely right. Jugurtha's predilection for night attacks and surprises shows that the Numidians didn't have the numbers to engage the Romans in a set battle. Their strength lay in speed, delay, persistence and geography. And besides, night battles of any size or importance in the ancient world were extremely rare because of the difficulty in ordering troops and the impossibility of controlling them unseen.

As he approached winter quarters, Marius's scouts informed him of the enemy, but almost immediately the Gaetulian and Moorish horse appeared and began their attack, which was loose, and without any real order, "more like a bandit attack than a battle."[9]

The Romans had no time to form up to receive them, and the horse and foot became mingled. Some kept the enemy at bay until their comrades were properly armed. As the battle developed, the footsoldiers ranged themselves in circles to stand off attacks from all sides. Marius led a troop of cavalry and took a pair of nearby hills, one with a large spring and the other big enough for a camp and steep enough to offer good protection. Marius ordered Sulla to guard the spring that night with cavalry, and then he gathered his men little by little and led them up the larger hill at a jog. Night was falling and the kings were obliged to break off the attack. Night had helped the Romans more than them. The enemy passed the night in jolly disorder in the ground about the hills. Their incautious behavior heartened the Romans, who watched them from the heights. The consul wished to lull the enemy and ordered the men to remain quiet, as well they might be inclined to do anyway.

At dawn the trumpets sounded above the sleeping enemy and the Romans rushed down upon them shouting. The attack caught them quite unprepared; they had no proper camp in the Roman style to help stand off an attacker, and the soldiers routed them. This battle shows clearly that while disciplined soldiers may be caught off-guard by troops of barbarians, once brought back into order their enemy could not match them. Usually, discipline trumps fervor.

Marius continued the march toward winter quarters, but in a square formation—a Roman tactic in particularly dangerous circumstances—the soldiers on the outside, the baggage and attendants on the inside; it was probably not much different, if at all, from the defensive formation Metellus had used on his first foray into Numidia two years before. It must have been a slow march, but the formation would discourage attack from any side. To maintain discipline and hearten the soldiers Marius himself made rounds of inspection in his marching camps. He was wise to maintain discipline and lead by example.

On the fourth day of the march scouts came back to the marching column from all directions; the enemy was approaching from all sides. Marius stopped the column and kept it in the defensive square formation until he could determine whether the attack would come from any particular direction. It came from three sides: Jugurtha against the head of the column, Bocchus the rear and others against Sulla on the right. It was a sharp battle in which, apparently, Jugurtha was surrounded by Roman cavalry, but managed, as always, to slip away. It ended as a Roman victory, said to be resounding, but not in itself conclusive. In effect the Numidian state was Jugurtha himself, and until he was captured or killed the war would drag on.

There was, however, one happy result for Marius from the battle outside of Cirta to compensate for the now usual strategically ineffective Roman victory: The Moorish king sent envoys to Marius five days after the battle to treat for peace. Apparently Bocchus was losing confidence in Jugurtha and the prospects of the war. Of course, one could hardly be sure of the offer; Bocchus had dealt with Metellus and nothing had come of it.

Marius took his chance, or more properly took a chance with his lieutenants. He had too, of course, for he needed experienced men to visit the king. He sent his legates Sulla and Aulus Manlius to hear the king's proposal. The two Romans, however, decided to push things a bit and took it upon themselves to discuss matters with the king rather than to merely listen and report. Sulla was to do the talking; he was the more eloquent, which was to be expected of a patrician with a good classical education.

Sulla encouraged Bocchus toward peace, and the king agreed to send envoys to the senate, but he wavered later under the influence of men at his court who were sympathetic to Jugurtha. Sulla and Aulus stayed on at Bocchus's court, where they could hardly have been comfortable in the hands of a barbarian king who was incapable of holding to a decision.

When his legates returned from treating unsuccessfully with Bocchus, Marius left his winter quarters with light infantry and horse to lay siege to a fort that Jugurtha had garrisoned with Roman deserters. He left Sulla in charge of the army at Cirta. Marius's continuing actions may have alarmed Bocchus, for he began again to seek peace. As envoys he chose five trusted relatives and sent them on their way to Marius with instructions to continue on to Rome if they thought this advisable. They had complete discretion to make peace.

His unfortunate envoys were attacked along their way by Gaetulian bandits, who left them practically nothing. Nevertheless they proceeded toward Cirta, where Sulla received them. They must have had little more than the clothes on their backs, and so would have appreciated Sulla's kindnesses when he received them. For he took this as an opportunity to treat them graciously and win them over during Marius's absence, which lasted more than a month.

Marius carried the siege and returned to Cirta, where, learning of the envoys, he called a council at Utica consisting of the provincial prefect, Lucius Bellienus, and all the senators who happened to be in the province of Africa, and ordered the envoys to go there with Sulla. The council agreed to the envoys' request to visit Rome, and three of them sailed off accompanied by the quaestor Cornelius Octavius Ruso, who had come to Africa to deliver the troops' pay. Two of the envoys were sent back to Bocchus to inform him of the situation.

At Rome the envoys were told that Bocchus would have Rome's friendship when he had earned it. Apparently an offer to cease hostilities was not enough. From the standpoint of its dignity the senate could hardly ask him to betray his ally in some way, but it is difficult to see exactly what else the senators could have meant. In any event, this vague injunction could only have spurred Bocchus to act as he later did.

When he learned of the senate's position, Bocchus invited Sulla to meet him and discuss their mutual interests. Sulla obliged and left with a bodyguard of horse and a number of light soldiers so that he could travel quickly: archers, Balearic slingers and a cohort of Paelignians equipped with velite equipment—helmet, shield, sword and javelins.

On the fifth day of Sulla's march, Bocchus's son Volux alarmed the Roman expedition when he appeared with a large number of horsemen. Sallust says they numbered a thousand, but this round figure seems high. The Romans prepared to fight, but the Moors were not in any order— they weren't arrayed for battle—so that when the first of the horsemen approached the soldiers and claimed they were not there to fight, but to escort, the Romans took them at their word, a dangerous thing if they numbered as many as Sallust says. The Moors and Romans went along together the rest of the day.

That night in the camp Volux learned, doubtless from a scout, that Jugurtha was in the neighborhood. What Jugurtha was doing is unclear. He may have been moving about the countryside to see what opportunities there were for him, but he'd proved himself shrewd many times, and it's probable that he was either shadowing the Romans or Volux to learn what was going on. He certainly had men at Bocchus's court who could have informed him that the Moorish king was speaking with the Romans—Sulla and Aulus's visit could not have been a secret to him—and he must have known that Volux had gone off with a large troop of horsemen. In any case, he was nearby and he was a threat.

Volux advised Sulla to flee. The legate refused; his forces, though small, were not negligible. We cannot know the exact number, but he did have his bodyguard of horse, a cohort of light infantry—five hundred to six hundred men—and his archers and slingers. It seems probable that he may have had a good seven hundred or even a thousand men with him. The light horsemen of the area, whether Moors, Numidians or Gaetulians, were mounted javelineers. If Sulla could trust Volux—and this wasn't entirely clear—he also had a number of them to help defend him. His slingers and archers could easily outrange Jugurtha's light horse, and his Paelignians, as veterans, would have been a match for quite a number of barbarian infantry, even though their equipment was lighter than a legionary's. Sulla did, however, agree to march by night. He ordered the men to build fires, as though they were passing the night in camp, and then marched out in silence about midnight.

After Sulla and the Moors had marched the night through, Jugurtha was discovered two miles ahead of them. The general opinion was that Volux had led the Roman forces into a trap, and Sulla agreed. He would not agree, though, to a demand by a number of his men that they kill Volux for it. Instead he ordered Volux and his men out of the camp for their evident hostility in bringing him to this pass. Volux argued with emotion that he wasn't in league with Jugurtha, who was acting in his own interests. He proposed a rather daring plan: that he accompany Sulla in a march through Jugurtha's camp.

Camp is no doubt too good a word for it—it was probably just a loose bivouac. Jugurtha's force was not big and he was evidently not prepared for a battle. The king's son argued that Jugurtha depended too much on his father Bocchus to allow Sulla's embassy to be attacked with Volux himself as a witness. As a political argument it had its points. Sulla accepted it, but bolstered it with speed: They marched immediately for Jugurtha's position so that he wouldn't have time to react. They passed through his camp without incident, and reached Bocchus a few days later. Sulla established his camp near that of Bocchus.

Once there Sulla began the underhanded business that passed for diplomacy in the area. We can be fairly certain of what happened because Sulla wrote of it in his memoirs. They are lost, but Sallust read them and made use of them in writing his account of the war.

Sulla was not the only envoy at Bocchus's court. When Jugurtha learned that Bocchus was dealing with the Romans he sent an envoy of his own, a man named Aspar. This meant, of course, that any negotiations between the Roman and Moor were apt to be noticed—and reported—even if their import wasn't known. Jugurtha must have been extremely suspicious by now, but he wasn't in a position to do much. As Volux had observed, his future depended for the most part upon Bocchus. He had lost too much over the course of the war: towns, men, the loyalty of his closest followers and money. He had so far eluded capture, but the steady Roman pressure was slowly bringing him to bay.

Sulla had some cause for disquiet himself. Bocchus sent Sulla a certain Dabar, one of his followers, to tell him that he and the king should meet openly in front of Aspar. This would presumably allay the Numidian envoy's concerns. It seems that Sulla could not have been convinced by this argument. Nothing could be done in front of Aspar, and Bocchus's request suggested that he merely wanted to delay things. This excuse for delay may have meant that Bocchus couldn't decide who to betray to whom: Jugurtha to Sulla, or Sulla to Jugurtha. If Marius found his legate in the Numidian's hands he would be severely compromised: holding a hostage of Sulla's importance might allow Jugurtha to wring concessions from the consul.

Sulla agreed to meet Bocchus in front of Aspar, but proposed that the meeting be something of a sham; they wouldn't conclude anything at it. In fact, he dictated the response that Bocchus would give to his demands. The next day the meeting was held and Sulla put the question to him whether he wanted peace or war. As agreed, Bocchus told Sulla that he would answer him in ten days. Both men returned to their camps. Their business was not concluded, however, for Sulla went to Bocchus in secret during the night and put his terms to him: that Bocchus's promise to withdraw beyond the Muluccha River, which formed the boundary between Mauretania and Numidia, was insufficient to buy peace. He would have to do something to benefit the Romans more directly—he would have to give Jugurtha to them.

The king protested, arguing that he could not break his treaty to Jugurtha and that if he did so he would alienate his own people, who liked the Numidian and had no affection for the Romans. Sulla argued with him, cajoled and no doubt threatened him with further war until the king agreed to the betrayal.

Another meeting followed the next day, this time between Bocchus and Aspar, who was told that Bocchus was not in a position to make peace with the Romans both for himself and on behalf of Jugurtha. Sallust tells us that the envoy, delighted at the news, left for Jugurtha's camp. He returned eight days later saying that his king was willing to cooperate but that he mistrusted Marius. He explained that Jugurtha had tried to make peace before but that things had fallen through. And it was true, though the Romans had had little to do with these failures. He thought, though, that he could see a way to force the Romans to keep to whatever terms they made or that he could extort.

The plan was simple. When the three of them met to discuss peace, Bocchus would seize Sulla and hand him over to Jugurtha. Bocchus agreed to this. In a subsequent meeting with Sulla, he made the same promise to seize Jugurtha.

In the end Bocchus kept his promise to Sulla. On the morning of the peace conference Bocchus rode out to a hillock with Sulla; men lay in wait about it. When Jugurtha appeared, unarmed and with only a few followers, he was rushed and his men killed. Sulla took him back to Marius.

This bit of treachery ended a war full of betrayals, skirmishes, haggling and sieges. In itself it had been rather a pointless affair—the Romans didn't even annex Jugurtha's territory. But it had made Marius's reputation and begun Sulla's career. More than that it had accelerated the senate's eclipse at the hands of the mob and the powerful men who could turn it to their advantage.

Meanwhile, Roman armies were being defeated in the north as the barbarians fought them in the Alps. Marius, contrary to constitutional custom, was elected consul in his absence for 104. He should have been in Rome if he were a candidate, and he should not have been reelected so soon after his first consulship. But the people would not be thwarted and the senate, to its loss, would not oppose them.

CHAPTER 8

Trouble in the North

IN 109 B.C., WHEN METELLUS HAD SET OFF FOR NUMIDIA, THE Cimbri and Teutones had circled back from their jaunt through Gaul. They had been a threat for years, in fact since they had defeated the consul Gaius Papirius Carbo in 113. After Carbo's defeat another barbarian tribe, the Celtic Tigurini,[1] joined themselves to the Cimbric–Teutonic alliance and ventured into Gaul with them. Near the frontier of the Gallia Transalpina, the new Roman province, they came up against an army led by a consul of 109, Marcus Junius Silanus. Doubting the outcome of a battle, they offered to submit to military service on behalf of the republic in return for land. The senate declined the offer, and the Tigurini defeated Silanus in an engagement, and as with the case of Gaius Papirius four years before, the barbarians did not follow up their advantage. In spite of these defeats, Roman prestige was still too great. The Cimbri and Teutones continued west through Gaul (Gallia Comata, the land of the long-haired Gauls—those outside of the Roman province), while the Tigurini broke off and raided in Gallia Transalpina, provoking a revolt of the Volcae Tectosages, a Celtic people subject to the Romans.

In 107 another Roman, Lucius Cassius Longinus, advanced to recover the situation. This man was Gaius Marius's colleague in the consulship and the man who, as praetor, had accompanied Jugurtha on his murderous little trip to Rome. He followed the Tigurini toward the Spanish border, where he was defeated and killed in an ambush. The Roman army was permitted to retreat after passing under the yoke.

Since Gallia Transalpina (the area lying between the Alps and the Pyrenees) was no longer threatened—the Tigurini, after their victory, did not return—the consul of 106, Quintus Servilius Caepio, was able to re-

111

duce the Volcae Tectosages and seize their capital, Tolosa.[2] There they found quite a haul of booty, some of it reputedly left by Gauls who had sacked Rome more than two hundred and fifty years before. There were said to be a hundred thousand pounds of gold and ten thousand pounds of silver, without a doubt an immense exaggeration, but nonetheless it must have been a large sum. Somehow it all managed to disappear before it reached Rome. Caepio was suspected, but nothing was proven.

Now all of these defeats (and doubtless the missing Tolosan treasure) suggested to the commons that there was a certain amount—probably a good deal—of senatorial bungling. The office of consul, and with it the most important military commands, was being traded among the best families and awarded to noble military incompetents, which had resulted in repeated defeats, the loss of soldiers drawn from the common people and the very real possibility of an invasion of Italy. The people grew uneasy.

If the Romans had long memories about the wars against Carthage, they also had long memories about northern barbarians, and with cause: In 186 the Romans had turned back a Gallic incursion, apparently with only a show of strength, and in 166 a band of Gallic invaders had been defeated by the consul Marcus Claudius Marcellus. But neither of these incursions amounted to much beside the rout of the Roman army by the Gallic Senones at the river Allia in 390 B.C.,[3] and the subsequent sack of Rome, spoils from which may have made up some of Caepio's missing Tolosan treasure.

The Gallic sack was legendary—the material from which the Roman character was made. Her greatest general, Camillus, driven by petty jealousies into wrongful exile; the great chieftain Brennus[4] of the Gallic Senones and his terrifying horde sweeping away the Roman army in one determined charge. After the battle, it was said, many Romans fled to Veii, some eight miles away, an Etruscan city they had conquered and left in ruins. There was talk of abandoning Rome and beginning again in conquered Veii. The anniversary of the battle was considered unlucky for centuries.

A number of determined Romans had held the Capitoline Hill, while older senators dressed themselves in their togas and magisterial robes and sat upon curule chairs in the forum, stolidly awaiting the entry of the Gauls. When the Gauls came upon these old men they were astonished at their calm dignity. Finally, it is recounted, a warrior touched the beard of Marcus Papirius, and the old man struck him across the head with a staff. The Gaul killed Papirius and, coming to themselves, as it were, the rest moved through the town slaughtering the grave old men.

The Romans maintained that the Gallic Senones were never able to take the Capitol—a sneak attack during the night was thwarted when the geese sacred to Juno gave an alarm. Still, the Capitoline defenders had to watch their city burn around them and, driven by hunger, paid a heavy indemnity to send the Gauls away. Roman pride was salved with a tale that the exiled general Camillus led an army of allies and Roman survivors from the Allia against the retreating Senones and defeated them north of Rome.

Whatever the truth behind this sequel, Camillus is credited with a pair of military reforms in direct response to the Gauls' chief weapon, the long sword. To help meet a second Gallic invasion thirteen years later he ordered the army to equip itself with iron helmets in place of their customary bronze in order to break the long Gallic swords or shed their blows. He is also said to have introduced the bronze binding at the top of the Roman *scutum*, so that they could not be split by sword strokes. The Romans later reverted to bronze helmets (the softer metal is easier to work), but they kept a metal binding on their long shields, a reminder of Camillus and their ancient Gallic enemies.

So now northern barbarians evoking ancient legends loured from the Alps, and the aristocracy had proved less than able to meet them. In fact, the Romans would take one more drubbing at their hands, worse than any that had gone before.

The senate responded by dispatching one of the consuls of 105, Cornelius Mallius Maximus, with a newly conscripted army to join Caepio, who was still in the north after the reduction of Tolosa, having been made proconsul after the expiration of his consulship. Mallius's legate, Marcus Aemilius Scaurus, was soon beaten while leading a force against the Cimbri, and this defeat was all the worse because the barbarians took him prisoner. Defeated Scaurus may have been, but he still carried himself with the pride and high-handedness appropriate to a Roman general when he was brought before them:

> . . . and he was called by them into their council, and when he discouraged them from going through the Alps to reach Italy because, he said, the Romans could not be defeated this way, he was killed by Boiorix, a wild youth.[5]

As for Mallius, he had difficulty keeping his men in hand, and they fell into slack discipline. Furthermore the consul and proconsul did not cooperate; it seems to have been predominately Caepio's fault. He resented Mallius's authority as consul and allowed his dignity to interfere with his duty, and hence with the public good. It was exactly the sort of thing the commons despised in the nobility. Cassius Dio writes:

> Servilius [Caepio] became the cause of many evils to the army by reason of his jealousy of his colleague; for, though he had in general equal authority, his rank was naturally diminished by the fact that the other was consul. After the death of Scaurus, Mallius had sent for Servilius; but the latter replied that each of them ought to guard his own province. Then, suspecting that Mallius might gain some success by himself, he grew jealous of him, fearing that he might secure the glory alone, and went to him; yet he neither encamped in the same place nor entered into any common plan, but took up a position between Mallius and the Cimbri, with the evident intention of being the first to join battle and so of winning all the glory of the war.[6]

Although Dio presents this as a conflict of personalities, there may have been something more to Caepio's attitude. He had successfully fought the Tectosages, and his men were tried; Mallius's were untested. Caepio was insubordinate, but he may have felt justified and may have convinced himself that he was better able than Mallius to handle the situation.

However Caepio may have reasoned it out with himself, it doesn't excuse the disaster that followed hard on his irresponsibility. The commanders acted separately in a large action near Arausio[7] on October 6 of 105, and the barbarians were able to deal with the armies separately, driving each back upon the Rhone. The casualty figures were grossly exaggerated,[8] but Cary and Scullard rate it as the worst Roman defeat since Cannae in 216 B.C.[9]

It would be an understatement to suggest that the commons were displeased. The senators must have been equally so, for it put them at the mercy of the rabble. They had in their hands the best army of the ancient world—the best organized, the best supported—and one with a long tradition of defeating opponents as wily as Hamilcar Barca, as brilliant as Hannibal and as persistent as the Macedonians. The public quite rightly suspected that Roman losses must have been the fault of the generals rather than the common soldiers. After the defeat of Caepio and Mallius, they had had enough.

The people demanded Marius as consul. This was reasonable enough given the circumstances. With the death of Scipio Aemilianus, he was Rome's most experienced general, he was popular with the soldiers and he had cast himself as a "new man," and the public favored him for it.

Unfortunately, the constitution was getting in the way—according to the *Lex Villia* no man could be consul twice until ten years had passed.

The people were quite prepared to flout the law—they'd flouted others when they'd had the power to do it: They had forced the senate to snatch the Numidian command from Metellus in 107 and hand it to Marius, while before that it had supported Tiberius Gracchus's bid for the treasure of Pergamum to support his land reforms. In fact, they had chosen Scipio Aemilianus as consul when he was underage so that he could put an end to the siege of Carthage. They wanted Marius as consul for 104 and they would have him.

The senate was in a poor position, though it was largely of its own making. True, the law of Gaius Gracchus prevented them from assigning provinces to the consuls they saw fit; there was little they could do about this clumsiness. But the consuls elected during the crisis were, with the exception of Mallius, men of the old families, and this shows that the senate still had a firm grip on the elections. Of course they might have seen to it that men who had already proven themselves militarily competent were elected consuls. We can't know why this wasn't done, though we may guess that it was the result of internal politics among the patrician families. The Scipiones had grown preeminent during the last generation, and the Metelli had done so recently. Likely the senatorial families were sparring among themselves to keep the honor of the consulship and its power of command distributed more widely, or at least away from families they judged might grow too powerful.

By this time the republic was governed by about twenty families, and they were jealous of their estate—they constantly formed alliances with each other to advance or protect themselves. Couple this with an attitude that has been common among nobility at all times and everywhere—that an aristocrat is naturally competent at whatever he sets his hand to—and one may account for the string of military blunderers who had destroyed half a dozen armies. The senators would readily fight among themselves about whom to support—with family considerations coming first, concern for the state second. In fact, it might be proper to say that the senators—the nobility and the patricians—thought of themselves as the state. What was good for them was good for Rome, and in this sense the interests of the state could not come second, for according to this view they were the same.

But the senators and the great families did not see to it that experienced generals met the German tribes. A victory over the Cimbri and Teutones might have left the senate in its dominant position, but they must have seen this too late. In the end the commons again elected Marius as a consul for 104. And they elected him in his absence (he was still in Africa), another unconstitutionality. Still, the senate capitulated; it had to in the circumstances. But with every submission to the people its grip on the state weakened, and in the end its authority would fall away more or less completely.

Marius had returned late in 105 as consul-elect and celebrated his triumph over Jugurtha. This triumph was an official parade, sanctioned by both the senate and people, in which the victorious general, or *imperator,* travelled across Rome in a two-horse chariot. He wore the purple triumphal toga that only a triumphant general was permitted to wear. He was accompanied by his soldiers in their tunics; they did not march through the city in arms. The parade included the display on litters or carts of the spoils of war. Marius is reported to have displayed 5,775 pounds of gold and 287,000 pounds of silver. Whatever the actual figure, it must have been substantial. Carts were pulled along bearing large paintings that depicted for the crowd the progress of the campaign. Prisoners of war marched along so the people could see what their enemies looked like. Marius's foremost prisoner was Jugurtha himself, who walked before the consul's chariot for everyone to see. After having been displayed to the crowd he was taken to Rome's prison, the Tullianum, where he was killed.

After the triumph Marius entered the senate house in his purple toga—the first man ever to do it—and it was a gesture that deeply offended the senators. Though he thought better of it, and left intending to return in a purple-edged white toga, it is not clear why he made this offensive gesture. He was no doubt elated by the parade and the adulation of the crowds. But gravity and form were extremely important to Romans—and probably more so to Marius, who had been raised in the old-fashioned atmosphere of a country town—and so it is hard to see his entrance as anything but a deliberate snub to the senate and a display of his successes and the position he must have seen himself winning: that of chief man in Rome. He knew that both the Numidian command (which the people had given him) and the people's support in the wake of German defeats of the nobility had elevated him, and his triumphal clothing worn rudely in the senate house would leave no doubt among the senators that here was a man powerful both in his own right and because of his support among the commons. At the same time, it should be noted that Marius's later conduct did not show that he regarded himself as opposed to the senate in principle. Instead, it showed that he desperately wanted to be accepted by the nobility and to be preeminent among them;

he cultivated the people, and they saw to it that he rose, but it was high office that Marius wanted, not revolution.

The quarrel between Sulla and Marius, which seems to have arisen at this point, should be seen against this background. Their discord was supposedly sparked by Sulla's boasts that he, not Marius, had been responsible for Jugurtha's capture. This is a convenient explanation, and Plutarch gives us a bit of detail:

> Thus was the first occasion [the betrayal of Jugurtha] given of that fierce and implacable hostility which so nearly ruined the whole Roman empire. For many that envied Marius attributed the success wholly to Sulla, and Sulla himself got a seal made, on which was engraved Bocchus betraying Jugurtha to him, and constantly used it, irritating the hot and jealous temper of Marius, who was naturally greedy of distinction, and quick to resent any claim to share in his glory, and whose enemies took care to promote the quarrel, ascribing the beginning and chief business of the war to Metellus and its conclusion to Sulla; that so the people might give over admiring and esteeming Marius as the worthiest person.[10]

The story of the seal seems true enough—a small detail used to bolster a simple explanation—and Sulla's son later minted a coin with the same scene on it, but there was probably more to their quarrel, which years later had even led a few of their partisans to the brink of fighting. The aristocracy, constantly sparring for position—and shifting alliances to do it—may have decided that Marius was powerful enough and needed curbing. Sulla, a young patrician and an active, popular and successful soldier, was just the man to counterbalance Marius's populist power. He was one of them: urbane, educated (Marius disdained Greek) and a strong supporter of traditional, aristocratic power. His actions, when years later he had grasped the ultimate power, would favor the senatorial party. His views and inclinations would have been known to the aristocracy early in his career, and it would have been with their tacit support that he taunted Marius.

But the consul had little time for that now; his first order of duty was to attend to the army. Marius brought veterans from Africa and raised new proletarian troops. The continued enrollment of the *capite censi* alleviated the problem of raising yet another army, and it helped fix the character of the army as a professional organization instead of a militia. These poor men depended on the army for everything; it was their life. From it they got regular pay, a chance for booty, an ordered life and sense of purpose, however limited, and they had a patron in their general. As the senate never made any effort to take care of mustered-out soldiers, it would be in the hands of the generals to look after their men with donatives and, if possible, grants of land for veterans to settle on at the end of their service. Marius understood this; he looked after his men and they knew it. He was a great patron, and not just of landowners, merchants and tradesmen. Many of his clients were armed, trained and battle-tried veterans, useful men in an emergency. Marius doesn't seem to have realized the implications of this himself, but they weren't lost on Sulla. He was watching the development of the professional army with interest and forethought.

*   *   *

Although there was doubt about the identity of the northern invaders for several decades after their appearance at the end of the first century A.D., when the Romans became better acquainted with the German tribes, as they did under the Empire, they came to know whom they had fought. Tacitus makes this clear in a passage written some time before A.D. 98:

> This very coastline of Germany near the Ocean the Cimbri hold, now a small people, but great in glory. The wide vestiges of their ancient fame remain, on both sides [of the Rhine] the camps and areas by whose circumference you may also measure the mass and might of the people and the proof of such a great expedition.[11]

Still, in Sallust's time, some sixty years after the conflict, the common opinion was that these people were Gauls. Since Sallust had been an associate of Julius Caesar and a quaestor of his, his opinion must have been conventional. The lingering confusion about the tribes' ethnicity may perhaps be traced to their alliance with the Gallic Tigurini and other minor Celtic tribes. There were negotiations at times between the barbarian alliance and the consuls in the field, but probably no Roman at this time spoke German, though many Italians must have known Gallic languages because of their contacts with Gauls in recently acquired Transalpine Gaul and because of the old Gaulish settlement in Cisalpine Gaul, now a Roman province. Some of the soldiers from this area, though now Roman allies, must have been, in effect, Romanized Gauls themselves. If the powerful German tribes negotiated behind a screen of Gallic intermediaries—which seems likely—then the Roman confusion is understandable.

Busying himself with the army, Marius carried through a number of reforms as did the surviving consul of 105, Publius Rutilius, who had hired *lanistae*—trainers from the gladiatorial schools—to instruct soldiers in swordplay. This probably marks the beginning of the practice of training soldiers with double-weight weapons against a stake. The fourth-century Roman writer Flavius Vegetius discusses this practice in his military handbook *Epitoma Rei Militaris:*

Formerly, as is found in books, recruits were trained in this way: they wove shields of osier in the manner of wickerwork, so that the wicker had twice the weight that a common shield was accustomed to have. Likewise they gave the recruits wooden clubs of double weight in place of swords. In this way they were drilled at stakes not only in the morning but in the afternoon. The use of stakes was not only applied to soldiers, but generally to gladiators. Never does either the arena or the field prove a man undefeated by arms unless he has been carefully drilled at the stake. Individual stakes are fixed in the ground by each recruit so that they cannot shake, and so they rise six feet. Against this stake, just as against an adversary, the recruit drills himself with this wickerwork and club as with the sword and shield, now as though attacking the head and face, now threatening the flanks, meanwhile he attacks the knees and chops at the legs; he pulls back, attacks, leaps forward; he tries against the stake with all his drive, with all his fighting skill, just as though against a real adversary. Through this practice caution is retained so that the recruit may stand against the threat of wounds without exposing any part to injury.[12]

As individual fighters, this training must have improved them markedly. But Marius was interested in larger and more basic reforms; for example, he shortened the baggage train accompanying an army by making the men themselves carry much of their equipment. Whether he came up with this idea himself or only enforced a regulation that had fallen away isn't known, but from this day onward the legionary marched in his armor carrying his weapons, his helmet hung by a thong from his neck. A satchel of personal belongings, several days' rations, a pick or a mattock to dig out the camp, and a pair of sharpened stakes for fortifying it were strapped to a pole.[13] This he carried over his shoulder, the weight of it resting on the rim of the long shield slung across his back by a leather strap around his chest. Although the weight each soldier carried was significant, it cut down on mules, carts and drovers.

The length of a consular army on the march cannot be known for certain, but at the turn of the last century the German military historian Hans Delbrück noted that 30,000 Prussian soldiers on the march, with their supply train, extended fourteen miles.[14] This analogy is certainly imperfect, but it seems likely that a Roman army of 20,000 must have extended roughly as much, and a good deal of this length would have been made up by the supply train, which had to be policed and guarded. To the extent that Marius could shorten it, it was easier to direct and less vulnerable.

This meant, of course, that the legionary now carried a great deal of weight while marching. Calculating from ancient accounts, some say that the soldiers now carried eighty to a hundred pounds of equipment on the march, but the higher figure, at least, seems unlikely. How could the average soldier of the period himself have weighed enough to carry this load every day? Many of the soldiers of that period may have weighed considerably less than one hundred and fifty pounds themselves. Still, the soldier must have carried considerable weight, and they were called—and called themselves—*muli mariani,* "Marius's mules."

As Marius continued to command and fit out his proletarian army, the equipment of the soldiers became uniform. Probably at this time most, if not all, legionaries wore mail shirts. This may already have been the case with Marius's proletarian soldiers whom he had fitted out for the Numidian War.

It was at this time the spear used by the third line *triarii* was given up: All troops now carried the heavy javelin, the *pilum,* which, we are told, Marius improved in 101 B.C. before his engagement with the Cimbri. The long iron shaft had previously been attached to the wooden haft with a pair of iron rivets, but Marius had one of them replaced with a wooden pin meant to break when the javelin struck; the buckled weapon couldn't then be thrown back.

Marius abolished the *velites,* or light troops, at least among the Romans, and made them into heavy infantry like the rest, and he took to engaging professional light troops such as slingers from the Balearic Islands and archers from Crete. Still, it seems likely that the Italian allies, at least, may have continued to contribute cohorts of light soldiers armed with swords and javelins because such troops are always useful, and their role could not have been taken by slingers and archers—or perhaps ordinary legionaries shed their mail shirts and operated as light-armed troops when circumstances required.

Marius didn't neglect the legion's *esprit de corps* either. He assigned to each legion a special emblem, the eagle standard. This was a silver eagle perched on a tall shaft and treated as a sort of cult object imbued with the spirit of the legion itself. Each century and maniple had always had its own standard (and continued to do so), such as a pegasus or a minotaur, but the legion itself had not had one. Marius's aim of raising the spirits of the army would have been more easily accomplished if he could harness the natural credibility of the common soldiers, and besides the standards helped give the legions a sense of identity they had previously lacked—all the more because legions until this time were frequently dissolved after campaigns and reformulated. They had always been numbered, but the numbers could be reassigned yearly. The introduction of the eagles demonstrated that a legion, like the increasingly professional soldiers who served in them, might be kept on an active footing. From this time on a legion seems to have retained its number.[15]

Marius's reforms were certainly undertaken with the view of changing Roman tactics to meet the northern barbarians. There are no detailed reports of the tactics of the Cimbri and Teutones, and so we cannot say whether the manipular Roman formation was fit to meet their attack. The Germans, like the Gauls, attacked in something of a rush. The Gauls favored a long sword with which they took great slashes. The Germans of the period did not have much skill in ironwork—unlike their Gaulish contemporaries—and must have used fewer swords. Tacitus, writing two hundred years after the Cimbric war, makes it plain that it was still the case in his lifetime. He attributed this—wrongly—to a dearth of iron in Germany, and said:

> Not even iron is abundant as is gathered from the kind of weapons. Few use swords or large spears: they carry spears, or frameas in their language, with a short narrow point, but so sharp and handy that with the same weapon, just as the situation demands, they fight close up or at a distance.[16]

In other words, they used a handily short spear. However, after having defeated half a dozen Roman armies, these Germans must have been much better equipped than their cousins back home and probably more adept at tactics.

We might infer, then, that the maniple was not the best formation to deal with determined barbarians. Though they were capable of independent movement, the units themselves were fairly small and shallow, and too numerous to command easily; the formation was a great advance on the earlier phalanx, but its flexibility may have been more or less limited to making a clean advance. Men in maniples, because these units were small, may not have had enough morale to stand up to a concerted charge by barbarians who, frankly, terrified them by reputation, appearance and mystery. They may have been swept away here and there, causing an entire line to buckle or fall away from the breach. This would have been a smaller problem when facing the civilized opponents of their day who fought in ordered ranks, usually in the Macedonian way—in large phalanxes that depended for their effect on the soldiers keeping their ranks in good order. But barbarian warriors who, through indiscipline, had a more fluid line may have posed a problem for the Romans. Marius addressed this problem by a basic change in tactics.

Until now the Roman line had been composed of maniples—pairs of centuries advancing side by side—each block probably six men deep and twenty or so across the front. Now, however, the army would fight in larger battalions: cohorts. The cohort already existed; a cohort was a group of men supplied by the Italian allies under their treaties with Rome. They did not furnish actual legions—only Rome did that—and so these allied cohorts were joined together with other allied cohorts and broken into maniples to form allied "legions" fighting side by side and in the Roman manner with the proper Roman legions.

Marius took these cohorts as his model: He joined three maniples together into a larger tactical body. In effect he had changed an administrative unit into a battalion. For administrative purposes the maniples within a cohort retained their designations as *hastati, principes* and *triarii*, though of course there was no longer any distinction in their equipment, purpose or position in the field; they all fought together wherever they were put. There is some debate whether Marius was actually the first to use cohorts as battalions, and indeed Sallust says that Metellus set four legionary cohorts against the Numidians at the battle of Muthul. Sallust was writing much later though, when the cohort had been the basic tactical unit of the army for decades. So it is possible that maniples had been joined into cohorts for combat from time to time, but certainly from Marius's time onward the cohort was the smallest fighting unit. In any case, Marius's exclusive use of them, even if they were not his own innovation, was a military change of the greatest importance.

So now the smallest tactical unit was three times as big as a maniple. The size of such a cohort depended on the size of the legion, which varied over the history of the republic. The later imperial legion seems to have been standardized at 4,800 men, and we know from Polybius that in times of emergency republican legions might be expanded to 5,000. Marius's legions are often said to have contained 6,000 men each, and in that case his cohorts were of 600 men. Others argue that the Marian legion was of the same size as the later imperial legion.[17] Whatever the exact figure, they must have been in this range.

Usually cohorts, like the maniples before them, were arranged in a three-part battle line, most often with four cohorts in the first line and three in the second and third. Because of their size, these larger battalions were in a position to defend themselves—indeed they were large enough to operate independently.

The advance to battle in lines of cohorts must have followed the old manipular model: an approach with smallish gaps in the line to ensure that troops reached the enemy without disorder, maniples and cohorts from the second line coming forward to fill in large gaps during the advance, and perhaps cohorts from the third line filled in gaps in the second as units moved forward into the first line. Now that the units were larger and could operate by themselves, cohorts might be sent out to guard the flanks as Caesar would do at the battle of Pharsalus fifty years later when he faced Pompey's more numerous cavalry and feared envelopment. Caesar explains the maneuver in his own words, speaking, as he usually does, in the third person:

> When he [Caesar] noticed this, which we have already explained, fearing lest he be outflanked on the right wing by the great number of cavalry, he quickly drew some individual cohorts from the third line and from this made a fourth and opposed it to the horse and explained what he wanted to happen and warned them that the day's victory rested in the valor of these cohorts.[18]

Or cohorts from the second or third lines could extend the formation by moving out parallel to the first. This gave a wider front to threaten the enemy's flanks. Many such maneuvers were possible.

These reforms, of course, took time and Marius was fortunate to have it. The barbarians still declined to cross into Italy; even after the Romans' stunning defeat at Arausio they stayed away for three years and so Marius could spend his second consulship, that of 104, training his troops. His discipline was severe and inevitable, but he is said to have bound his men to him through a rough justice, which is well illustrated by an anecdote.

An officer named Gaius Lusius had made unsuccessful sexual advances upon a subordinate of his named Trebonius. Ordering the soldier to appear at his tent one night, he made an attack upon him that Trebonius repelled with his sword, stabbing Lusius to death. It seemed unfortunate for Trebonius that Gaius Lusius was Marius's nephew. The soldiers must have expected a certain and unpleasant end for him, but when the consul tried him for killing his nephew, Trebonius explained his situation and Marius, instead of punishing him, rewarded him with a crown that he himself placed on the soldier's head. Marius probably invested Trebonius with the *corona civica,* a high decoration awarded only for saving the life of a fellow Roman on the battlefield, and the irony of the award was a calculated appeal to the grim humor of the common soldiers. Marius knew soldiers, and it's doubtful if his action didn't get the results he expected: higher morale when they saw the consul as a protection against officers, even of his own family—and a greater determination to meet the standards of the old Roman discipline that applied to every man regardless of station. Whatever his private feelings in the matter, Marius knew the importance of this and he knew that this judgment would endear him to the men. It must have recalled to them the ancient stories of Manlius Torquatus, the consul who had executed his own son for disobeying orders on campaign.

Though the barbarians stayed off, the threat of them lingered, and the commons, in fear of them, reelected Marius consul for 103, again in violation of the *Lex Villia.* It was his third consulship, and as a consecutive consulship it was even more unconstitutional. Fewer and fewer props to the constitution remained, and the power of the senate continued to weaken.

Meanwhile the Cimbri had crossed Gaul and fought unsuccessfully against the Celtiberians along the border of Spain. The Spaniards' success encouraged some of them to revolt against Roman rule as the Volcae Tectosages had done in Gallia Narbonensis. The Teutones, around the same time, had entered northern Gaul beyond the Roman province. The two tribes, however, began to wander back toward Roman territory, and it became apparent that they and the Tigurini had decided to attack Italy on three fronts: the Teutones from Gaul, the Cimbri down through the Alps and the Tigurini through the Julian Alps into the area around modern Venice. Rome disposed her armies accordingly: Marius advanced to Gaul, his consular colleague Catulus tried to hold the passes of the Alps, and Sulla, now Catulus's quaestor, stood with an army farther east near the Julian Alps, prepared to meet the Tigurini.

CHAPTER 9

The Northern Campaign

THERE IS VERY LITTLE THAT WE KNOW ABOUT THE ACTUAL fighting. It would be an interesting story: Marius and Catulus against the barbarians details of the marches, tactics and so forth. Unfortunately, details are few and probably suspect.[1] Still, the broad outline of events is clear enough, and some things can be fairly inferred, for instance, Marius's march to Gallia Transalpina in 103.

The trip was long, and though the army travelled quickly for the time—about fifteen miles a day—it wouldn't have done so every day. The heavily laden soldiers had to rest now and again, and we may be sure that from time to time there were unexpected problems that required a halt. So we can be fairly certain that the army marched for about two months to reach Gallia Transalpina, but this was very good speed for an ancient army, and it could march this fast because of the road system the Romans had constructed since their first great highway, the Via Appia. Trade was certainly helped by these roadways, but we mustn't lose sight of the fact that their primary purpose was to accommodate the army. These roads were the arteries along which Rome's strength travelled wherever it might be needed, first in Italy and southern Gaul, and finally throughout Europe. The armies took the roads, avoiding wasted days or even weeks in drawn-out columns going this way and that to find passable ways; those ways had all been made for them by dogged Roman civil engineers. These roads were about four feet thick, having been dug into the earth and filled with several layers of different materials, and they were paved with large stones that resisted centuries of weather and wear.[2] Some still exist in Italy and France, topped nowadays by asphalt to withstand automobile traffic.

Once in Gallia Transalpina, Marius established his base in the Rhone Valley at Arelate,[3] where he was beset not by the Teutones or the Ambrones who had joined them,[4] but by problems of supply, a threat no less serious to the army than the barbarians he was preparing to meet. Vegetius says rather elegantly: "Very often, indeed, want rather than battle destroys an army, and hunger is more savage than steel."[5]

How was hunger to be avoided? The military historian Archer Jones states that sixty thousand pounds of supplies were necessary every day to feed an army of twenty thousand men; it took a small ship to carry that burden.[6] Marius, whose army was larger, depended on a steady shipment of provisions by sea. Ships were not a problem: Roman publicans (knights, of course) would ship supplies to the army. Rome's armies seldom lacked provisions, but the mouth of the Rhone was too silted to let ships pass upstream. Overland transportation was nearly impossible; hauling heavy loads any distance by land was simply impractical in the ancient world, as land carriage of goods cost about thirty times as much as it did by sea,[7] and even if cost had been no object, a wagon train could hardly have handled the tons of supplies that he needed every day. Unlike the barbarians, Marius couldn't despoil the countryside for supplies, for it was Roman territory.

Marius, Roman that he was, applied civil engineering to the problem: He set the troops to digging a canal from the sea, which bypassed the silted mouth of the river. The remains of this Fossa Mariana have been discovered through underwater archaeology and it appears to have been between five and eight miles long. Plutarch suggests that the exercise was meant, as much as anything, to harden the troops, which of course it must have done, but there is no question that his logistical situation spurred him to it. Plutarch's treatment of Marius's canal is more an excuse for a quaint lesson about Roman military discipline than anything else.

So Marius solved a logistical problem and at the same time did a favor for the knights—always great supporters of his. The canal made trade into the Rhone Valley easier and pleased the knights because of their interest in the economic development of the new province. The incident also shows the benefit of using the army to construct public works: It helped to develop provincial economies and exerted a civilizing influence quite apart from its military duties.

Marius had spent the year 103 further breaking in his new army, but in 102 he had to face the Teutones. Plutarch, more interested Marius's character than in the details of his campaigns, simply indicates that the Germans encamped in his neighborhood, but that the consul bided his time and refused to attack. His purpose was to observe the enemy carefully before engaging and to familiarize his men with Germans, of whom they probably had an almost superstitious dread. To this end he kept his men about the camp even though, we are told, the soldiers railed against him for doing so, even in the face of attacks on the camp itself, which Livy characterizes as severe: "Gaius Marius the consul defended his camp when it was attacked by the Teutones and Ambrones with all their strength."[8] Yet after weeks or even months of preparation the consular camp would have been particularly well fortified and the attacks, though dangerous, may have been psychologically useful in breaking in the new soldiers and dispelling, to some degree at least, their fears.

Furthermore, Marius cannily used the natural credulity and superstition of his soldiers to his advantage. Back in Rome his wife Julia had discovered a seeress, a Syrian named Martha, who had had the temerity to address the senate and offer to inform it about future events. The senators were not amused. Afterward she

> betook herself to the women, and gave them proofs of her skill, especially Marius's wife, at whose feet she sat when she was viewing a contest of gladiators, and correctly foretold which of them should overcome. She was for this and the like predictings sent by her to Marius and the army, where she was very much looked up to, and, for the most part, carried about in a litter.[9]

Marius used this Asiatic oddsmaker to bolster his soldiers' spirits: He had her conduct sacrifices clad in scarlet, holding a little golden spear, no doubt coaxing her to predict a Roman victory.

Marius's fellow consul, Lucius Catulus, had meanwhile advanced into the Alps, but then pulled back behind the Adige River when he found he could not hold them against the Cimbri. As Delbrück notes, in the days before modern mass armies, mountain ranges could not be held indefinitely—there were never enough soldiers to guard every pass, every defile and track. In time, a defender would always be outflanked.[10] As late as the nineteenth century, when European armies had grown to proportions the ancients could never have fielded, Napoleon averred that deserts, not mountain ranges, made the most difficult natural obstacle.[11]

So Catulus's mistake was a strategic one. With about 25,000 men he should not have really expected to keep the Cimbri bottled up in the mountains, especially when there were so many passes for them to choose and so many ways for them to slip around Roman troops isolated from each other in passes and valleys. Perhaps Catulus saw his strategy as a sort of delaying action, but even so he should have been prepared to fight them eventually. As it developed he was in the end supported by Marius's army, but that was nothing he could have relied on in 102.

It is clear that Catulus's retreat to the Adige was disordered, probably as a result of speed, and it seems likely that the Cimbri may have gotten onto his flanks or come close. The consul's withdrawal may in fact have become a flight as he could not get far enough ahead of the enemy to reestablish a proper front. Plutarch casts these events in a flattering light. He states that Catulus, unable to keep his men from fleeing, took up a standard himself and led his men in the retreat so that it would be seen as his disgrace, not the soldiers', so highly did he hold Rome's honor. This story, though, feels as though it has been recast to favor the consul.

After Catulus pulled back to the Adige he built fortifications on both sides where it might be crossed and threw a bridge over the river to let him come to the defense of soldiers holding the fortifications on the far side, but in spite of the preparations things did not go well for him. He could no more hold the Adige than the Alpine passes and had to pull farther back, eventually crossing to the south bank of the Po. A cohort left to guard a fort on the Adige, unable to retreat with the rest of the army, put up a gallant resistance to the Cimbri and then made a fighting retreat of their own, eventually reaching Catulus's army as it rushed south. The action of the this cohort appears as the only bright spot in the defense of the Adige.[12]

In Gallia Transalpina, meanwhile, Marius had his hands full with the Teutones and Ambrones, who began to march south toward the coast, heading for Italy. Plutarch says that they were so numerous that they passed the Roman camp for six days. Delbrück reasonably dismisses this by asking, if it were true, why Marius did not attack the attenuated column as it passed by. We should probably view this colorful detail simply as an illustration of their large numbers, and as an inexact way of stating that Marius chose to follow them and attack only when he saw fit. After the barbarians had struck out for Italy, the consul set after them.

> As soon as they were passed and had gone on a little distance ahead, Marius began to move, and follow them at his leisure, always encamping at some small distance from them; choosing also strong positions, and carefully fortifying them.[13]

As Plutarch tells us, he avoided open battle, but by staying close to the Germans in terrain well fitted for the defense, he could threaten them in some safety, and he probably used his strategy to curb their foraging.

The barbarians and the shadowing Roman army moved into the vicinity of Aquae Sextiae,[14] the colony established twenty-five years before by Gaius Sextius Calvinus at the start of the campaigns in Gallia Transalpina. At the end of a day's march, Marius followed his custom and began to establish camp on high ground over a stream, beyond which lay the Teutones and Ambrones. Following the usual order of things, four military tribunes would have overseen the construction of the camp's four walls, built up from the earth dug from the trenches surrounding the camp. Legionaries would have been digging these fosses under the direction of their centurions while the cavalry, light troops and probably a number of legionaries stood ready to drive off any attack.

As the soldiers went about the task of fortifying the camp, servants and military slaves, *calones* and *lixae*, went down the slope to the river to fetch water. They went armed of course—with axes and with swords and javelins too—since the German camp lay across the river and some of the barbarians were down at the water themselves. It may not have been unusual for opponents to meet each other under such circumstances, each side tacitly putting up with the other so long as they could keep apart, however, sometimes a fight would erupt as had happened at the Battle of Pydna in 168 B.C. when Roman and Macedonian camp followers came to blows at a river and were reinforced by their soldiers until a full-scale battle followed. Something similar happened near Aquae Sextiae that day. The Ambrones left their camp to help their fellows at the river, and some contingents of Italian allies and Romans went down the slope to meet them as they crossed the stream. While at Pydna the battle was conclusive even though it had escalated and developed more or less accidentally from a mere skirmish, in this case it was not. Plutarch tells us that the barbarians were thrown back against the river and suffered a significant defeat, but he may have exaggerated since the larger and decisive battle was fought two days later.

This action, however, did have one result that might have been useful had the fighting continued the next day: The Romans were unable to complete their camp fortifications before nightfall. They still held the height where the half-finished camp lay, and the Germans had retired, but the security the soldiers were accustomed to—and upon which the commander relied to keep his men rested and confident—was not there.

There was, however, no attack upon the camp during the night. The barbarians evidently had had enough fighting during the engagement at the river, and they spent the next day ordering themselves for a battle. Marius took that day to do the same. He put a number of cohorts, perhaps five or six—they are said to have numbered 3,000 in all—under a lieutenant of his, Claudius Marcellus, and ordered them to slip into a wooded area nearby and hold themselves through the night in preparation for battle the following day.

The balance of the army Marius led out the next day on the height before the camp, sending his cavalry out ahead to skirmish with the Teutones and provoke them into action. We don't know the disposition of the infantry, though in default of any information on this detail we can imagine them in the conventional *acies triplex,* or three-line formation, the one most generally used.[15] He is said to have instructed the men "to stand still and keep their ground; when they [the barbarians] came within reach, to throw their javelins, then use their swords, and joining their shields, force them back."[16] Whether he instructed them this way or not, the advice reflects the usual Roman practice of disordering the enemy with javelins, knocking them with shields and closing with the sword. It differed only in that the troops were to stand fast and receive the enemy charge instead of themselves advancing.

The command, in fact, is essentially that given by Pompey the Great at the Battle of Pharsalus in 48 B.C.,[17] and the reasoning behind it is about the same: that the enemy would disorder themselves during the advance—"the steepness of the ground would render the enemy's blows inefficient, nor could their shields be kept close together, the inequality of the ground hindering the stability of their footing."[18] Plutarch, writing many years after both battles, may be suspected of cribbing from Caesar's account of Pharsalus to fill in that of Marius, but if the battle at Aquae Sextiae was indeed fought at the top of a rise, then Marius must have seen it as the sort of defensive–offensive battle that Pompey judged Pharsalus to be.[19] It would only have been prudent to await the enemy's attack from his superior position and then advance down the slope on a disordered enemy.

The Roman cavalry are said to have drawn the Germans into an attack; if this was the provocation, then they must have retreated before the enemy and then dispersed to the Roman flanks, leaving the field clear for the infantry. The Teutones and Ambrones attacked uphill, were met and driven slowly down the slope by the legionaries and then, while fully engaged, were struck from behind by Claudius Marcellus's cohorts emerging from the woods. The Germans, caught between the two forces, dissolved and were utterly defeated. The usual incredible figures are given for the killed and captured,[20] but whatever the exact numbers, the Teutones and Ambrones were finished as a threat to Rome.

After the battle Marius selected those enemy weapons and armor he thought would best flatter the triumph he knew would be declared for him, and he piled the rest up to burn in thanksgiving for the victory. Plutarch tells the story that as Marius stood in his purple-bordered toga, torch in hand, about to set the barbarian equipment alight, horsemen were seen approaching. When they were received they informed Marius that he had been elected consul yet again. We may doubt such perfect timing, but it's probably true enough, as Plutarch goes on to tell us that Marius learned soon afterward of Catulus's withdrawal to the Adige under Cimbric pressure. It may have seemed that Catulus would hold the Adige since Marius did not go directly to him in Cisalpine Gaul. Instead he was called back to Rome for a time. We don't know his business, but no doubt there were affairs of various sorts for him to attend to. Perhaps he had been recalled to receive a triumph; he was voted one, but he declined to celebrate it until the Cimbri were beaten—leaving it in trust, as it were.

Had Catulus's situation appeared desperate Marius might have hastened to him directly from Gaul with his army, instead of travelling to the city. Probably the approach of winter seemed likely to slow or put an end to Cimbric campaigning for a while, even if they had advanced as far south as the Po Valley. They had certainly done this by the summer of 101, when Marius was in his fifth consulship with his former legate Manius Aquilius as his consular colleague. By this time Marius had ordered his army from Gallia Transalpina to Gallia Cisalpina and across the Po into Italy proper[21] to join the troops of Catulus, whose powers had also been extended as proconsul. Combined, the armies are reported to have numbered 55,000, and this seems a credible figure as Plutarch took it from the memoirs of Sulla, which are unfortunately lost.[22]

Sulla joined the two consuls, apparently leaving his army at the Julian Alps farther east to bottle up the Tigurini. It was an uneasy trio. Plutarch's report of their battle against the Cimbri is confused, as we'll see later, and almost certainly this is because of political in-fighting between Marius and Catulus. The latter was abetted by the patrician Sulla, who clearly took Catulus's part, doubtless out of both a personal dislike of Marius and a natural bias toward the senatorial aristocracy, whose dangerous and bloody champion he would be. There was dissension between the consul and the proconsul after the battle, and years later back in Rome Marius would have a hand in Catulus's death. It's no wonder, then, that Plutarch's description of the battle against the Cimbri is unclear, or that his account of Catulus's earlier retreat shows evidence of two different traditions.

The battle with the Cimbri took place on the Campi Raudii near the town of Vercellae,[23] which was probably itself near modern Ferrara. First, Plutarch's story. He tells us that Catulus commanded his army in the center of the battle line while Marius divided up his troops and put them on the flanks. Plutarch took this from Sulla's memoirs, and there's no reason to doubt this assertion, though Sulla's bias comes through when he imputes an ignoble motivation to Marius:

> Sulla, who was present at the fight, gives this account; saying, also, that Marius drew up his army in this order [with his troops on the wings], because he expected that the armies would meet on the wings, since it generally happens that in such extensive fronts the centre falls back, and thus he would have the whole victory to himself and his soldiers, and Catulus would not be even engaged. They tell us, also, that Catulus himself alleged this in vindication of his honour, accusing, in various ways, the enviousness of Marius.[24]

Plutarch then goes on to relate that the Cimbric infantry came out in good order in a large square (more probably rectangular) formation, a favorite of German tribes. Their cavalry advanced upon the Romans and drew off "to the right" to "get them [the Romans] between themselves and their infantry, who were placed in the left wing."[25] This is hard to understand, even apart from the question of whose right and left are being talked about. How could drawing Roman troops ahead and to one side put them between those horsemen and the infantry? The account must be garbled. But next comes the interesting part of the description and the oddest:

> However, in the engagement, *according to the accounts of Sulla and his friends,* Marius met with what might be called a mark of divine displeasure. For a great dust being raised, which (as it might very probably happen) almost covered both the armies, he, leading on his forces to the pursuit, missed the enemy, and having passed by their array, moved, for a good space, up and down the field; meanwhile the enemy, by chance, engaged with Catulus, and the heat of the battle was chiefly

with him and his men, *among whom Sulla says he was;* adding, that the
Romans had great advantage of the heat and sun that shone in the faces
of the Cimbri. [emphasis added][26]

The source of this interesting detail is Sulla and his friends, Sulla
adding—as much to aggrandize himself as to establish his credibility—
that he was with Catulus in the thick of the fighting while Marius and
his troops marched ineffectively about, blinded by dust. Despite this
weird maneuvering, the battle was won over the Cimbri at tremendous
cost to them. They were utterly broken, and Catulus ended up with
their standards, which he used to bolster the claim that he was the principal winner.

What can be taken away from this account? A few things at least
make sense: Roman troop numbers, their disposition, Catulus's position
in the center and Marius's position on one of the flanks. These don't
seem in any way unlikely. Furthermore, we can probably accept Sulla's
claim that most of the hard fighting was done in the center by Catulus's
troops. Both Catulus and Sulla had an interest in claiming this—senatorial pride was at stake—but there must have been some truth in their
version of events if they judged that the story would be accepted, and
the odd part of their account, that Marius somehow missed the enemy
and wandered about the battlefield, suggests that they are putting the
worst face they can on some independent maneuver of his. We should
recall that the new cohort-army could maneuver well and that cohorts
under Claudius Marcellus had delivered a successful rear attack upon
the Teutones at Aquae Sextiae.

The day of the battle fell shortly after the summer solstice, which
should have been hot, just north of the Po. Were the consul and proconsul camped together as sometimes happened, or were they apart? They
were close enough to support each other in any case, and that morning
the soldiers were called out and divided themselves into their centuries,
probably by *contubernia*, hence squad by squad. The wide ways in the
camp between the protective walls and the squares of tents allowed this,
and regular streets such as the *Via Quintana* and the *Via Principalis* allowed efficient communication between various parts of the camp.
Roman forethought in camp construction allowed the army to organize
itself before it left through the four gates. When the time came to move
out, the commander, whether Marius or Catulus, must have advanced
out of the *porta praetoria*, which faced the enemy, accompanied by his
bodyguard and by the legions. The allies probably marched at the same

time through the side gates, the *porta principalis dextra* and *porta principalis sinistra*. We can expect that the allied cavalry went out the back of the camp, through the *porta decumana*, and once out that it divided into two bodies to pass around either side of the camp and appear on the flanks of the allied soldiers as both of them joined the Roman legions in front of the camp. The camp itself was guarded, probably by a number of fit soldiers, both legionaries and light-armed troops, and no doubt by any injured or infirm men who could still help hold a rampart, and by the camp workers, the *lixae* and *calones*.

We can assume that the battlefield was fairly wide because of the numbers involved, at least on the Roman side, and Plutarch's account of the Cimbric cavalry maneuver—whatever it was exactly—suggests that it probably had few obstacles. The approach to the battlefield was probably not long; the heavy infantry that made up by far the majority of the Roman forces wore their armor and their pace toward the battlefield would have been moderate, in order to save them for the accustomed charge and hand-to-hand fighting to come.

If the troops left the camp by the four ways described they would naturally have found themselves in six parallel columns heading to the field: two columns of Roman legionaries in the center, a column of allied heavy infantry on either side of them (legionaries in all but name) and the cavalry on either flank, ready to repel an unforeseen attack. Again this would have been the square formation, *agmen quadratum*, like that Metellus and Marius had used in Numidia, handy for going into battle order quickly.

In the field the Romans customarily took the center, the allies fought on either side of them, and the cavalry was posted on the wings. This may have taken a little maneuvering unless the consuls' armies had consolidated and marched to the field together.

As the troops reached the battlefield they would, depending on their approach, go from column into line, either through a flank march or perhaps merely by halting and turning to face the enemy if their approach had allowed them to do this. Without knowing exactly where the Roman camp or camps were, nor the battlefield, we cannot even guess about this, beyond saying that the Romans must have reached the field in good order through their adherence to method, the heavy infantry of the Roman legions and the allied cohorts spread, probably into three lines of cohorts, perhaps two, the light soldiers in the field before them, and the cavalry on the flanks.

Without knowing the depth and hence the frontage of a cohort one cannot say how wide the Roman front was on the Campi Raudii, even if we do know the size of the army and that it was the Roman practice to allot a soldier three feet within which to fight.[27] Still, its magnitude can be guessed at in a general sort of way if the combined army of Marius and Catulus did number 55,000 men and if a cohort were twelve men deep and forty or fifty across the front, which seems reasonable.

The front of the combined army consisting of four Roman legions and the equivalent in allies should have been thirty-two cohorts wide, giving a front close to a mile across, and close to a mile and a half with the cavalry and light troops on the flanks. The horse may have been very small, perhaps limited to Roman and Italian allied cavalry since we do not hear specifically of any others, thus about 1,400 in all, but this seems too few.

Its depth is hard to guess: There may have been a hundred yards between each line to allow easy movement, to prevent the communication of disorder from one line to another, to allow the exhausted, wounded and killed to be brought back from the front, to give room for light soldiers after the battle had opened, and to allow messengers and runners and unengaged cohorts to move about freely.

Catulus, Marius and Sulla had some eighty cohorts to direct, apart from light troops and cavalry. Although there was later a squabble about who was the true victor, and this suggests a command divided to some extent on the battlefield, some division was necessary, though there may have been less subordination than either Marius or Catulus wished. Probably each man was responsible, in some way, for directing more than two dozen cohorts—and cavalry and light troops as well—all of this from three or four hundred yards to the rear of the actual fighting.

The Cimbric warriors probably did not outnumber the Romans significantly, if at all, and a rectangular formation implies great depth, so it was probably not as wide as the Roman front. It almost certainly had no reserves as the Romans did with their second and especially third battle lines. So, shorter across the front and without a reserve to meet unforeseen contingencies, the Cimbri were vulnerable to flank attack and to possible envelopment if they were not able to carry the battle quickly.

The three Roman commanders knew this, of course. If the enemy didn't break at the first Roman charge, then a steady resistance in the center might allow the legionaries to work around one flank or the other. Something might be done with the third battle line too, as Caesar would do later at Pharsalus: It might be used independently either to protect the Roman flank from the Cimbric cavalry or even to maneuver independently against the enemy flank, if the soldiers could be led once the excitement of battle was spreading.

With this scene set, we might put in what little detail we can take from Plutarch's account and mix it with what is known of conventional Roman battles. First, the Cimbri probably began to advance, since their advantage lay in warlike enthusiasm and in their foreign appearance and reputation for victory. It would have begun at a walk, and then worked up to a jog, the men trying to keep their single, unwieldy formation as coherent as they could. Men must have rattled each other, parts crowded, others thinned, any man who fell sent confusion back to the end of the formation. They likely screamed and beat weapons on their shields to work up their courage and dishearten the Romans.

Any Roman light troops out skirmishing ran back to the flanks and out of the way. The Roman generals gave the signal to move the standards forward, the command sent by horn blasts so that each cohort received it at the same time. The three battle lines moved ahead at a walking pace, each cohort advancing alongside its neighbors under the direction of its centurions. To help the soldiers recognize them, the six centurions of each cohort were distinguished from the common soldiers by helmets with transverse crests, brushes across the helmet from ear to ear so the soldiers could follow "not only their standard, but also the centurion, who had an emblem on his helmet."[28] The soldiers were ranged behind him by *contubernia,* or squads.

The centurions and their lieutenants, the *optiones,* kept their eyes on the men and on the neighboring cohorts. Those centurions in the second line also watched the cohorts in front of them. If one cohort crowded into another and a gap opened, then a maniple or cohort from the second line jogged up to fill it. No disorder travelled along the line.

It may have been necessary at some point for the advance to stop and the cohorts to align themselves before the final approach.[29] Any gaps could be filled at this time too. And then, at the signal, the soldiers began their charge, probably a short jog of perhaps forty or fifty yards; running with armor, shield and heavy javelin in hand while in a formation must have been out of the question. As Romans approached the enemy, they would cast their heavy javelins, perhaps at a distance of twenty yards or so, and then draw their swords and prepare to close. This means the soldiers probably came to a near halt, perhaps involuntarily, to be sure of their neighbors. As usual du Picq puts it best:

> At the moment of getting close to the enemy, the dash slackened of its own accord, because the men of the first rank, of necessity and instinctively, assured themselves of the position of their supports, their neigh-

bors in the same line, their comrades in the second, and collected themselves together in order to be more the masters of their movements to strike and parry.[30]

At or about the moment of contact, the narrow gaps between the cohorts were filled naturally by men from the rear ranks, and so the two opposing lines stayed face to face, so long as one didn't break and allow itself to be struck in a suddenly exposed flank. After an initial contact there may generally not have been much fencing—much posturing, more likely—and at a few points, at different times the line probably advanced a few steps up to the enemy and clashed at swords' point.

Ancient battle accounts make it clear that by far the most killing took place during the flight after one side had broken and was run down by the victors. Winning armies, occasionally, lost almost no one. This indicates that there was relatively little killing during the actual face-to-face combat—very little sword-fighting, in other words. The strategy seems to have been to maintain a cohesive front, to menace the enemy and outlast him. If he lost his will, or began to melt away (usually from the back), he was lost. Where possible though, it was useful to find or make a breach in the line, sweep his flanks or surprise him.

On the Campi Raudii it's likely that the Roman army advanced against the Cimbri in this way, and that the lines wavered back and forth, but did not break, and the centurions near the front urged their soldiers forward and pressed them to come to actual blows, crossing swords themselves when they needed to lead by example. At any place where the line thinned as soldiers pulled out from exhaustion or injury, another cohort would be sent to brace them.

At some point, we are told, the Cimbric cavalry advanced, wearing armor and fantastic helmets and swinging heavy swords,[31] apparently against one of the Roman wings (we are not told which) and swept to the "right" (we are not told whose right) in feigned flight to draw away part of the Roman line. This tactic is said to have succeeded, though because our source ultimately is Sulla, Marius's personal enemy, we must consider that he may be misrepresenting events. We might look at it another way. At the advance of the German cavalry it would have been quite natural for Marius to take a few cohorts from his third line and pull them away from the battle formation entirely, setting them obliquely to meet and repel them. It would have been a sensible enough move, for cavalry could not defeat trained heavy infantry—horses will not charge into steady men. It would be easy, however, for Sulla to later characterize this defensive maneuver as the withdrawal of soldiers belonging to his political enemy.

But could there be even more to such a maneuver? Recall that Marius defeated the Teutones by hiding half a legion in the woods and then sending them against the barbarians' rear. If we suppose that Marius took a number of cohorts out of the formation (perhaps incidentally driving off the Cimbric horse), at a distance far enough from the battle to allow him to form the battalions into a line without interference, he could then have attacked the Cimbric flank while it was held in place fighting those soldiers commanded by Catulus and Sulla. Again Caesar at Pharsalus comes to mind: His six detached third-line cohorts defeated Pompey's cavalry when it attacked his flank, and then went on to attack Pompey's infantry in the flank and rear.

Ancient battles were brief, often taking two or three hours.[32] If Marius maneuvered this way it may well have taken him some time to do it, time during which, as Catulus and Sulla later claimed, they were in the thick of the fighting. Besides it seems unreasonable to suppose that Marius marched about blind in the dust while the rest of the army did the fighting. A flank attack of this sort while the Cimbri were occupied with the bulk of the Roman army could account for the Roman victory, which, it turned out, was as decisive as that against the Teutones and Ambrones.

Given only Plutarch's account of the battle, the details cannot be known. But if the fight went this way, then it was one that could easily be misrepresented later, when circumstance might offer it, by any of the combatants at the expense of his partners, and therefore result in a garbled account. In fact a dispute arose immediately between Marius and Catulus concerning the battle. There happened to be officials from the city of Parma in camp at the time of the battle, and they were asked, at least by Catulus's men, to judge whose army had been the more responsible for the victory. After the fight,

> The ordinary plunder was taken by Marius's soldiers, but the other spoils, as ensigns, trumpets, and the like, they say, were brought to Catulus's camp; which he used for the best argument that the victory was obtained by himself and his army. Some dissensions arising, as was natural, among the soldiers, the deputies from Parma, being then present, were made judges of the controversy; whom Catulus's men carried about among their slain enemies, and manifestly showed them that they were slain by their javelins, which were known by the inscriptions, having Catulus's name cut in the wood.[33]

A victory of this scale would tremendously enhance reputations, whether that of Marius, or Catulus or Sulla, and, by association with the latter two, that of the senate as well, which needed a bit of polish. A lot was at stake in Rome, too much perhaps for an accurate account of the battle to survive competing interests.

The victory itself was not in doubt; the usual inflated casualty figures tell us that: 120,000 to 140,000 killed and 60,000 captured.[34] Of course these numbers should be reduced drastically, and though it's difficult to say how much, they are at least an indication that the Cimbri had been utterly broken, as is Tacitus's statement, given earlier, that in his time they were a small people living in Germany.

As a capstone to these two great battles—near Aquae Sextiae and on the Campi Raudii—Sulla was able to drive the Tigurini back into the Alps whence they disappeared as a threat. It was time for the great men to return home. It was time for politics as usual at Rome.

CHAPTER 10

After the Wars

AT ROME, MARIUS AND CATULUS CELEBRATED A JOINT triumph over the barbarians. Plutarch suggests that Marius wanted it for himself alone, but that he was uneasy about what Catulus's men might do if they were denied the privilege, so the consul and proconsul compromised; therefore the decision must have been made in the field, though it was technically the senate's prerogative to grant the honor.

In the eyes of the public, however, the victory was Marius's; they hailed him as the "Third Founder of Rome" after Romulus himself and Camillus—the old saviour from the war with Brennus—and conferred a sixth unconstitutional consulship on the heels of the fifth. This, Marius's penultimate consulship, though an unprecedented honor, was useful to him practically because he would use it to settle his veterans on land of their own. The proletariat had followed him, and he meant to do right by them as he seems to have done in 103 through Lucius Apuleius Saturninus, a tribune who had helped him to his fourth consulship the following year.

During that tribuneship of 103, while Marius was training his army against the Germans, Saturninus passed agrarian legislation giving land in Africa to veterans of the Jugurthine War, so it is clear that they were in alliance by then. Saturninus was known as the tribune behind the popular vote that sent Cornelius Mallius Maximus into exile after the disaster at Arausio, while his colleague Gaius Norbanus prosecuted Mallius's incompetent comrade Servilius Caepio, and after some rioting achieved a conviction that sent him, too, into exile in Smyrna.

To the same end Saturninus also effected the passage of a bill establishing courts made up of knights, to try "offenses against the dignity of

Rome"—by which was meant military incompetence—this would help in the future prosecutions of military blunderers such as Mallius and Caepio, who had had to be driven into exile, respectively, through prosecution under an inappropriate statute and by popular vote. The tribune reinstated Gaius Gracchus's grain distribution, though he may have taken this latter measure during his second tribunate of 100, a tribunate to which he arrived through violence. For violence was Saturninus's tool, one he had used as early as his first tribuneship when he had set a gang against one of his fellow tribunes who opposed his land distribution law of 103.

In the following year Mithridates VI, King of Pontus, sent an embassy to Rome, and Saturninus—now a private citizen—took the opportunity to insult it. Common feeling in Rome about this Asiatic king was doubtless hostile because he had seized the friendly kingdoms of Galatia and Cappadocia while Rome fought the Germans. Still it was injudicious to affront his ambassadors: He was a very powerful man and was frankly as unscrupulous as Saturninus had shown himself to be. Saturninus was, however, a domestic nuisance—only later would he be a domestic threat. Rome had to deal first with King Mithridates whether she wished to or not, and it was better that he were not offended. The senate had been cautious about engaging in a relatively minor campaign against Jugurtha; friction with a powerful, civilized kingdom at the other side of the Mediterranean was even less attractive.

Mithridates had come to power after his father's death in 121 B.C., locking up his mother and murdering his brother. He was no scantling despot: Half-Greek, half-Persian, his original realm was Pontus, an Asiatic kingdom bordering the Black Sea and the Roman province of Asia. He had greatly increased his territories when, shortly after his accession, the Greek cities of Bosporus and Chersonesus, located on the northern coast of the Black Sea, asked his aid in repelling the raids of nomadic Sarmatian and Scythian barbarians from the steppe. He so successfully responded that the whole of the northern Black Sea coast fell to him and he established a capital there at Panticapaeum. The revenues from the area and its use as a recruiting ground increased his power further and led him to build a large fleet; more territorial expansion followed, and by the time of his embassy's visit to Rome, Mithridates was one of the most powerful kings in Asia.

He was also a wily opportunist, as he had shown by seizing Galatia and Cappadocia in 104 while Rome was busy defending her northern frontier against the Germanic tribes. He must have felt no qualms in sharking up these territories since the senate, which had conferred some Phrygian territories on his father in 129, had revoked them when Mithridates took the throne. Thus, the senate had many delicate things to discuss with the king's envoys; freelance provocations by private citizens like Saturninus were not only uncalled for, they could be damaging. Saturninus was put on trial for his life, but he stirred up the mob and got himself acquitted.

In 102, the former tribune's troubles continued. Marius's old patron Metellus Numidicus, now one of the censors, tried to strike Saturninus from the roll of the senate, doubtless as undeserving to sit with that institution given his violent propensities, but the former tribune loosed thugs against him and drove him to the Capitol for safety. Metellus's fellow censor, more reasonable or more realistic than he, kept Saturninus on the list. Saturninus, though, had became accustomed to brutality—it worked so much more quickly than argument and solved so many difficult problems. When he ran for the tribunate of 100 he hired killers to murder a rival named Nonius, who was running against him. Plutarch blames Marius for conniving in the murder, but other ancient historians are silent on this, which suggests that this aspersion on Marius's character is untrue; certainly his later actions following another of Saturninus's murders show that, while he tolerated a certain amount of ruffianism in order to help his troops, he didn't countenance murder.[1]

When Marius ran for the consulship of 100, one of the candidates was old Metellus Numidicus. Marius's old patron was always in the way and, worse, he was a model of all the patrician virtues: He was courageous, dignified, grave, competent and diligent. He had the interests of the state at heart and there was no sham in him. Not that Marius was himself a pure opportunist and without ability, but he always seemed to see the main chance when it came to his immediate advantage and he would always be a "new man" and without the traditional entrenched support of a patrician. He would be forced to take his support where he could, and that would vary from time to time. In the end this left him with a reputation for changeability—even duplicity—which was less a reflection of his character than of the fact that he had no political ideas beyond joining the charmed circle of patrician–noble authority and coaxing the mob to adulate him. He was bound to be a man of unsteady policy.

But issues of character had little to do with the election of consuls for 100, at least insofar as Marius was concerned: The people wanted him again. The only issue seems to have been who would be his partner in the consulship, and money helped to decide that. Plutarch tells us that Marius "by this bribery kept out Metellus and had Valerius Flaccus given him as instrument, rather than colleague, in the consulship."[2] But if he was re-

lieved of sharing his office with his old patron, he was still uneasy of
Metellus, whether through feelings of guilt over the way he had trumped
him and taken the Numidian command, or because he feared the old
man's enmity. The Metelli were still the most illustrious patrician clan.
Who, besides the Metelli, could claim so many great men in recent mem-
ory? According to Velleius Paterculus, "For in less than twelve years during this time the Metelli were consuls or censors or triumphed more than
twelve times."[3] Marius, even in the midst of his sixth consulship, and with
the prestige of having recently saved the republic, had to watch this clan.

Marius, however, had a pair of willing associates: the tribune Saturninus and his comrade the praetor Gnaeus Servilius Glaucia. Though it
seems a bit odd, at the height of his power Marius relied on these men
rather than directly on his own prestige when it came to passing legislation for the benefit of his soldiers. Saturninus, in the end, was able to do
it, using his accustomed force, but Marius might have looked after the
soldiers peaceably and could have changed the state in a number of ways
that might have stabilized it, and yet he did not. The general was an inept
politician and, beyond solving immediate problems that might face him,
he was a man of no broad political aims.

While helping the veterans was Marius's goal, it ought to have been a
goal of the senate too. Traditionally, the senate had made no provisions
for discharged soldiers, letting them drift back home after their service,
often to sink into poverty. Marius fought to see that this wouldn't happen
to the veterans of the northern barbarian campaigns; he had used Saturninus to look after some of his African veterans. But ultimately it was
the senate that shirked this duty. It failed to recognize the new professional army for what it was: an organization with interests apart from the
nobility, even from the city mob in Rome; an organization that could be
coaxed, perhaps, to see itself firmly as part of the body politic if the senate showed genuine concern for its welfare.

As the most powerful man in Rome, Marius might have done something about it—taking up the cause of the discharged veterans generally,
for instance, thus making the senate face the issue squarely. Instead he
dealt with the issue only as it concerned him: He set Saturninus to getting
land for the men who'd fought with him in the north. It was an ad hoc solution that showed that Marius, though he might hate the great families
who controlled the senate, was no different from them in that he could see
no further than they. The army, which Marius had sharpened and profes-
sionalized, at first for expediency and then out of necessity, could now be
as much a political instrument—or even an autonomous political force—

as the commons at Rome itself. The ramifications of this ought to have been dimly visible to both the senate and Marius—but they were not.

The senators chose to do nothing to bind the army to itself and use it as a pillar of the state; instead they turned away from this issue as though it didn't exist. Soon the army would be not a support, but a battering ram at the door of the senate. The senate couldn't see this because there had been little if any tension between the army and the state so long as it had been a militia first defending and then pushing Rome to prominence during the first three centuries of the republic. The interests of the people and senate had often been quite different, of course, but the army hadn't been in the mix as a separate entity. Now that time had passed; the soldiers revered their eagles, took pride in their legions, gave their loyalty to their commander and depended on him to look after them, but the senate ignored these developments. Saturninus, however, showed that he was aware of the soldiers' utility as a political prop; like them, he was a man of violence.

Saturninus hated Metellus; he had the censor to thank for trying to drive him out of the senate, though he had deserved it. He may also have feared the censor because he had used murder to win the tribuneship. Marius too had little affection for his former patron, and having slandered him to win the consulship and deprive him of the command against Jugurtha, it was in his interest to neutralize him. Working together, the men found a way to couple their interests against Metellus with Marius's concerns about land grants, through a clever piece of legislation that would aid the soldiers and discomfit Metellus. Furthermore, Saturninus would not only ingratiate himself with the most powerful man in Rome, but also with those whom the law settled.

Saturninus set to work on a land bill that, beyond the distribution of land to veterans, also provided for the establishment of several colonies of veterans who were to be given Roman citizenship. Lands were to be doled out in Transalpine Gaul from territory recently held by the Cimbri, and provision was made for colonies in Sicily, Achaea and Macedonia. The senate, which had shirked any responsibility to provide for mustered-out veterans, actively opposed the bill through their clients among the proletariat in the city. Part of their opposition to the law may have arisen from one of its humiliating provisions:

> It was provided also in this law that, if the people should enact it, the senators should take an oath within five days to obey it, and that any one who should refuse to do so should be expelled from the Senate and should pay a fine of twenty talents for the benefit of the people.[4]

One of the effects of this provision was to maneuver Metellus into exile. It is unlikely that this provision was really intended for that, for it would have been a roundabout way to accomplish it. Instead it might be seen as a proof of the strength of the tribune and his supporters, for here was a reversal of the usual order of things: a bill to be approved under duress by the senators after passage by the people—not a bill to be approved in the senate and then accepted by the people.[5] Because the cost to any senator who refused the oath would be enormous, the bill was a sort of contract of adhesion, and so it was natural that the senators decided to thwart its passage through the efforts of their clients.

Besides obligation to their patrons, the mob was jealous of its Roman citizenship and was as unwilling to extend it as in the days of Gaius Gracchus, and Saturninus had, therefore, to oppose the sway of both patronage and pride if he were to carry the legislation. The solution was to appeal to that part of the electorate who had the greatest interest in the success of his program: men who had served in the army and now looked forward to the chance of property. "Apuleius [Saturninus] appointed the day for holding the comitia and sent messengers to inform those in the country districts, in whom he had most confidence, because they had served in the army under Marius."[6] Many of these people answered the tribune's summons and came to Rome to cast their votes.

The day arrived when the matter was to be put to the *comitia* for consideration, and Saturninus was ready for his opponents. "Those who attempted to prevent the passage of the laws proposed by the tribunes were assaulted by Apuleius [Saturninus] and driven away from the rostra."[7] During the commotion the bill's opponents (the clients of the nobility, and the mob) claimed to have heard thunder, and in the face of thunder the Romans were prevented by tradition from finishing this sort of business. Saturninus and his followers, though, wouldn't be put off by the weather. In response to this recalcitrance, the city dwellers, who feared the passage of the law, "seized whatever clubs they could lay their hands on, and dispersed the rustics."[8] The first case of violence of this sort, that involving Tiberius Gracchus, had waited ten years for a sequel in the death of his brother. Now Saturninus had made violence a commonplace at political assemblies.

The rustics, however, didn't stay dispersed. Saturninus led these old soldiers back against the city mob and quite naturally these veterans bested the townspeople and carried the bill. It remained now for the senators to swear obedience to it; now had come the time when Saturninus and Marius would see if Metellus was still made of the old stuff. Would he, as the tribune and the consul hoped, stand on his principles and suffer exile, or would he concede and lose face? Plutarch says Marius decided to grease the way with a bit of trickery, though Appian's version of events differs, suggesting that what happened afterward was not entirely clear.

Plutarch tells us that the senate had debated the land law's oath-taking provision at the consul Marius's suggestion. Marius then played a canny trick on Metellus and the senate when he gave the impression that he himself would refuse the oath. Metellus agreed with this, certainly as a matter of principle but bolstered, one supposes, with the support of his political enemy who seemed now to oppose the tribune who had carried the bill that was, after all, in Marius's favor. The senate was in agreement with both men, and Marius dismissed them.

On the fifth day after the law's passage Marius called the senators together. As consul, Marius was the first to speak to the gathered assembly and he, in contrast to his earlier statements in the senate, agreed to swear to the law "if so be it were one, a proviso which he added as a mere cover for his effrontery."[9] Whether or not Marius compromised the senators into swearing to uphold the law, or whether they were more willing to do so than Plutarch's account indicates, the rest of the senate followed his example, except Metellus, who stood on principle. Despite the entreaties of his friends who recalled to him the penalties of refusing to take an oath in favor of the land bill, the old patrician resisted, as Plutarch says: "telling those that were with him that to do a wrong thing is base, and to do well where there is no danger, common; the good man's characteristic is to do so where there is danger."[10]

Appian tells a slightly different story, and it too reflects poorly on Marius, though in a different way. Instead, Marius seems to scheme against the people and Saturninus (his very supporters) rather than the senate. The result was not far different, but his actions are a bit more subtle as he gulls Metellus into standing openly against the law. Appian tells that Marius suggested to senators this way out of their situation:

He saw a way, however, to avoid it, and he proposed the following trick—to swear that they would obey this law as far as it was a law, and thus at once disperse the country people by stratagem. Afterward it could be easily shown that this law, which had been enacted by violence and after thunder had been reported, contrary to the custom of their ancestors, was not really a law.[11]

The story of tricking Metellus may be anti-Marian embroidering from a later time after Sulla had taken supreme power and Marius and his supporters had fallen into disgrace. Yet since this was a serious political struggle, it is not unimaginable that Marius and Saturninus saw the oath provision of their land bill as a probable way of damaging Metellus in the eyes of the people, if not actually driving him into exile, as it in fact did. But what other motive could Marius have had to encourage the senate to cooperate with and then repudiate the land law when the balance of power shifted? If he were to provide for his veterans and if he had connived in Saturninus's use of them to throw the vote in their own favor, any action on his part to undo Saturninus's work seems inconsistent. The explanation may be that Marius was playing both ends against the middle: He seemed to cooperate with the senate, thereby maintaining his pull in that body, all the while hoping that the legislation, once enacted, would stand anyway. He may have acted as a sort of double agent in telling both the aristocrats and the people what they wanted to hear, reckoning to come out on top when the people, under his confederate Saturninus, prevailed.

Marius led the senators to the Temple of Saturn, where quaestors generally gave oaths, and he and a coterie of his followers were the first to swear to uphold the law. The rest of the senators did the same with the exception, as might be expected, of Metellus. The following day Saturninus tried to have the ex-consul arrested and taken from his home, but other tribunes protected him, and this caused Saturninus to call out his "country," actually veteran, supporters to help him vote Metellus into exile. Metellus found himself surrounded and defended by the city folk who carried daggers; probably many of them were clients of some sort, though probably not all—there must have been a good deal of resentment among the city mob for the soldiers who had travelled to Rome and robbed them of their vote. But, Appian tells us:

> He thanked them and praised them for their good intentions, but said that he could not allow any danger to befall the country on his account. After saying this he withdrew from the city. Apuleius got the decree ratified, and Marius made proclamation of the contents of the decree.[12]

Metellus duly went into exile on the Greek island of Rhodes, where, as so many Roman gentlemen did while banished, he spent his time in philosophy. He was given a great welcome there.

With the land-and-colony law now enacted, soldiers began to be settled on properties, and thus Marius's immediate concern was taken care of. Yet Plutarch assures us, without much detail, that in consideration of Saturninus's actions he "was forced to connive with Saturninus, now proceeding to the very height of insolence and violence, and was, without knowing it, the instrument of mischief beyond endurance."[13] The interesting feature of this sentence is its assertion that Marius was an unwitting confederate of the tribune, at least as far as damage to the republic was concerned. It seems an odd assertion of naivete in a man of Marius's experience and station, and yet it may be true. He seems to have been a schemer—consider his treatment of Metellus in both the Jugurthine War and in the matter of Saturninus's land bill—and he could see practical ways to seize his immediate goals if there is any truth in the allegations that he bribed his way to the aedileship as a young man, and later to his sixth consulship. Exactly what would have constituted bribery may be an open question since in Roman politics patronage was used by most men to help them reach high office, but he was clearly accused of having crossed the line, whatever it may have been.

Politically, then, he was something of a tactician, but not, apparently, much of a strategist; recall his actions as tribune when he managed to delight and then anger both the senate and the commons. His deference to Saturninus may well be true a combination both of a feeling of obligation and the lack of any long-range plans. He was then at the top of the Roman world and that was enough. He had reached his goal, and the idea of pursuing any real political program was foreign to him. This was less a flaw in his character, probably, than a reflection on his traditional upbringing. The Gracchi, after all, were the first to propose radical changes and to try pushing through programs with serious permanent effects. Before them, the political history of the republic appears more a series of cobblings as the senate and the people remade the government slowly, a step at a time to meet various exigencies. Marius, as a country-knight, had old-fashioned attitudes, one of which was to get to Rome and rise as high as he could, not to remake the state like a Gracchus. Put another way, political strategy, as opposed to tactics, probably had little meaning to him.

*   *   *

A second slave war that had erupted in Sicily in 104 ended in 100 B.C. Manius Aquilius, Marius's erstwhile legate during the campaign against the northern barbarians—and his colleague as consul in 101—had taken some of the veterans down to Sicily and beaten them. Aquilius himself took the signal action of meeting one of the slave leaders in single combat and killing him. Though Aquilius himself was badly wounded, the scars defended him in a later extortion trial. His attorney, Marcus Antonius, ripped Aquilius's tunic from his chest to display his battle scars; he was acquitted at once.

For Marius there was an event that would help him later as well. A wealthy lady named Fannia and her husband, Tinnius, had divorced, and Fannia demanded her dowry back. Tinnius denied it to her on the ground that she had been adulterous, and Marius sat as judge on the case. After a trial on the issue, he found that Fannia had indeed been loose, but that Tinnius knew about it and had condoned her behavior when he married her knowingly and stayed with her. The consul decided in Fannia's favor on this ground and ordered her dowry restored. He nonetheless fined her the inconsiderable sum of four small coins to shame her for her behavior. He would meet Fannia more than a decade later, and while Plutarch suggests that she might have been ill-disposed to him because he had disgraced her in the judgment, in fact she was of great help to him; as events would later show, the dowry was more important to her than a brief humiliation.

In the meantime Saturninus and his friend the praetor Glaucia had set their sights on offices for 99. As praetor, Glaucia was forbidden to run for the consulship as he wished, but after years of so much constitutional irregularity he saw no obstacle to it; the real problem as far as Saturninus and Glaucia were concerned was that the praetor might lose the election to the populist Gaius Memmius, the tribune of 110 whose inflammatory speeches had set the commons against the nobility during the Jugurthine War. It was at his suggestion that Jugurtha had been brought that year to Rome to answer charges about his conduct. Saturninus sank to the crudest method available to rid his friend Glaucia of this competitor: He had him killed.

Saturninus's elevation to the tribuneship of 101 had given him immunity from prosecution for his earlier murder of Nonius until the expiry of his office, and he had probably been clever enough to muddy the circumstances of the murder itself so that he could not be directly blamed. His ruffians had chased Nonius from the *comitia*, where he had been haranguing the crowd against Saturninus and Glaucia, and they had stabbed him when he fled to an inn. Saturninus's complicity might be assured, but his guilt was probably difficult to prove, and would be more so after he had served a year as tribune.

Yet Memmius's murder was far more serious. He had been unpopular with the senate in the days of the Jugurthine War; he was probably something of a follower of Marius. Still, Saturninus and Glaucia's actions, by their unacceptably violent cast, were undermining the electoral procedure and the very legitimacy of the tribunate. It was clear that Saturninus and Glaucia were willing to do whatever it took to maintain themselves as leaders of the mob. The Gracchi, by contrast, had been mild reformers.

The senate met to discuss the actions of Saturninus and Glaucia and issued, as it had in response to Gaius Gracchus's protest against the repeal of his colonial law, the *senatus consultum ultimum,* the instruction to the consul to take whatever action was necessary to protect the state. In this case it meant that Marius must put down his lieutenants. Now, this may not have been such an unpalatable decree; Marius was not a revolutionary, at least not consciously, and Saturninus and Glaucia's actions must have embarrassed and offended him deeply. If these conscienceless men were tolerated they would inevitably curb the power and privileges of the nobility, of which Marius was now one, and they might compromise him in particular since he had been a patron of sorts to them. On the other hand, these men had supported him in reaching his immediate and narrow political ends. To bring them to heel was to diminish his prestige, and he must have known it. Still, he was consul and he honored the senate's decree and set out against Saturninus, Glaucia and their supporters. Plutarch says:

> . . . he did bring his soldiers into the Forum, and driving the insurgents into the capitol, and then cutting off the conduits, forced them to surrender by want of water. They, in this distress, addressing themselves to him, surrendered, as it is termed, on the public faith.[14]

To protect these insurgents, Marius locked them up in the senate house itself, the Curia Hostilia, but he was unable to ensure their safety. An enraged crowd rushed the building and scrambled onto its roof, where they snatched off the roof tiles and stoned many of the prisoners to death, among them the two ringleaders. The immediate crisis was over, but Marius, to some degree at least, had lost standing. He had turned on former supporters and shown himself unable to protect them against the mob.

Perhaps in part because of some loss of standing, Marius was willing to leave the city for a while on a tour of the east as some sort of envoy, in late 99 or early 98. He may have hoped that his reputation would recover in his absence, if indeed it had ever really suffered much. He was elected augur or diviner in his absence in 97, which suggests that he had in fact remained popular, or that any loss of standing had been brief. Plutarch, however, suggests that there was another reason behind Marius's junket:

> There was now an edict preferred to recall Metellus from banishment; this he [Marius] vigorously, but in vain, opposed both by word and deed, and was at length obliged to desist. The people unanimously voted for it; and he, not able to endure the sight of Metellus's return, made a voyage to Cappadocia and Galatia, giving out that he had to perform the sacrifices which he had vowed to Cybele, but actuated really by other less apparent reasons.[15]

Marius in fact went to Pessinus in Phrygia to carry out his religious obligation; perhaps he managed to pass through Cappadocia and Galatia as well, as Plutarch suggests. It would certainly have been useful to Rome if he had, as these were kingdoms that Mithridates, King of Pontus, had snatched while Rome was contending with the northern barbarian alliance. The "less apparent reasons" Plutarch suggests for Marius's visit were to stir up trouble in the area and provoke Mithridates to war. Plutarch harshly describes the Roman's character:

> For, in fact, being a man altogether ignorant of civil life and ordinary politics, he received all his advancement from war . . . and hoped that by setting at variance some of the kings, and by exasperating Mithridates, especially, who was then apparently making preparations for war, he himself should be chosen general against him.[16]

Rome was unhappy with Mithridates, but whether she desired war so soon after the conflict with the northern barbarians is unlikely. However, it's difficult to see Marius's visit as anything less than a spy mission under the protection afforded a Roman diplomat. Though Plutarch tells us that Marius used his chance to provoke and upbraid the King of Pontus—"O king, either endeavour to be stronger than the Romans, or else quietly submit to their commands."—the intended effect was probably to dissuade the king from any further territorial grabs by showing him that he was now an object of Roman attention. Rome did not go immediately to war with Mithridates; in 96 the senate only demanded that he remove himself from Cappadocia.

After his mission, Marius returned to Rome, where things remained fairly quiet for about the next five years as the senate enjoyed the ascendancy it had gained after Saturninus and Glaucia had been put down pursuant to its decree.

During this time Sulla advanced his political career. In 98 he ran for the office of praetor, but was defeated despite his growing reputation. He blamed his defeat on the Roman mob, who, he claimed, punished him for not running for the aedileship first on his way to the praetorship, because they would have gotten from him fabulous "shows": contests between gladiators and combats between wild animals and hunters. The excuse seems flimsy since he lavished enough promises and money on the people to get himself elected in 97. Perhaps he had simply been too frugal the first time around. Certainly he must have spent a good sum in 97, as one of the Caesars dryly remarked to him that he was right to call his praetorial authority "his own" as he had bought it.[17] In 96 Sulla was sent off on the next leg of his political and military career: He was sent east to deal with piracy and Mithridates, King of Pontus.

CHAPTER 11

The Italian War

MARIUS'S FORTUNES MIGHT HAVE SEEMED IN DECLINE; THERE were no great wars for him to prosecute, and we lose him for a while. Perhaps he passed some time in trade with his knightly friends and clients. Sulla, however, found in the next few years a chance to enhance the name that he had diligently worked to lift from obscurity. It was Mithridates who let him do it. He had snatched Cappadocia shortly before Sulla was sent east as a propraetor in 96 to Cilicia on the coast of Anatolia. Sulla had apparently gone to check piracy, a perennially favorite pastime of the Cilicians, but had also to install Ariobarzanes on the Cappadocian throne. The King of Pontus had already been told to give up that country and Paphlagonia as well, but the senate's command had not, by itself, proven enough.

Sulla marched off on his mission using only local levies. He drove Gordius—Mithridates's governor—out of Cappadocia and installed Ariobarzanes on the throne. No doubt Sulla played things with his usual skill, and he must have used the campaign to gather intelligence about Mithridates, his forces and the lie of the countries roundabout. This was crucial, for Mithridates was unable to control his ambition—as he had demonstrated so often. Sulla knew there would soon be open war between Pontus and Rome and he could learn things through this little action.

In one regard, perhaps, things didn't turn out as well as Sulla might have hoped. During his little campaign, Sulla's forces had clashed with those of Tigranes, king of Armenia. While nothing came of it directly, Tigranes threw in his lot with Mithdridates: he married his daughter.

Meanwhile Sulla advanced to the Euphrates, where he met Orobazus, an emissary of King Arsaces of Parthia; he was the first Roman to hold a meeting of state with a representative of this powerful nation. The subsequent history of these peoples would be charged with war, though this meeting was peaceful enough. It did, however, have a rough sequel for the Parthian ambassador.

> At the time of which reception, the story is, that, having ordered three chairs of state to be set, one for Ariobarzanes, one for Orobazus, and a third for himself, he [Sulla] placed himself in the middle, and so gave audience. For this the King of Parthia afterwards put Orobazus to death.[1]

Arsaces apparently thought his minister had been slighted and thus the royal dignity. The King of Parthia did not share the view held by a seer in Orobazus's employ. This man is said to have looked upon Sulla and opined that he would become a great man; the wonder, so he said, was that he wasn't already the greatest. The days of his supremacy had not yet arrived, but he had done remarkably well. But in spite of his successes—or perhaps because of them—Sulla returned home to a prosecution.

Plutarch tells us that he was accused of "having exacted a vast sum of money from a well-affected and associate kingdom."[2] The implication is that Sulla extorted money from Ariobarzanes in return for setting him on the Cappadocian throne. While this charge may have been true, we may be suspicious: Sulla was a defendant in the extortion court, which was so often a weapon of the knights against the nobility. We can't know the truth of the allegation, not least because the merits of the case were never addressed. The prosecutor Censorinus dropped the matter, no doubt under pressure from the senate and its allies. It is interesting to note, however, that the former consul Publius Rutilius Rufus was condemned shortly after this in 92 of extortion in Asia—in spite of his model conduct there. He was clearly a victim of anti-senatorial bias in the extortion court: He spent his exile in Asia, remaining a popular man, among those whom he was accused of abusing. Sulla, whether guilty or not, would have been a tempting target for populist knights.

*   *   *

The year 91 B.C. saw the tribuneship of Marcus Livius Drusus, son of the tribune of the same name who had worked so diligently against Gaius Gracchus. Father and son could hardly have been more different in political outlook: The elder had been a tool of the senate while the younger was a reformer along the lines of Gracchus. He was farsighted enough to know that the allies grumbled at Rome's treatment of them and, like Gaius Gracchus, he meant to do something for them.

The younger Drusus was a wealthy man and boastful, calling himself the "patron of the senate," and the story of how he built his house on the Palatine Hill displays another aspect of his character. Drusus's architect said that he could build him a house in such a way that no one could look into it. Drusus replied, "If in fact you have the skill, build my house in such a way that no matter what I might do, it could be seen by everyone."[3] Drusus's pride in his uprightness displays a certain happy priggishness, but his rectitude was not in doubt.

Drusus saw two reforms as necessary: a curb on the extortion courts and the extension of the citizenship to the Italian allies. The shameful trial of Publius Rutilius Rufus had shown that the knights could, through main strength, condemn innocent senatorial governors, but the trial was more than a blot on Roman jurisprudence: It infringed on the ability of the senate to govern provinces fairly and not merely for the benefit of equestrian tax farmers. Gaius Gracchus's transfer of the extortion courts from the control of the senate to the knights was proving a mistake; not only had it not helped him politically, it had blunted senatorial power without any good effect on the republic as a whole.

But reform would have to come after catering a bit to the mob. Accordingly, Drusus put into effect a corn law and his father's old law regarding colonies. Following these sops to the mob he proposed a law to empanel the extortion courts equally from senators and knights, or else something even more radical: that 300 knights be enrolled in the senate and that the courts be manned from this enlarged senate. The historians are unclear on this point. Whatever the exact nature of the measure though, he meant to render the courts more fair and protect the senate.

Drusus's actions were misconstrued. Neither the senate nor the knights were happy with the proposed legislation. Among the knights there were many who were more interested in continuing the extortion courts in their own hands, as they were such a useful tool, and though there was some support among the more farsighted, the senators were more generally jealous of their position and too clubby to allow newcomers. "Thus it came to pass that both the senate and the knights, although opposed to each other, were united in hating Drusus."[4]

The measure, however, was carried by force in the fashion now customary where controversial legislation was concerned. The issue of Italian citizenship came next.

Drusus had succeeded in forcing his earlier measures through, but he could not do so with his plan to enfranchise the Italians, for the Roman mob opposed the extension of citizenship. Some of the Italians, however, were not content to let the matter rest in the hands of the Roman proletariat; the Marsic[5] noble Quintus Pompaedius Silo approached the city with several thousand armed retainers, determined to get the citizenship by overawing the senate. He was talked out of his plan, probably with the assurance that the senate would work to confer the desired rights if petitioned peacefully. Drusus apparently had nothing to do with Pompaedius's expedition, but Pompaedius was his friend and the damage was done: Drusus was suspected of working with the Marsian.

Drusus's troubles continued: The consul Lucius Marcius Phillipus moved to have Drusus's colonial and judicial legislation nullified as having been achieved unconstitutionally. The ground for this was probably that it had all been passed together in violation of a law that forbade different measures to be tacked together in the same bill.[6] Drusus argued cogently that to annul his legislation was not in the interest of the senate: doing so would undo his judicial reform and put the senators back into the power of the knights, who would continue to run the extortion courts. The senate, however, turned a deaf ear to his plea and undid his work.

The senate's victory over Drusus was not enough in some quarters, and this animus bred a plot. A number of Umbrians and Etruscans were let into the city. These provincials mistrusted Drusus on the ground of his colonial legislation, and those who had invited them were rewarded with Drusus's subsequent assassination, which, Appian implies, was their doing. Coming back from the forum (as Velleius Paterculus says) or while conducting business in the atrium of his house (as Appian has it), Drusus was stabbed by an unknown assailant. He died a few hours later with friends gathered around him. He maintained his pride to the end when he asked a fair question: "When," he said, "relatives and friends, will the republic have a citizen like me?"[7] It would be a long wait.

Drusus's death would soon trigger the most dangerous war since that against Hannibal—more dangerous, probably, than Marius's against the German tribes a decade before. Rome could count upon her allies when she faced the northern barbarians; soon, however, she found herself, quite literally, at sword's point with many of them.

But the revolt still lay in the future. In the meantime Drusus's death formed a pretext for more political in-fighting as the knights sought to compromise the senate. They convinced the tribune Quintus Varius to propose legislation against anyone who might help the Italians get citizenship. The bill was vetoed by other tribunes (doubtless at the senate's behest), but these officers were induced to rescind the veto when faced with naked daggers.

A number of prominent senators who had supported Drusus were haled before the court. Cotta made a good defense but then slipped into exile, as had Mummius, who had gone before he could be brought to trial. Drusus's death and the treatment of his senatorial allies convinced the Italians they would get nowhere; the time had come to take things into their own hands, hands that had probably been ready for some time. Rome meanwhile concerned herself with the political struggles between senate, knights and mob, a colorful example of which was the struggle of Sulla and Marius over a set of trophies sent by King Bocchus of Mauretania showing Jugurtha taken by Sulla. When Marius tried to have them removed, Sulla's supporters opposed him, and the city might have dissolved into an uproar if events hadn't overtaken the squabble.

There was some whiff of rebellion in the air, for Rome sent agents among the Italians to see what they were about. The Italian cities were busy exchanging hostages as part of their union. One of these agents saw a hostage being taken to the town of Ausculum and he alerted a praetor, a certain Servilius. Servilius and his legate, a senator named Fronteius, visited the town. The townspeople, fearing that their preparations had been discovered, murdered the Roman officers and all the Roman citizens in the town and went into open revolt.

The Romans themselves would call the ensuing war the "Marsic War" after the Marsi, who, with the Paeligni, were among the first to revolt. Soon, however, the list of allies in revolt was long. In addition to the Marsi and the Paeligni, Rome found herself facing the Vestini, Marrucini, Picentines, Frentani, Hirpini, Pompeians, Venusini, Apuleians, Lucanians and her traditional enemy, the Samnites. Rome's Latin allies, who had more privileges than others, remained loyal to her with the exception of Venusia, but she had lost control of Italy from Umbria in the north to Calabria in the south and east to the Adriatic Sea.

The rebellious confederation sent envoys to Rome to express their grievances, but the senate would not have them; instead it told them to put aside the rebellion and then send ambassadors. The erstwhile allies responded by mustering soldiers and raised an army said to be 100,000 strong.[8] Again, as with all ancient troop figures, this was doubtless an exaggeration, but this time the number may not be too far off; it would correspond to four consular armies, while Rome and her remaining allies are said to have matched the figure.

It is hardly a surprise that Velleius Paterculus would write of the war as a terrible catastrophe for the republic:

> So changeable and unhappy was the fortune of the Italian War that two years in a row two Roman consuls, Rutilius and then Cato Porcius, were killed by the enemy, the Roman army was routed in many places, and one took up the military cloak and remained a long time so clothed.[9]

Though in revolt from Rome, the confederation paid her the compliment of organizing their government along Roman lines. Corfinium, about a hundred miles east from Rome, was the Paelignians' main city, and this was chosen as the confederates' capital, and all rebels were now citizens of it. Renamed "Italica," it hosted a senate of five hundred; a pair of consuls and twelve praetors were duly chosen and Italy was divided into two provinces, each given to a consul in the Roman way. The northwestern province was given to Quintus Pompaedius Silo and the southeastern went to the Samnite Gaius Papius Mutilus; each was given six praetors as lieutenants to help them conduct the war. And they knew quite well how to conduct the war—as they themselves complained (and explained), "through all the years and all the wars they sent twice as many of themselves as soldiers and horsemen,"[10] and now these soldiers and horsemen were ranged against Rome and her Latin allies.

The consuls for the year 91, Sextus Julius Caesar and Publius Rutilius Lupus, left the city to meet the enemy themselves. Caesar went south against the Samnite Mutilus, Lupus to the north against Pompaedius. Once again the senate had chosen as leaders men without great military experience—the senate might have chosen Marius for one of the highest commands, though perhaps, even in this dangerous time, it could not bring itself to invest a man who had already been six times consul with such power. In the end the senate muddled along, letting internal politics prevail.

The senate was not entirely irresponsible however: it freed slaves and enrolled them in the army to guard the western coast, recruited Gaulish auxiliaries and hired Numidian, Mauretanian and Spanish horse and the usual Cretan archers. With her remaining allies Rome may in fact have raised as many troops—perhaps one hundred thousand—as Appian credits to her. Furthermore, though unwilling to put proven generals at the highest level of command, the senate did attach such men to the consuls as legates: Gaius Marius to Rutilius and Sulla to Caesar, with lesser men as well.[11]

The forces of the Italian rebels and the Romans were variously divided up and the campaign began, as so often was the case, badly for the Romans. The Paelignian Vettius Scato defeated Caesar in an engagement, killed a number of his men and advanced to Aesernia, a town ninety miles east of Rome. The capture of Aesernia was important as it lay on a road running between the Samnite and Marsic countries and prevented easy communication between them. Vettius, after a time, was able to starve it into submission.

The Samnite commander Marcus Egnatius took Venafrum, and Publius Presentaeus, another rebel commander, defeated Gaius Perpenna, one of Rutilius's legates, who was commanding some ten thousand men. Four thousand were said to have been killed and the bulk of the equipment from the rest captured, suggesting that the surviving Roman troops escaped through flight. Rutilius stripped Perpenna of his command and gave his troops to Marius. Licinius Crassus, a legate of the consul Caesar, lost eight hundred men in an action in Lucania at the hands of another rebel commander, and the rest shut themselves up in Grumentum for safety.

Gaius Papius Mutilus continued with his successes: He took Nola, Slabiae, Minurvium and Salernium, enrolling slaves and prisoners into his army. More towns submitted as he ravaged the countryside about Nuceria to the north of Rome, following which he settled into the siege of Acerrae. Lucius Julius Caesar, a brother of the consul Sextus, attempted to relieve the town with an army containing thousands of Gaulish auxiliaries as well as Numidian horsemen. Mutilus, knowing this, displayed a son of Jugurtha, named Oxynta, to Caesar's troops, and a number of the Numidians came over to him. Caesar dismissed the rest of his Numidians and shipped them home as untrustworthy.

Mutilus attacked Caesar's camp and broke into it, but Caesar's cavalry made a sally from the gates and drove off the enemy. The consul was able to save himself, but he withdrew afterward, unable to force Mutilus to lift the siege.

Marius's experience along the river Tolenus was equally colorful. Rutilius and the old veteran (Marius was now in his sixties) were operating along the river, across which was an army under the command of Vettius Scato. Both the consul and Marius threw bridges over the Tolenus, probably with a view to catching the rebel between their two armies. Vettius encamped near Marius's bridgehead, but laid an ambush upriver near Rutilius. He caught the consul's army before it had completely crossed the bridge, and drove many of the Roman troops into the river.

Bodies floating downstream alerted Marius that an action was taking place, so he crossed the river against the opposition of Vettius's troops, won his way clear to the other side and seized the rebel camp, which was not well defended. Vettius, though he had defeated the consul, was forced to withdraw for want of supplies. Marius's victory, however, was marred by Rutilius's death in the first engagement.

The consul's body was taken to Rome, where there followed so much lamentation that the senate decreed that, in the future, the dead should be interred where they were killed lest others be discouraged from military service. Following the Roman lead in this matter, the rebels resolved to do the same.

Sextus Caesar served the remainder of his consulship alone—he was too occupied with the war to hold a consular election. Rutilius's troops were divided up between Gaius Marius and another of Rutilius's legates, Quintus Caepio. The shock caused by the loss of a consul in battle was balanced somewhat at least by the further concentration of troops under Marius's command. And in fact those who found themselves under the old general were the more fortunate, for the Marsic general Pompaedius defeated Caepio in some sort of ambush.[12] The commander himself was killed with many of his troops and the survivors, as before, were then attached to Marius's army. It was clearly to the benefit of the state that Marius's command should be large, but it was growing at a high price: the defeat of lesser commanders.

Marius seems to have fought with his accustomed caution and deliberateness, refusing to leave his fortified camp if it didn't suit him, much as he had done when faced with the Teutones a decade before. Plutarch gives an anecdote about this.

A story is told that when Publius [Pompaedius] Silo, a man of the greatest repute and authority among the enemies, said to him, "If you are indeed a great general, Marius, leave your camp and fight a battle," he replied, "If you are one, make me do so."[13]

Marius knew both when to fight and when not to.

The rebel general Marius Egnatius had rather more luck against the consul Caesar than Pompaedius had with Marius. He defeated the consul's large army and forced him to flee to Teanum. He was reinforced and marched from there to the relief of Acerrae, which he had unsuccessfully tried to relieve before. Once there he settled his men in camp and the two commanders, Caesar and Mutilus, faced each other in a stalemate without fighting.

Rome's interests were meanwhile being infringed outside of Italy. Mithridates, ever the opportunist, seized Cappadocia once again—and Bithynia too—with the help of his new son-in-law Tigranes, king of Armenia. Rome could watch, but she could do nothing as yet: Her governor in Asia had a few troops, but so long as Rome was embroiled in war with her allies, she hadn't enough military power to right things.

There was some good news from the Marsic War, though. Marius and Sulla, attacked by a Marsic force, defeated it, Sulla apparently being granted a triumph for killing more than six thousand of the enemy. This enhanced the reputation that had been growing since his exploits in Numidia and Asia.

Gnaeus Pompeius Strabo, whose son would be Julius Caesar's great rival decades later, laid siege to Asculum, where the revolt had first flared. Gaius Vidacilius, whose hometown this was, advanced to its aid with eight cohorts and instructed the townspeople to burst out against Pompeius's troops while he attacked, but they failed to do so. He made his way into the town notwithstanding, but saw that it would fall. His end was singular: He killed his political enemies for stopping the townsfolk from attacking as he had ordered. He then constructed a funeral pyre for himself in a temple, feasted his friends, took poison and then leapt onto the pyre, which he commanded his friends to light.

Sextus Caesar—his consular authority extended after his term had ended—won a victory over some 20,000 of the enemy, and he continued the siege of Asculum, where he was replaced by Gaius Baebius when he died of disease.

Toward the end of 90, however, the senate became alarmed by stirrings among the Etruscans and Umbrians. Any further spread of the uprising might be more than she could handle, and so the senate saw to it that Roman citizenship was extended to the Etruscans, Umbrians and Latin allies. This kept the revolt localized and eventually furnished the means to end the war, though at the very price it would have taken to avoid the conflict altogether. Roman citizenship was extended not only to those allies who had not taken up arms against Rome, but to those who agreed to lay them down. This eventually damped down the fire of the rebellion and strengthened Rome's hand. Paterculus implies that those who received the citizenship sent troops on her behalf and Appian says explicitly that the Etruscans did so.

Nonetheless fighting continued into 89 when, as Paterculus has told us, Rome lost the consul Porcius Cato, killed fighting the Marsi. But this was not a bad year for Lucius Sulla: For his actions he would be elected to the consulship in 88. Perhaps it was at this time that, as he led an army out of Rome, a flame reportedly burst out of the ground near Laverna. Seers declared that it meant "a person of great qualities and rare and singular aspect" would take the government and settle things.[14] Sulla, remarking on his blond hair—and likely thinking of his blue eyes and wine-marked complexion—said later that he was that man.

Back in the field, Sulla met the rebel Lucius Cluentius near Pompeii—a city in revolt. Cluentius provoked Sulla by pitching his camp insultingly near, and the legate attacked in haste without waiting for the return of troops he had sent foraging. Cluentius was able to send Sulla into retreat, but with the return of his foragers Sulla was able to save his situation and defeat Cluentius, who then moved his camp to a more prudent distance. The two armies met again after Cluentius had received a reinforcement of Gauls, but these men lost heart when, before the armies met, a huge Gaul challenged any comer to a duel. A small Marusian soldier accepted and killed his challenger; the Gauls began to flee and Sulla attacked Cluentius's crumbling front. The legate killed many in the pursuit and drove the rest toward Nola, where the citizens, fearing the Romans might break in after the rebel troops, opened only one gate to them; Cluentius died fighting outside the walls.

Sulla next moved against Aeculanium, a wooden-walled town of the Hirpini, and forced a surrender by laying combustibles about the walls and setting them alight. He allowed the plunder of the town as an example, but spared those who surrendered, thus bringing the Hirpini under control. He then turned his attention to the Samnites and took the city of Bovanum. The summer over, Sulla returned to Rome to stand for the consulship.

While Sulla was back in the city, other Roman generals were successful in the field. Pompeius Strabo subdued, among others, the Marsi, who, with the Samnites, had formed the basis of the revolt. Gaius Cosconius burned Salapia. Cannae surrendered to him and, while he suffered a reverse at the hands of Trebatius and was driven into the town for protection, he made good his situation thereafter. A river kept apart Cosconius's and Trebatius's forces and the latter suggested that the two armies meet on one side or the other to settle matters. Cosconius agreed to let Trebatius pass over to his side, but decided that victory was worth some dishonor: "Cosconius withdrew, and while Trebatius was crossing attacked him and got the better of him, and while he was escaping toward the stream, killed 15,000 of his men."[15] As usual in these battles, the defeated lost by far their greatest numbers as they fled.

After Cosconius's victories, but probably as a result of Pompeius bringing the Marsi to heel, the rebel capital was moved from Italica to the Samnite city of Aesernia, where the government was reorganized. Power was allotted between five praetors, the most famous of them the Marsic leader Pompaedius Silo.

Silo, however, was killed in 88 in battle against the forces of Caecilius Metellus Pius, son of old Metellus Numidicus. Metellus took Silo's remaining contingents into his own army, and we may see the effect of the extension of citizenship working here. We do not know the details, but grants of citizenship coupled with military victories brought the war largely to an end by 88. Some fighting continued for a while in the Samnite country and Lucania, but, as Appian tells us, even these latter people appear to have gotten Roman citizenship later on. An abortive attempt by a pair of rebel commanders to cross into Sicily was countered by the timely action of that province's governor.

And so by 88 B.C. the war was over, but for a few small areas, such as Nola, a town in Campania near Capua. But the price of Rome's victory was the granting of citizenship, which had it been granted sooner would have prevented the war altogether. And yet that grant was not what it might once have been. Although the new citizens of Italy far outnumbered the old, they were carefully distributed among eight new tribes so that they could not outvote the Romans of the thirty-five earlier tribes.[16] This would be a cause of dissension later, and an opportunity for Gaius Marius when he sought command in Rome's newest war, that against Mithridates.

CHAPTER 12

Civil War

MANIUS AQUILIUS, MARIUS'S OLD COMRADE-IN-ARMS AND fellow consul, had been sent east in 89 B.C. to confront Mithridates and drive him back to his own territories from which he had advanced into Phrygia, Bithynia and, as usual, Cappadocia. Rome did this as soon as she felt the tide of the Italian War turn in her favor. Aquilius joined local Greek militias to the Roman troops of Lucius Cassius, governor of the province of Asia, and threw Mithridates out of recently conquered Cappadocia and Bithynia and installed Nicomedes as king of Bithynia. Aquilius, though, went beyond his brief and extorted money from Nicomedes for the liberation of his kingdom, but he could not pay it. Therefore, under pressure from the Roman general, he was made to raid Pontic territory. Mithridates complained, but took no retaliatory measures.

With the close of the Italian War there was the usual civil strife at Rome, this time between debtors and creditors. The former argued against the taking of interest on loans on the ground that an ancient law, now fallen in abeyance, forbade it. This was true enough, but custom had by now sanctioned the taking of interest and the creditors stood on their rights from this perspective. A praetor named Asellio was given the unenviable task of reconciling the parties. Whatever his solution, it must have been a compromise, and the debtors would have none of it. He was struck by a stone while sacrificing to Castor and Pollux in the forum. Dropping the libation bowl, he sprinted for the Temple of Vesta, but was headed off. He turned from there and managed to reach a tavern, but found no safety there—his throat was cut. No one was brought in for the crime. As Appian explained, the creditors saw to this.

Yet the Asellio scandal was a minor incident in view of what was to come. Soon it would not be the debts of private parties at issue, but the command of a great war. For what could be a greater prize to men such as Marius and Sulla?

For there was to be war with Mithridates; it was certain by 88, and Sulla, who was now consul, would have the greatest chance at it. Emboldened by Nicomedes's successful depredations against Pontus, Aquilius invaded Galatia without senatorial approval. Aquilius worked together with Lucius Cassius, the governor of Asia, and with Nicomedes of Bithynia. The Romans moved forward along three fronts: Cassius advanced into Galatia, a Roman legate, Quintus Oppius led troops into Cappadocia and Aquilius himself advanced to intersect Mithridates as the king approached Bithynia. The Romans would have done better to keep their forces together.

Nicomedes and his Bithynians were the first to come up against the king's army. Mithridates himself was leading the greater part of his troops, the advance guard of light infantry and cavalry moving ahead under the command of the brothers Neoptolemus and Archelaus and under his own son Arcathias. The armies met on a plain alongside the river Amnias. The fight began over a hill on the plain that both sides reckoned worth having, and it was decided in favor of the Pontic force by the light infantry, the cavalry and a number of scythed chariots even before Mithridates's phalanx had reached the field.

The Bithynian defeat surprised Aquilius, made him think better of the advance, and probably caused him to rethink the wisdom of provoking the war, as he had done, without any real authority. He began a retreat but was caught along the way and forced to fight a battle that resulted in a sharp defeat. Aquilius continued his retreat; Nicomedes and Cassius joined the remnants of their forces in retreat as well, and the three men finally dispersed, Cassius to Apamea, Nicomedes to Pergamus and Aquilius to Rhodes. The various kingdoms and territories of Asia Minor now belonged once again to Mithridates: Bithynia, Cappadocia, Mysia, Phrygia, even the Roman province of Asia. To crown this stunning reversal, Aquilius the former consul fell into the hands of Mithridates, who, according to Appian, had him killed by the colorful expedient of pouring molten gold down his throat as a punishment for greed.[1] It is hardly surprising that Velleius Paterculus vividly characterized Mithridates as

> . . . a man of whom one did not hold silent nor speak without caution, sharp in war, especially courageous, great sometimes through luck but

always through spirit, a leader in counsel, a soldier in action, through hatred a Hannibal to the Romans.[2]

The king followed up his defeat of Aquilius with a device that showed as well as anything that particular mix of cunning and practical viciousness that made him such a serious opponent. After Rome had declared war upon him, he sent letters to the Greek cities of Asia, which were by now thoroughly disgusted with the Roman tax farmers who had been set on them since the days of Gaius Gracchus. In these letters he commanded that on a set day and hour they should murder all the Romans living among them. In return he promised them a remission of taxes for the next five years. Mithridates's appeal to their pent-up frustration, sweetened as it was by a financial incentive, succeeded as he had hoped and many were killed. Even more important from a strategic standpoint, these cities were now fully committed to him in the coming war. He now got ready to meddle in Greece to compound his successes.

In a sense Marius had been preparing for the war as well. After the Saturninus debacle he had toured Asia and visited the king of Pontus, and even now he hoped for command of the army in the new war in spite of his age—he was over seventy. To that end he would go out to the Campus Martius, the traditional military practice field outside and to the west of the city walls, to exercise and practice coursing. Plutarch equivocates when he declares that the old general was "still nimble in his armour, and expert in riding; though he was undoubtedly grown bulky in his old age, and inclining to excessive faintness and corpulency."[3]

When pressed to explain why, at his age and with so many accomplishments, he still wished to go to this war, he is said to have replied that he wished to "teach his son to be a general."[4] It was more likely that the old general chafed in retirement. He had stepped down from command during the later stages of the Italian War pleading age and fatigue, but the glory and booty of a successful campaign in the richest area of the ancient world were undoubtedly great inducements. Be that as it may, he was unlikely to be given the opportunity—the senate had not, for example, put him in chief command of the Italian War, and it was unlikely to do otherwise than assign the conduct of the new war to whichever of the two consuls should be given the province of Asia by lot in the accustomed way. As it happened, Asia, and hence the war, fell to Sulla as consul.

But would the decision stick? Would the usual constitutional procedures be honored after forty years of populist demagoguery and political violence? Violence was now a commonplace tool even in the passage of salutary provisions—those on all sides of an issue were prepared to such recourse, and so it is no surprise that Marius might hope to repeat his political success of 107, when the tribunes had taken the command of the Numidian War from Metellus and given it to him. Perhaps it might happen again.

Marius's opportunity lay in the dissatisfaction of the Italians, the new Romans who had found their citizenship a rather dilute thing as they had all been allotted to eight tribes (and hence eight votes), the old Romans thus easily outvoting them with their thirty-five tribes. The new Romans had as their champion the reforming tribune Publius Sulpicius, who proposed to reform the tribal system and enroll the new citizens in the thirty-five old tribes so that their right to vote would not be utterly vitiated. The proposed legislation was predictably unpopular with the older Romans because the great mass of Romans were new, and if they were distributed fairly they could outvote them.

So Sulpicius needed further support for his reforms, which must have been opposed by part of the senate as well as the mob. We know this because he went about with a bodyguard of young knights said to number six hundred and known as the "anti-senators." It follows further that there must have been some significant support for his measures among the knights generally if his supporters were so blatant in bearding the senate. What their interest might be is hard to say as we look back so far; probably they reckoned that flooding the old voting tribes with the new citizens would make them harder for the nobles to control through their traditional client–patron relationships. The knights, who were becoming more and more a distinct class, might then assert themselves against the senate with support of a mob that was growing less and less beholden to the senatorial families. The more powerful families, trying to keep their slipping grasp on the voters, would share the Roman mob's interest in excluding the newly admitted citizens and could appeal successfully both to the rabble's interest in keeping the vote in its hands and to any residual ill will against the new citizens on account of the Italian War.

Sulpicius knew where to look for support: to old Marius the *novus homo*, the "new man." He could count on the general's hunger for command in the coming Mithridatic War to make him an ally, and Marius's thousands of veterans constituted a vast clientage. The tribune's plan was simple enough: Push through the law to register the new citizens in the old tribes, and then, while they were dominated by pro-Marian sentiments, push through a law to lift the command of the war from Sulla and confer it on Marius.

As the date of the vote approached the city was flooded by the new citizens come in support of Sulpicius. Many of these would have been Marian supporters if not actual clients. The Roman mob met them with violence and riots ensued, growing worse from day to day. Sulla and his consular colleague Quintus Pompeius responded by proclaiming a ban on public business. These magistrates had the right to do this, but Sulpicius took the position that it was improper as a mere tactic to prevent the vote. He may have been right; though Appian says that Sulla had no inkling of Marius and Sulpicius's plans about the war, it seems that a patrician as astute as Sulla, whose world was the circle of the Roman nobility, would have seen what his enemy's support of Sulpicius meant.[5]

In any case, Sulpicius called on his supporters to go armed to the forum and he confronted Sulla and Pompeius, demanding that they lift the ban on public business. "A tumult arose, and those who had been armed drew their daggers and threatened to kill the consuls, who refused to obey."[6] Pompeius got away somehow while Sulla temporized, saying that he needed time to seek counsel. His adviser, as it would turn out, was Marius.

Sulla went to Marius's house, as one story goes, apparently for protection. Sulla himself, in his memoirs, asserts that he was dragged there at sword's point. Whichever was the case there must have been great pressure applied to him to get him there, to the very lion's den, and it would be fascinating to know what passed between them, but there is no surviving account. Marius did prevail upon Sulla to allow public business; it may not have been difficult to persuade him, for some followers of Sulpicius had already murdered the consul Pompeius's son for railing against them too vigorously. The murder touched home: The young Pompeius was Sulla's son-in-law.

Marius probably did not broach the subject of the Mithridatic command. Though a bluff character, he knew Sulla well and it seems unlikely that he would have pushed the aristocrat on this issue. Marius needed the consul's unwilling cooperation in the matter of allowing the vote, and though he could get what he wanted by suggesting to Sulla that it was in his interest to protect himself from the unfortunate violence of Sulpicius's supporters, there was no point in taunting the consul. Better to get done the business at hand.

Whether he knew Marius's ultimate purpose and gulled the old man with cannily feigned ignorance, or whether indeed he thought the citizenship vote was the only matter to concern him, we cannot know. Sulla did, however, leave the city and go to his command just as though he were to lead his legions off to fight Mithridates. Given the innovation and enormity of the actions he would soon take, though, it seems hard to believe that he hadn't considered taking them, if occasion warranted.

Sulpicius put the vote through and Marius was subsequently chosen as commander against Mithridates.

The news reached Sulla at his headquarters at Nola, near Capua,[7] where his troops had been putting down some of the last flickers of the Italian War. When a pair of tribunes whom the senate had dispatched to take the army for Marius arrived, the temper of the troops was evident: They stoned them. In response Marius killed some Sullan supporters back in Rome and had their property seized, which he could do as he had cowed the senate.

Sulla's troops were no less unhappy than he was at the prospect of having the war taken from them. Though war in poor countries like Spain appalled citizen-soldiers, the contrary prospect of losing a chance at war and booty in the richest part of the world had much the same effect on the increasingly professional armies. Sulla's legions saw themselves faced with the possibility that Marius would bring his own legions to Asia, and that the spoils would be theirs. This fear was useful to Sulla and he depended upon it. Appian says that he did not openly urge his soldiers to remedy their situation, but this can hardly have been true. At the very least he must have encouraged them in subtle ways. His actions against the Marians were quick and sure, not the product of haste and improvisation. It was determined: The army would march against Rome herself.

Marius and Sulpicius were completely unprepared. Even though constitutional scruples had been going by the board for some decades, still the general and the tribune did not foresee the possibility of open military action against the state by a duly elected executive of the highest rank. Here was treason to take their breath away: Sulla and six legions marching north from a mere hundred and twenty-five miles away.

They were not the only men whom Sulla had shocked deeply—all of his higher officers, one quaestor excepted—resigned their commands and hurried to the defense of the city. It may have been their appearance that made it clear to the Marians what was happening, but there wasn't time to do much. Once started, Sulla's army, marching fifteen or twenty miles a day, could reach Rome in a week and a half.

The former consul and his minion Sulpicius prepared to defend the city, but hadn't the time to scrape up many troops. If Marius had been as unscrupulous as Sulla, he might have called up his veterans during his earlier troubles over Sulpicius's bills and mustered them into an army; if he had been as astute as his opponent he might have prevented the consul from reaching his troops at Nola, but he was not and did not. Again Marius showed himself to be a clumsy and short-sighted politician, or perhaps one old-fashioned enough to trust in the honor of a patrician, even an enemy. But times had changed. Violence often settled matters in the forum, where in earlier times at least the guise of civil procedure was maintained. Now an army would decide things.

This does not mean that Sulla didn't have some interest in the welfare of the state, subordinate as that interest likely was to his own advancement through the happy ending he expected in the war with Mithridates. His later actions would show a serious concern in the state, even, paradoxically, in its constitution, but nothing could efface the example he would make at the head of his army.

The senate sent a deputation to meet Sulla on the road. They asked him why he led an army to Rome and he answered that it was to save her from tyrants. Thus he gave a bit of a patriotic gloss to his march, but it could hardly have been convincing to any, particularly to the "tyrants" themselves, Marius and Sulpicius. Two more deputations were sent, and to each he gave the same answer, though to the third he said that he would meet Marius, Sulpicius and the senate in the Campus Martius and come to some agreement with them, though neither Marius nor Sulpicius would have dared such a meeting.

But if Marius and Sulpicius were dismayed at events, the same could not be said of Sulla's co-consul, Pompeius, who came from the city to join him. Despite Sulla's unheard of advance, and despite Pompeius's high office, he was prepared to support Sulla fully. His hatred of the Marians, if not a product of the murder of his son, was certainly intensified by it, and this may explain his willingness to connive in Sulla's actions.

Meanwhile, Marius and Sulpicius labored unsuccessfully to gain time as Sulla advanced. They sent another delegation under color of senatorial authority and instructed Sulla not to establish his camp closer then forty *stades,* about four and a half miles, of the city. Sulla agreed, pretended to begin laying out his camp on the spot, and then, when the envoys had left, he took to the road once more, sending two legates, Lucius Basillus and Gaius Memmius, to take the Esquiline Gate, while he hurried after.

He soon reached Rome and disposed his army around it. With one legion he himself occupied the Esquiline Gate on the eastern side of the city, while Pompeius took the Colline Gate to the north. A third legion took the *pons fabricius,* which led across the Tiber on the west, and a fourth remained at some undisclosed place outside the walls—most probably occupying and defending Sulla's camp. The city was now enveloped on three sides, and Sulla advanced through the Esquiline Gate.

The citizens resisted—some doubtless out of affection for Marius, but many no doubt out of horror at the enormity of Sulla's action. They pitched things from rooftops down upon the soldiers below until Sulla threatened them with fire and began to set buildings alight.

Marius and Sulpicius resisted as well. The Marian forces met Sulla's men in the Esquiline Forum just south of the Esquiline Gate, and the ensuing battle was "the first regularly fought in Rome with bugle and standards in full military fashion, no longer a mere faction fight."[8] If the Marians fought in the streets under standards like soldiers, this means that Marius and Sulpicius had been able to put together some scratch force, evidently of Marius's veterans, despite the press of time. Although the Marians acquitted themselves well enough, numbers told. Sulla called in more troops from his camp and sent them down the Suburran Road, which ran west along the northern edge of the Esquiline Forum, and they began working their way around the Marian flank. The Marians, fearing that they would be surrounded, fled the city; Rome was now Sulla's.

Sulla, now more a tyrant than the opponents whom he had so dubbed, took up the task of running Marius and his followers to ground. Soon cavalrymen were sweeping through the country in search of the fleeing general and his cronies. Sulpicius was caught and killed, but Marius was more elusive. He had begun a flight with all the elements of an overwrought adventure story: narrow escapes, pathos, triumphant return and, finally, revenge.

After fleeing the city Marius reached his country estate of Solonium south of Rome, and began to prepare for the worst. He sent his son, the younger Gaius Marius, off to enlist the help of his father-in-law Mucius while he himself made his way to Ostia with his son-in-law Granius. From there he sailed off in a ship that had been fitted out for him by a friend. His ultimate goal was Africa, where many of his veterans from the Numidian War had been settled as colonists.

The younger Marius, meanwhile, reached his father-in-law's estate when Sullan cavalrymen approached; Mucius's overseer hid the younger Marius in a cartload of beans driven past the horsemen. The young man, his escape made, was able to get aboard a ship bound for Africa, where ultimately he was taken in as a guest of Hiempsal, king of Numidia. This

Numidian might be expected to protect the young Marius since his position on the throne had been a direct result of the elder Marius's defeat and capture of Jugurtha.

Old Marius had less luck at sea. A storm came up that drove his ship ashore near Circeii, south of Rome. Without any provisions and apparently any real plan, Marius and his party ranged through the area. As Plutarch says: "For the land and sea were both equally unsafe for them; it was dangerous to meet with people, and it was no less so to meet with none, on account of their want of necessaries."[9] In the end Marius and his followers headed south along the coast on foot in the direction of Minturnae, but before they reached it they saw and were themselves sighted by a troop of Sullan horsemen, who galloped after them. Marius and his party, seeing two ships sailing close to the shore, ran down to the beach and swam to them. Granius and the others were taken aboard one of the vessels, while Marius, heavy and old, struggled with the help of two servants to reach the other. Granius's boat sailed to the nearby island of Aenaria, but the boat that Marius had reached did not pull away so quickly. The cavalrymen had come onto the beach and were shouting for the crew to put Marius ashore or toss him overboard, and the crew havered. Plutarch says "the masters of the ship, after frequent changes, in a short space of time, of their purpose, inclining first to one, then to the other side, resolved at length to answer the soldiers that they would not give up Marius." All the same, his troubles were not over.

Indeed, Marius was in the midst of them, for the crew of the boat, though they had refused the horsemen, were in fact still undecided. Sailing south along the coast, they put in at the mouth of the Liris River near the city of Minturnae and told the old general to go ashore and rest; they would sail some time later, so they said, when the wind arose inland. Marius debarked and lay in a field to rest; the sailors raised anchor and sailed off, "as thinking it neither honourable to deliver Marius into the hands of those that sought him, nor safe to protect him."[10] It was an attitude he would meet with again.

Now Marius found himself in much the same position as he had shortly been in: exhausted, hungry, hunted and without any means to escape Italy. But his situation was worse: He was now without any followers.

Knowing that his hunters might be anywhere, Marius hid himself in the swamps outside of Minturnae, going so far as to strip himself naked and hide in a pool with only his face above the water. He was found nevertheless and suffered the indignity of being dragged naked and muddy from the water, summarily bound and marched to Minturnae to execution. It looked to be a pathetic end to the savior of Italy, a man who had been six times consul.

At Minturnae the *duumviri*—the two mayors, as it were, of the town—were bound by Sulla's legislation to kill or surrender the old man, but found themselves, like the sailors before them, unwilling to commit themselves. They lodged Marius under house arrest at the home of the divorcée Fannia, whose case Marius had considered back in 101. Plutarch tells us that she "was supposed not very well affected towards him," but this wasn't true—and really, one could hardly have expected her to be ill-disposed to him given that Marius's judgment had been, from the standpoint of her property, entirely in her favor. So, we shouldn't be surprised that, as Plutarch goes on, "But Fannia did not then behave like a woman that had been injured, but as soon as she saw Marius, remembered nothing less than old affronts; took care of him according to her ability, and comforted him."[11] Marius had the good fortune, at least, to be detained in the house of a supporter.

Comfortable he may have been, but he was still in great danger, for the *duumviri*, though they had difficulty coming to the decision, finally resolved to kill him. However, none of the townsfolk would consent to do it. The stories differ about who was lumbered in the end with the murderous task—Plutarch says it was a Gallic or Cimbric horseman,[12] Appian a Gaul, and Velleius Paterculus says it was a public slave, but the thrust of the story doesn't differ in any of the versions. Paterculus tells us that:

> Sent to kill him with a sword was a public slave of the German nation who by chance had been captured by this victorious general in the Cimbric War; when he recognized Marius, expressing with a great wail his indignation about the fall of such a man, he dropped the sword, and ran from the jail.[13]

This event may have had something of a superstitious effect on the *duumviri*. Reversing their position, they gave Marius money and clothes and put him aboard a vessel to take his chances elsewhere.[14] He was able to sail to Aenaria, where he found Granius and his other followers, and together they set sail for Africa. Appian, by contrast, tells us that the Minturnians didn't do so much for him, but that they merely put him out of the town, and that Marius overpowered a fisherman, stole his boat and reached an island (apparently Aenaria), where he found friends to sail to Africa with.[15] Paterculus tells us that Marius encountered his own son near Aenaria as well,[16] but both Plutarch and Appian are agreed that the younger Marius had in fact fled to Numidia. Since he left Italy by another and earlier ship it seems Paterculus may be mistaken on this point. These divergences in his story suggest that legends have grown up around Marius's travails, but though they differ in their colorful details, in the main they recount the same story.

Marius and Granius headed for Africa, but were forced stop at Eryx in Sicily for water, where the local quaestor attacked the landing party and killed several of them. They sailed next to the island of Meninx, and it was here that Marius learned that his son had escaped and gone to King Hiempsal of Numidia. From Meninx, Marius reached the province of Africa, where he hoped to enlist the help of Sextilius the governor, a man who had no connection with him, but a man who, as it turned out, would take the government line in the same equivocal way that the sailors and the Minturnian *duumviri* had done.

Appian says that Sextilius would not let Marius land; Plutarch says that Sextilius sent a deputation after Marius had landed to warn him away. He would, he said, put the senate's decree of outlawry in effect should the old general not sail away. Paterculus gives the most pathetic and poetical account of all, stating that he "endured a poor life in a hut in the Carthaginian ruins, with Marius regarding Carthage and she watching Marius, each able to be a solace to the other."[17]

To reconcile these accounts we should probably believe that Marius did, in fact, land and camp unhappily in the ruins of Carthage (the handiwork of his old superior Scipio Aemilianus), and that he was sent off some time later when Sextilius realized what he was about, or had judged him too great a danger to tolerate. Compelled to move on then, Marius went west to Numidia, probably not far from the border of Africa, where he might stay in touch with the veterans of the Numidian War, whom he had settled during his consulship of 106 and who were therefore his clients. It was probably the presence of so many Marian veterans that had induced Sextilius to tolerate Marius and send him along rather than seize him promptly as he was obliged by law to do.

Marius was now joined by his son and a number of their principal followers who had slipped from Hiempsal's court; the king had done his best to delay their departure, and this had made it reasonably plain to the younger Marius that they must flee while they could from a monarch who was about to surrender them to the Sullans.

And so, the heart of the Marian party—the old general himself, his son and a handful of their close supporters—spent the winter of 88–87 in a dangerous, perhaps pathetic state, cobbling together whatever forces they could to oppose the Sullans. This meant, now that Sulla had shown what he was willing to do, that the rules of the game had changed radically. The Marians, for their own survival, would have to follow Sulla's example and capture the city.

*   *   *

Back in Rome Sulla concerned himself with constitutional reforms, an odd thing, perhaps, for one who had just marched against his own country. It may seem a paradox that he, the first Roman to take an army against Rome, should busy himself with legal reforms of a fundamental nature, not mere laws forced through the assembly to the detriment of opponents. It seems, then, that Sulla was at once a tyrant and a constitutionalist. True, he outlawed Marius, Sulpicius and twelve others of the nobility whom he regarded as the most troublesome of his opponents; their goods were seized and anyone who caught them might kill or drag them before the consuls. But the rest of his measures, though hardly less subtle, were radical and undercut the means by which popular politicians had appealed directly to the public.

Sulla and his colleague Pompeius reestablished the rule that no measure should be brought to a vote before it had been laid before the senate—a practice most notably ignored by Tiberius Gracchus in his haste to reform some fifty years before. Of more significance, though, was this reform: Legislative voting would now be done, as it had been hundreds of years before, by century. In this way the knights and wealthier classes could once again control the voting through the disproportionate allocation of centuries.

As for the senate, which had declined in numbers, Sulla enrolled three hundred new members. This would extend the senate's influence and help furnish men to sit as judges in the various courts. It is difficult to say how far he could pack the senate in his favor, but doubtless he enrolled among the new senators friends and men he thought would be broadly useful to him.

He did not leave the tribunate unchanged either. This office was hobbled by a rule forbidding those who took it from rising to the higher offices—this discouraged capable men from the tribunate.

Sulpicius's legislation, among which was the distribution of the new citizens into the old tribes, was stricken as having been illegally pushed through—certainly a defensible argument, even though the result of the legislation had been just.

The result of all this business was to curb popular politicians and to channel the power of the state into the hands of the senate whence it had been slipping since the days of the Gracchi. Though it must be said that any reforms that prevented civil disturbances would allow Sulla to go east and prosecute the war against Mithridates without having to glance over his shoulder, the extensive and basic nature of these Sullan reforms speak of a real interest on his part to remake and strengthen the state. But it was all from a man who had shown that he judged himself to be above a constitution. His example had been of the very worst kind, and the Marians had learned from it. Their chance would come soon when Sulla left for the east.

CHAPTER 13

Sulla, Marius and Mithridates

IN 88 B.C. MITHRIDATES WAS AS ACTIVE IN PURSUING HIS interests as Sulla. He had many of the Greek cities of Asia Minor in his pocket, though cities in Lycia,[1] such as Patara, resisted him. It was time now to woo and threaten Greece proper. The island state of Rhodes, however, was determined to stand steady for Rome. Those Romans who had escaped the Asiatic massacres made their way there, as did Lucius Cassius, the ousted governor of Asia, now bereft of his province. One of the more colorful sieges in ancient history began as Rhodes stood alone against the army and fleet of Mithridates.

The Rhodians strengthened their walls in anticipation of a siege, built siege engines and destroyed those parts of the town beneath the walls to deprive the enemy of them. Their mettle was shown not merely in the preparations they made for stubborn resistance, but also in the pluck with which they awaited the Great King: The Rhodians did not sit quiet waiting for the Mithridatic forces to arrive, but sent out their warships to meet the king's fleet. This was audacious as his fleet was said to number three hundred vessels; a hundred are reported as biremes, agile and quick, the rest larger and said to be closed in, which meant that the oarsmen were protected. This protection was generally afforded to larger galleys and so these vessels were probably quadriremes or quinqueremes, the standard battleships of the period. The Rhodian fleet, though smaller, was probably of the same kind, for a quinquereme is mentioned as well as biremes.

As the Mithridatic fleet approached, the Rhodians spread their galleys into a line, or lines, to face the oncoming enemy. As the principal weapon of a galley was its ram, galley fleets commonly advanced against each other in this way to protect the vulnerable sides and sterns of the vessels. Going head to head like lines of infantry, the ships would try to sweep alongside the enemy, snap their oars and then turn and ram helpless ships. Alternatively they might pass through the enemy line and try to turn and strike enemy galleys or, if they could, surround the enemy fleet and ram any that tried to pass through the cordon.

On this occasion the Rhodians set one flank near their island—almost certainly at the extreme eastern end where the city of Rhodes itself was located—and with the line extending north or northwest from that point; it was from this direction that Mithridates's fleet, sailing down from Asia Minor, could be expected. The Rhodians had set their right flank at the eastern point of the island to hinder any encirclement from that side, and held back a number of galleys for an attack on the flank. They must have been behind the left flank, which extended out to sea, and were probably stationed there to move out and prevent a run past the end of it. This disposition, as it turned out, was not sufficient: Mithridates, aboard his quinquereme flagship, ordered his fleet to extend farther out to sea, which it could do as it outnumbered the Rhodians. Fearing encirclement, the Rhodians pulled slowly back to the harbor and locked themselves in, probably with a harbor chain. Mithridates could not force the harbor, even after he had landed, and so he waited for footsoldiers to join him from Asia. The siege of Rhodes had begun.

Bottled up as their fleet was, the Rhodians still looked for chances to harry the Pontic forces, and on one occasion provoked an unexpected sea battle. They sent a bireme out to catch an enemy merchant vessel passing by. Mithridates's ships moved out to protect her and other Rhodian ships moved out too. The Rhodian ships, more adept at maneuver than the king's vessels, rammed a number of them and sailed back to harbor towing one of the enemy's triremes, replete with crew.

A second and equally dramatic episode followed when the Rhodians dispatched six fast ships to search for a quinquereme of theirs that they did not know had already been captured. The Rhodian flotilla, under its admiral Damagoras, soon found itself in a vulnerable position: Mithridates ordered twenty-five of his warships after the Rhodian half dozen. Damagoras prudently pulled away, refusing to engage. At nightfall, thinking that the action could not be pressed further, the Mithridatic sailors turned their ships away. Damagoras then attacked them, sank two galleys and chased two to the coast of Lycia before returning the following day. He had ridden out the night at sea—itself unusual for ancient galleys. The outcome, Appian tells us, was "as unexpected to the Rhodians on account of the smallness of their force as to Mithridates on account of the largeness of his."[2]

The king's poor luck at sea continued. Mithridatic infantry being ferried over in merchantmen and triremes were blown by a storm toward Rhodes. The Rhodians went out after them—perhaps the Mithridatic fleet was disordered from the storm—and destroyed a number by ramming and fire. They came home to Rhodes with four hundred prisoners. A small number, perhaps, to a king who could field tens of thousands, but a third humiliation at the hands of the plucky Rhodians must have been hard to bear. After an elaborate but abortive night attack, he decided on an assault from the sea. To this end the king had built a *sambuca*—literally a "harp." In fact this large apparatus was a sort of covered ramp to be run up against city walls. Soldiers could then rush up through it with some protection, and reach the top of the parapet.

This *sambuca* was fitted to a pair of ships and brought up from the sea while other boats carried soldiers and boarding ladders to help push the assault. The Rhodians were quite afraid of the huge thing, but the *sambuca* could not bear its own weight and fell apart. The Rhodians claimed divine help in the affair, reporting that a vision of Isis was seen pouring fire upon the great device. With this Mithridates abandoned the siege.

Mithridates then sailed off to nearby Lycia, where he began the siege of Patara, but seems to have run afoul of divine agency again. When, in order to get material for siege engines, he began to cut down a wood sacred to Latona—the mother of the twins Apollo and Artemis—he had a warning dream and gave up both cutting the trees and the siege itself. Instead he retired from the field and left the day-to-day business of the war to his generals. Pelopidas campaigned against the Lycians, and Archelaus—a Cappadocian, as was much of his army—set out to win or compel the obedience of the Greek states.

In 87 Archelaus took his fleet and began a politic attack upon Delos, an island dependency of Athens, which was then in revolt from her. He handed the island back to Athens and sent the Delian treasury to her under the charge of an ambitious Athenian named Aristion—together with two thousand soldiers to guard it. With this support Aristion was able to do what Mithridates had doubtless sent him for: He took over Athens to rule as the Great King's puppet.

Much else of Greece aligned itself—foolishly, as it turned out—with the king of Pontus. They were likely decided by some distaste of the Romans, who had exercised a protecting role for some time now, a role that kept the Greek states from constantly warring with each other, a freedom for which they seemed to chafe. And Mithridates was close and had large armies; though there was danger in snubbing Rome, the Great King's forces were already on Greek soil and he must be accommodated. The Achaeans, Lacedaemonians and Beotians came over to him, and while some of Greece declined to ally with Mithridates—places such as Euboea, Demetrias and Magnesia—his general Metrophanes pillaged their territories for it.

Macedonia was not neglected either: with the encouragement of the Great King, Thracians raided that Roman province.

*   *   *

While Mithridates was working his ways in Greece and Macedonia, Sulla continued, by his lights, to put the Roman house in order. Two of his supporters, his nephew Nonius and a certain Servius, ran for offices, but were rejected by the people, who elected others notwithstanding Sulla's wishes. This was a clear indication that the people were against him and his response was to pick the consuls for 87 with some care. One, Gnaeus Octavius, was a tractable man; the other, Lucius Cornelius Cinna, a man Sulla hoped tractable despite his Marian affinities. In fact, Sulla was suspicious of him, but the man had too much influence at Rome and so he thought it best to allow him the consulship in return for an oath of personal loyalty. He erred. "Thus Sulla himself, adept as he was at seeing through the minds of men and reasoning out the nature of things, made a grave mistake in the present instance and bequeathed a great war to the state."[3]

Sulla's next step was to protect his colleague Quintus Pompeius and to secure his hold a little more firmly on Italy. Pompeius was made proconsul of Italy and assigned the army of Pompeius Strabo, himself a proconsul with forces raised for the Italian War. Quintus Pompeius got to the army, but while assuming command he was murdered by the troops, Strabo resuming command. His complicity in the killing, if any, is unclear. All the same, whether he was responsible or the soldiers alone, it was a stunning crime: the death of a consul at the hands of Roman troops.[4] This was another example of the accelerating breakdown of order that was progressing throughout the late republic.

Sulla took no direct hand in following up the killing, and apparently no one was punished. Instead he left the city and got back to his troops, which were once again at Nola. These were soldiers he had cosseted during the Italian War and who had shown themselves willing to fight for him against the duly constituted government of their own state; there was little question of his safety while among them. He could turn his attention to the east; Mithridates held most of it, and was whelming what was left.

Rome's interests in Greece at this time were supported only by Bruttius Sura, a legate of Sentius, governor of Macedonia. This intrepid fellow led a small force into Greece where he engaged Metrophanes at sea, sinking a pair of ships. The latter pulled away, leaving Bruttius to take the island of Sciathus, which lies between the coasts of Thessaly and Euboea. This place was a Mithridatic stronghold and treasury for the enemy's loot.

Reinforced with a thousand men, Bruttius fought Archelaus and Aristion for three days near Chaeronea in Boeotia. He seems to have done well; Appian suggests that the result of the contest was uncertain, but Plutarch, whose hometown was Chaeronea, reports that Bruttius drove Archelaus to the sea. If so, this must have been to the strait between Boeotia and the island of Euboea on which stood Chalcis, to which Archelaus might have fled. This town was held by the Pontic forces and would often be a refuge for his troops. Whatever the exact outcome of the fighting, Archelaus and Aristion received reinforcements and Bruttius, judging himself too far outnumbered, made his way south to Attica, where he seized Piraeus, the port of Athens itself.[5] Athens, Archelaus and Aristion's base, was only about five miles away and connected to the port by the famous "Long Walls," so Bruttius showed he was extremely bold. Perhaps he thought to draw Archelaus out of Boeotia by seizing the port of Athens. Whatever his strategy, he was made to relinquish the port and get back to Sentius when Archelaus, whose fleet controlled the seas, got to the Piraeus after him. Archelaus then occupied the well-fortified port.

Sulla arrived in Greece at about this point with five legions, some extra cohorts and some cavalry. He reinforced himself with Greek allied soldiers from Aetolia and Thessaly and then marched south through Boeotia and Attica until he reached Athens and the Piraeus. He divided his army between the two places, concentrating his attention on the port; he thought defeating Archelaus of more immediate importance than taking Athens. Sulla's passage through Boeotia had recalled the area to the Roman side, though he developed a grudge against Thebes, its chief city, which he would act upon later.

Uneasy about the situation at Rome—and rightly so, as it turned out— he first tried to take the Piraeus by storm, but Archelaus's Cappadocians fought well and drove him back. Sulla realized that it would take siege-craft to reduce the place. He set to building engines and putting up a mound upon which to place them and from which to attack. He dismantled the Long Walls and used their materials for the mound.

Meanwhile Archelaus himself was not inactive. He made an attack against the workers and the engines, but Sulla had been informed beforehand by a pair of slaves in the Piraeus. They had hit upon a clever trick: They inscribed messages on lead bullets and slung them out to the Roman lines. Sulla learned from them about Archelaus's sally and was able to ambush his men.

Sulla was concerned about money as well as strategy. He had been sent off to Greece with very little, doubtless as a result of the costs of the Italian War, and to pay his way he seized the temple treasures of Epidaurus, Olympia and Delphi. Though it caused great dismay among the Greeks, Sulla would not be denied; he had to feed and pay an army that exceeded thirty thousand. Diodorus of Sicily goes so far as to say that Sulla seized these treasures for the war he foresaw back in Italy.[6] If so, he was either very perspicacious or very cautious: He would conduct war in Italy again, but that should not have been clear yet. Probably the immediate cost of the war was the ground of his action.

Archelaus, besieged as he was, probably worried less about money and he seems always to have been liberally supplied by his king. As Mithridates's fleet controlled the seas, and as Archelaus was sitting in a port, he was able to get reinforcements first from Chalcis, and then from the king. He himself fought in one sally, staying outside the walls so late that the gate was shut against him and he was taken up the wall to safety with ropes. But despite his bravery and his industry in building towers with catapults to answer those of Sulla, he was unable to force the Romans to retire, though Sulla went into winter quarters that year at Eleusis, up the coast to the north of Piraeus.

All the same, Sulla kept troops at the siege, though his cordon was perhaps not so strict; he thought it advisable to dig a deep ditch about his camp and down to the sea as a protection against Archelaus's cavalry (of which he always had a good deal). Although a permanent Roman camp of the sort for quartering soldiers through a winter would naturally have had more complete defenses than a marching camp, Sulla's concern about attacks—and there were some—demonstrates that Archelaus had some freedom of movement during the winter of 87–86.

And ships were a problem; Sulla needed them. Without a significant naval contingent it would be difficult to bring Archelaus to bay and impossible to interdict reinforcements. The problem, however, was that there wasn't much of a Roman navy at the time. Sulla asked Rhodes to send ships, but she was overmatched by the Great King's fleet and could not do so. Accordingly he sent his legate Lucullus on a mission to put together a fleet with what ships he could get from King Ptolemy of Egypt and the cities of the Syrian coast. Sulla had so little control over matters at sea that Lucullus had to shift from ship to ship as he headed for Alexandria to avoid detection and capture. He was gone for quite a while.

By 86 B.C. Athens had begun to starve. Sulla, informed by the slaves who slung informative bullets, was able to ambush a relief column Archelaus had sent toward the city; he seized the provisions and captured the soldiers. Archelaus by now had an inkling that someone was informing the Roman commander of his plans and he cannily used this to gain what advantage he could. He sent another supply column to the city, but against the chance that Sulla's men would move against it, he gathered his men at the gates to attack the Roman siege engines. As it turned out, Archelaus burned a number of the engines while Sulla was busy taking the supply column.

At this point Sulla must have had some concern about what had happened to the north. Mithridates's son Arcathias had successfully invaded Macedonia, defeated the few Roman forces there, and appointed governors of his own over the territory. He died of illness in Thessaly, which must have stopped the army for a while, but it was not far away and must have weighed on Sulla's mind.

Still, the fighting continued about the walls of Piraeus while Sulla contented himself with bottling Athens up tight and waiting for hunger to do its work. His siege mound, meanwhile, had risen high enough for him to bring his engines—probably rams and penthouses—against the walls. At this point, however, the ramp collapsed; Archelaus had been busy undermining it. Sulla repaired the mound but, following his opponent's example, set his men to mining as well and at some point the opposing soldiers met each other and fought underground.

By this time the Romans were finally able to bring rams up the mound and beat the walls, causing some breaches, while other sections of the wall came down as the result of Roman mining. A sharp fight followed, but Archelaus was able to keep the Romans from getting through the breaches, while during the night he put up breastworks behind the gaps. The Romans, despite their efforts, could not breach them: They had to attack on a narrow front and receive missiles from three sides as they pressed forward. Sulla decided that he would have to starve the Piraeus into submission, as he was doing to Athens, but it might be a long process insofar as Mithridates's ships could pass in and out of the harbor.

Athens, however, was already exhausted by hunger and offered little resistance when Sulla broke into it on the first of March 86. As Appian tells us:

The feeble defenders were soon put to flight, and the Romans rushed into the city. A great and pitiless slaughter ensued in Athens. The inhabitants, for want of nourishment, were too weak to fly, and Sulla ordered an indiscriminate massacre, not sparing the women and children.[7]

Cruelty like this was common enough when cities fell: Marius's treatment of the Numidians at Capsa is an example, though he spared the women and children, at least. That Sulla should display such remorselessness at Athens, however, is remarkable. Though its glory days were over, it was still one of the great seats of Western culture (and Sulla had himself been educated in the Greek tradition). Furthermore, while many Athenians probably dreamed of being free of Roman protection (and hence curbs on their freedom), the city seems to have been as much coerced by Aristion at the head of Archelaus's troops as moved by animosity toward the Romans.

We are told that Sulla stopped the killing at the behest of a pair of Athenian exiles and of senators who were accompanying him on campaign,[8] but he was a calculator; he had probably decided how much horror it was useful to inflict. The killing at Athens illustrates that Sulla could be quite indifferent to the sufferings of individuals as he worked toward his aims, in this case the reduction of Archelaus's main base and the satisfaction of his troops by looting, which he allowed. He did, however, order that the city not be burned.

Aristion and some of his followers reached the Acropolis, where they held on for some time, but Sulla merely hemmed them in with soldiers, knowing that in time they would surrender for lack of food and water. When they were compelled finally to surrender, Sulla killed Aristion, his guard and any who had had any power under the tyrant. "The rest he pardoned and gave to all of them substantially the same laws that had been previously established for them by the Romans."[9] In this he seems to have displayed something of the interest in legalities that he had at Rome.

Sulla now redoubled his efforts against Piraeus; he gave it his full attention and deployed more soldiers. He concentrated on the gap that Archelaus had protected with a breastwork and broke through it, only to find another behind it, and another, for the Cappadocian general kept putting up new ones as the old were taken. Yet Roman persistence, as usual, prevailed and Sulla took Piraeus on 15 March 86. Archelaus abandoned the port and took his army through Boeotia to Thessaly, where he joined and took command of an army led by a certain Dromichaetes (or perhaps Taxiles) as well as the army recently commanded by Mithridates's late son. The combined army was a colorful mix of eastern troops, among them Pontics, Cappadocians, Thracians and Bithynians.[10]

As for Sulla, he burned Piraeus in anger at the trouble it had given him, and with it a number of famous buildings. He then moved north toward the Pontic army that now was said to number 120,000,[11] as usual an inflated figure. Sulla had crossed to Greece with only five legions, some extra cohorts and horse, and though he moved north with a number of Greek and Macedonian auxiliaries, this army could not have been very large even if he had taken them all. Appian implies a figure of 40,000 for the Boeotian campaign, for having claimed for the Pontic army 120,000 he then says of the Romans that "they were in all not one-third the number of the enemy."[12] It seems, therefore, that Appian arrived at this figure through the unlikely assumption that Sulla marched out of Attica with his entire army—and that at full strength after a siege of several months that involved hard fighting.

It seems altogether more probable that Sulla left part of his force behind to hold Athens, Piraeus and Attica—say, three understrength legions (or their equivalent) and his unfit soldiers. He then advanced against the Pontic army with two legions, each understrength from a season of hard campaigning, intending to join up with his legate Hortensius, who led another force, probably of several cohorts.

In fact, Plutarch gives a much lower figure for the Roman forces: 15,000 infantry and 1,500 cavalry—and that after Sulla had been joined by Hortensius, who had slipped from Thessaly through rough country into Boeotia. Because Plutarch based his *Life of Sulla* on Sulla's own memoirs, his figure must be much closer to the truth. If so, then it follows that the Pontic forces were of such a number that a force of perhaps two legions, auxiliaries and cavalry could face them. After all, Sulla had the habit of success, which he had gained through his competence and not the luck to which he publicly attributed it in order to encourage his credulous soldiers. He could hardly have expected to meet and defeat an army of such incredible size, even though his army was homogeneous, experienced and practiced in Roman tactics and technique. Although it seems that Archelaus's army did outnumber the Roman, perhaps significantly, still it must have been of about the same order, though with more and probably better horsemen, as Mithridates could draw on the cavalry traditions of the east, of Thrace and of the tribes along the Black Sea steppe. For example, he had among his cavalry Scythians—nomad horsearchers who would have been unmatched as light cavalry. He also had a number of scythed chariots, horrid devices perhaps, though they had not proved useful against Alexander the Great at Guagamela in 331.

Sulla camped on the plain of Elatea; Archelaus was nearby. The Cappadocian general led his troops out repeatedly, but Sulla refused to engage, concerned about the lie of the land—it must have favored cavalry—and about the enemy's numbers. Plutarch says that, quite to the contrary, Sulla wished to engage the enemy, but that his men shrank from it, cowed by their appearance and numbers. He gives a splendid description:

> The clamour and cries of so many nations forming for battle rent the air, nor was the pomp and ostentation of their costly array altogether idle and unserviceable for terror; for the brightness of their armour, embellished magnificently with gold and silver, and the rich colours of their Median and Scythian coats, intermixed with brass and shining steel, presented a flaming and terrible sight as they swayed about and moved in their ranks.[13]

This is rhetoric and unlikely to be true, even if it is based on Sulla's memoirs, as it might be. It is easier to think that if Sulla did not engage it was deliberate, and if Plutarch's source is his memoirs, then he is passing on a Sullan explanation that flattered the general by heightening the drama of the occasion.

When Archelaus could not force an engagement, he began a withdrawal toward Chaeronea and camped in the neighborhood, which was unfavorable to cavalry. The terrain was rocky, the two armies were separated by a narrow plain that would not allow Archelaus to bring his numbers to bear, and the field sloped up and away from him. His carelessness in stopping at this place may have been due to Sulla's earlier reluctance to engage him, but whatever the reason, the Roman general knew he had found the right place.

Sulla put his army into the plain although he had learned from the Chaeronians that Archelaus had posted a good-sized force on Mount Thurium; he intended to use these troops to outflank the Roman left as it advanced. Sulla had already sent a legion and a troop of Chaeronean allies into Chaeronea itself to protect it, and two of their commanders convinced him that they could get above Archelaus's troops on Mount Thurium and drive them off. With this assurance he arrayed his men on the plain.

Because Plutarch's account is probably drawn from Sulla's own memoirs, we can see, with good assurance, how he deployed his men. Sulla almost certainly put his men into two lines, the *acies duplex*. Although

Plutarch does not explicitly say this, we can be almost certain of it for several reasons. Sulla's army was not large, and to get a front wide enough to prevent outflanking it made sense to array his men in two rather than three lines. Further, we hear that his reserves were divided between two commanders, Hortensius on the left and Galba on the right, and we know that during the action Hortensius was in command of five cohorts; it seems likely that Galba had the same number. Sulla himself took the right wing of the front line, his lieutenant Murena the left. All of this suggests an army of two legions— twenty cohorts, disposed in two lines of ten with a commander over each five. This is what we would expect if the infantry numbered, as Plutarch says, 15,000. The cavalry must have been on the wings; we do not know where the Greek and Macedonian detachments were. Sulla had to rely on his professional Roman troops in such a serious engagement; he may have kept these auxiliaries as a reserve, or they may have been used with the Chaeroneans for the attack on Mount Thurium. In any case, they were probably not many.

We do not know much about Archelaus's dispositions, apart from the fact that Taxiles was leading the right wing, and that the infantry was disposed in a phalanx, no doubt on the conventional Macedonian model found in those areas that were, or like Pontus had been, part of the Hellenistic kingdoms founded by the successors of Alexander the Great. So, Archelaus's infantry fought in close order with pikes of fourteen or sixteen feet. The cavalry was certainly on the wings, and the scythed chariots would have been disposed in front of the infantry, ready to race at the Romans.

Sulla had the advantage of the terrain; Archelaus had to advance up to him. Sulla also had the advantage of maneuverability since his army fought in cohorts, whereas Archelaus's phalanx had to keep in strict order to prevent gaps from opening along the line. For the Romans, it would be a battle of maneuver.

The fight opened as the Chaeroneans surprised Archelaus's troops on Mount Thurium. These rushed down in disorder, some falling from the heights, and spilled out near Murena's cohorts on the left wing. He cut some of them off, while others ran into Archelaus's line, causing some disorder. At this point Sulla advanced to take advantage of any confusion. This closed the distance between the armies and gave little room for the scythed chariots to get much speed and they were easily repulsed. The armies met, at first, only along the Roman left. We might expect that the armies along this part of the line came close to each other, some *pila* were hurled at the Pontic phalanx, and that there was some sporadic contact along the line as phalangites tried to press here and there against the legionaries' shields, while the legionaries tried to turn away the points so that they could work their way close. If they kept good formation, the phalangites could expect, by threat and sporadic contact, to push the Romans back. This part of the fight may have been something of a close stand-off.

Archelaus extended his right wing with a view to enveloping the Roman left. As his phalanx was suited to moving ahead, this flanking maneuver was probably carried out largely by cavalry. Appian says that he led this maneuver himself with the horse, and while his account of the battle is in some ways rather different than Plutarch's, in broad outline it is similar, and this assertion seems right in view of later developments.

Hortensius moved out with his cohorts from the second line to meet the flanking maneuver, but was forced to pull back to higher ground. Doing this he found himself pulling away from the rest of the Roman battle line and was in very real danger of being surrounded. Appian reports that Archelaus cut the Roman line in two and surrounded both parts; though this would seem an overstatement, he may be reporting an attempted encirclement of Hortensius's cohorts.

Sulla learned of Hortensius's position and came to his aid with a troop of cavalry. Archelaus suspected some movement as he watched the dust kicked up as the cavalry approached, and so he moved over against the Roman right, relieving the pressure on Hortensius. Plutarch says he hoped to catch the right wing without its leader; whether Archelaus could guess that much is unclear, but perhaps he saw that Sulla's standard had shifted.

Taxiles's section of the phalanx, known as the "Brazen Shields," now pressed forward in earnest against Murena. Sulla ordered four of Hortensius's cohorts to support Murena and took the fifth with him in support of the right wing. At this point Archelaus's right wing broke and fled. Sulla withheld pursuit until he knew that Murena had prevailed on the left, and then the Romans pressed forward on the enemy, breaking into their camp as they fled for safety.

Archelaus's losses are unknown; both Plutarch and Appian say he got away with 10,000 men. Sulla claimed to have lost only fourteen, of which two later reappeared. As usual with ancient battles, there must have been a complete disparity between the losses of the victors and the vanquished, but if Sulla's claim is substantially true this implies that the battle may not have been so hard fought, and if Archelaus got away with 10,000, then he must have come away with most of his army. All the same, he had to flee across the strait to Chalcis, and Sulla now held

Greece. From Chalcis Archelaus went to sea and ravaged various of the Greek coasts. Sulla had to bear this, as Lucullus had not yet returned—Sulla still had no ships.

Mithridates did not react well to the news of Chaeronea. He killed a number of men he thought might become disloyal if Sulla should approach, and he tried to murder the tetrarchs of Galatia and their wives and children. Three of the tetrarchs escaped and managed to raise an army in the countryside and drive Mithridates out of Galatia.

The Great King was more successful with the people of Chios. He had dispatched another general, Zenobius, with another army for Greece. Zenobius stopped at the island off the coast of Asia Minor and called a meeting of the citizens at which he demanded the children of the leading people as hostages. He had the city in his hands already; his demand was met. A letter from Mithridates accused them of communicating with Sulla; their punishment was a fine of two thousand talents. The townspeople got the money together, but Zenobius complained they had failed to raise that figure and set them to gather more. The fine paid, Zenobius then took the people into exile.

> Then he [Zenobius] stationed his army with drawn swords around the theater itself and along the streets leading from it to the sea. Then he led the Chians one by one out of the theater and put them in ships, the men separate from the women and children, and all treated with indignity by their barbarian captors. Thence they were dragged to Mithridates, who sent them to the Euxine [the Black Sea].[14]

Zenobius, notorious among the Greeks for this, met a well-deserved end shortly thereafter. Instead of heading to Greece, he led his army to Ephesus in Asia Minor—perhaps there were already rumblings of revolt in the area. The citizens agreed to let him in if he brought only a few attendants, a condition he unwisely agreed to. He intended to call an assembly at the theater, but the citizens got him to put it off for a day during which they planned their resistance, the example of Chios in their minds. They seized Zenobius, threw him in prison and then later killed him. The townsfolk manned the walls and supplied the town and then stood in open revolt from Mithridates. Tralles, Hypaepa, Mesopolis and other towns took Ephesus's lead rather than suffer the fate of Chios. Such an extremely dangerous decision suggests that they suspected he would punish them anyway, and this in turn is a hint that they may in fact have contacted Sulla.

Mithridates had success in bringing some of the cities to heel, but reflection led him to realize that he could hardly risk a continued insurrection: Sulla was defeating his forces in Boeotia and he had lost control of Galatia. In response he pronounced the Greek cities free (in what sense is unclear) and then forgave all the debtors in them, gave citizenship to those living there and freed the slaves. By this action he calmed those cities in revolt, or on the point of it, and created in them a faction of relieved debtors, new citizens and freedmen who saw Mithridates as the protector of their new privileges.

Conspiracies were another thing, however. There were a number that he dealt with brutally. But any relief he felt from his successes at ferreting them out could only be tempered by the knowledge that men were now willing to take the risk of plotting against him.

*   *   *

Whereas military defeats had led Mithridates into personal danger from his subjects, military victories had not improved Sulla's position with his countrymen. Immediately after Sulla's departure for the east, the consul Cinna had thrown aside any pretense of loyalty to him and introduced legislation, as Sulpicius had done, to distribute the new citizens among the thirty-five voting tribes. The old citizens opposed this and the two factions met in the forum with daggers. The consul Octavius rushed down with his followers and quelled the riot. Octavius supported the status quo—that is, not allowing the new citizens to be fairly distributed—and his followers killed a number of their opponents and drove them out of the city.

Cinna was determined to distribute the new citizens fairly and to pursue his opposition to the Sullans. He first offered the slaves freedom if they would assist him, but none would. The consul then went into the countryside and excited the Italians who had recently become citizens, gathering them into a makeshift army. He went south into Campania, where a Roman army at Capua was watching the locals (the Italian War still flickered there), and convinced them, the discontented Campanians and the army, to band together and join him. He next passed among the allied cities, which furnished him with troops and funds.

Cinna also sent a message to a man far away who followed with great interest what was happening: Gaius Marius in exile along the North African coast.

The senate, meanwhile, had stripped Cinna of his consulship on the ground that he had abandoned the city while it was in danger and had offered to free the slaves. To replace him as consul, Lucius Merula, the Priest of Jupiter, was chosen. The senate and the consul Octavius could see what was coming: another march on Rome. Sulla's example had swept away any scruples that ambitious men might have about attacking their country.

The government of Rome put itself in a state of defense: The walls were set in order, trenches were dug and troops were raised among the loyal, even among loyal Gauls to the north. Word was sent to Pompeius Strabo to come to the aid of his city, but he hesitated, bargaining for a second consulship.

Marius meanwhile returned from Africa with a few hundred supporters and a troop of Numidian horse. He landed in Etruria, declared the slaves free and walked through the countryside, leaving his hair long to recall his exile, stumping like a politician and reminding the people of his accomplishments and of his six consulships. Many flocked to him, including 6,000 Etruscans, and he soon had a sizable force. It likely helped him that Italy had been at war; many of the men were probably veterans of one army or another. The old general's forces soon formed a fairly serviceable army that he led to join Cinna's near Rome. The men divided their army into three parts and laid siege to the city. Cinna and his lieutenant Gnaeus Papirius Carbo established themselves by the city, Quintus Sertorius above it and Marius below. Sertorius and Marius bridged the river above and below Rome to cut off supplies and Marius took and looted Ostia, the port of Rome. Cinna dispatched troops to Ariminum to block the way of the Gallic soldiers that the senate had sent for.

The government had also sent for Metellus Pius, son of Marius's old commander in Numidia, who was keeping the Samnites down. He was unwilling to make peace with them on their terms, but when Marius learned of this he agreed to what Metellus had refused, and the Samnites became his allies.

Against these odds Rome had little chance. Pompeius Strabo had finally come to the aid of the city, but Cinna and Marius had now grown too powerful. A military tribune named Appius Claudius, charged with defending the Janiculan Hill, betrayed the city to Marius and soon he and Cinna were within the walls. Octavius and Pompeius managed to thrust them out, but it was not long before the city would be lost. Appian tells us that Pompeius and a number of nobles died of disease—a common scourge during sieges. The people recalled that Pompeius had delayed in coming to their rescue: At his funeral they seized his body and dragged it through the streets on a hook to display their contempt.

Marius plundered a number of towns to seize grain for his forces, and then advanced along the Appian Way. He and Cinna encamped a little over a mile from the city. By the fall of 87 the senate had lost heart and began to treat with the Marians. When their deputation arrived, Cinna asked whether they regarded him as a consul or as a mere citizen. They were nonplussed and departed. Cinna knew that he had the upper hand and moved his camp closer.

Shortly thereafter a second deputation arrived to tell Cinna that he was regarded as consul, and was free to enter the city. Marius, however, declined, saying that he could not enter Rome so long as he was adjudged an outlaw. The tribunes quickly arranged a vote to lift his banishment and that of all others for which Sulla was responsible.

Once in the city, Cinna and Marius began to attack and seize the property of those they regarded as political opponents. Octavius, they promised, would not be hurt, but in fact he was soon murdered and his head displayed on the rostra in the forum, the first head of a consul so treated.

Many were killed with the return of Marius and surely it was a bloody affair. How much was the direct responsibility of the embittered old man cannot be said. Opinions differ about the scope of the killing and to what degree it should be attributed to Cinna. Plutarch describes the killing in his usual colorful, if rhetorical way:

> When they had now butchered a great number, Cinna grew more remiss and cloyed with murders; but Marius's rage continued still fresh and unsatisfied, and he daily sought for all that were any way suspected by him. Now was every road and every town filled with those that pursued and hunted them that fled and hid themselves; and it was remarkable that there was no more confidence to be placed, as things stood, either in hospitality or friendship; for there were found but a very few that did not betray those that fled to them for shelter.[15]

Velleius Paterculus lends the events perspective by telling what the future would bring: "Nothing would have been crueller than this victory, except that soon came the return of Sulla. Not only was the free play of swords a savagery to the ordinary people, but the best and most prominent men of the state were punished in various ways."[16]

The old general Catulus, veteran of the Cimbric War and Marius's colleague in the consulship, committed suicide, as did the consul Lucius Merula, rather than face false charges in court.

The capstone of the violence was this: Cinna and Marius made themselves consuls for 86. The old general had reached a seventh consulship, which he did not enjoy long; he died within the month. It was a pathetic end for a man who had begun as a country knight, served his nation abroad and risen to become Rome's bulwark against the northern barbarians and against her allies in time of revolt. He had been a rough man, but until his return any harm he caused had been the result of clumsiness, of negligence at worst: taking the command of the Numidian campaign from Metellus, opening the army to the poor and teaching the soldiers to look to their general for protection, trying to wrest command from Sulla. But he ended his days very badly, more badly than could have been expected.

After Marius's death Cinna picked Lucius Valerius Flaccus as his colleague in the consulship, and together they put through a number of measures for the benefit of the commons. Cinna saw to it that the new citizens were finally enrolled among the thirty-five voting tribes, and Flaccus had a law passed that creditors must be satisfied with a quarter of the debts owed them.

The war with Mithridates was not forgotten: Flaccus was sent off to Asia with two legions to fight the Great King on his doorstep. Because Flaccus had little military experience he took with him as a legate Gaius Flavius Fimbria. It was a poor choice.

*   *   *

After the victory at Chaeronea, Sulla held a celebration at Thebes, Boeotia's chief city, but he did not hold it there through any affection for the Thebans; he held against them their earlier support of Mithridates. Therefore, he seized half of the Theban territory and dedicated it to Apollo and Jupiter, the revenue to be paid in compensation for the treasures he had taken earlier to support his campaign.

Some time thereafter Sulla learned of Flaccus's expedition to Asia. Although Flaccus could hardly fail to help Sulla, even acting independently against Mithridates, Sulla did not see him as an ally. He had surely been informed of what was happening at Rome. Perhaps there was some small comfort when a number of Flaccus's men, sent ahead to Thessaly, deserted to him. The rest, though they disliked Flaccus, were persuaded to stay loyal to the consul by the legate Fimbria and they continued east.

Meanwhile one of Mithridates's generals, Dorylaus, had landed in Boeotia with another army for Archelaus, which the latter joined to the ten thousand survivors of Chaeronea. Sulla marched to meet the Pontic

commanders near Orchomenus on the Boeotian plain. He approached
Archelaus, but saw that he had a large number of cavalry; Sulla decided
to deny the Pontic horse as much of its compass as he could. To do this
he dug wide trenches in the field to protect his flanks. The Cappadocian
general attacked the workers and drove them off. When the battle came,
it began badly for the Romans as the soldiers were fearful of so much
cavalry, but Sulla led two cohorts from the right wing and drove the
enemy from the entrenchments, and in the end the Romans prevailed. It
is probably this event that is romanticized in both Plutarch and Appian
when they state that Sulla seized a standard and ran in front of his troops
to encourage them as they quailed before the enemy. Appian tells us that
he cried to his troops: "If you are ever asked, Romans, where you abandoned Sulla, your general, say that it was when he was fighting the battle of Orchomenus."[17]

It seems to have been a sharp defeat for Archelaus and a very personal
one too: Diogenes, his son or his stepson, had been killed in the battle.
The defeated Mithridatic forces retreated to their camp, and that night
Sulla set pickets throughout the plain so that Archelaus could not slip
away to Chalcis as he had done after Chaeronea. The next day Sulla surrounded the enemy camp with entrenchments and then stormed it, Lucius Basillus, who had helped Sulla lead his troops against Rome, showing particular bravery for which he was decorated afterward.

Archelaus himself, however, was able to slip away and find a boat that
he took to Chalcis. Once there, he began to collect what units he could
from other regions.

After Orchomenus Sulla went into winter quarters in Thessaly to pass
the winter of 86–85. There he waited for Lucullus to return with ships,
but he could not learn where his legate was and so started building them
himself.

But Sulla had another problem too: He had been declared an enemy of
the Roman people at the behest of Marius and Cinna. He had surely
known it for some time, for, among other supporters, his wife Metella arrived with his children to tell him that his houses, both in the city and in
the country, had been burned and that the Marians were conducting a
purge. Clearly he would get no more support for this war, although that
would have been plain enough to a man like Sulla when he learned of
Flaccus's appointment to conduct the war against Mithridates.

Sulla had ambition and plans for Rome and, as would any man, he
had no wish to die at the hands of enemies. And he had made many
when he marched on Rome. Outlaw or not, he would not relinquish his

army, and his army was content with him. He had looked after them in the Italian War, and had looked out for them in this one. They were satisfied that he would look out for them when they returned home: They were his clients. As Appian says about Sulla and his outlaw status: "However, in spite of this he did not relax his authority in the least, since he had a zealous and devoted army."[18]

The year was now 85 B.C. and Sulla had a clear way east through Thrace and then over to Bithynia, where he could fight Mithridates in his own territories. This was as evident to Archelaus as it was to Sulla, and the Cappadocian general suggested they meet to discuss peace terms. Sulla was, of course, pleased; he knew he must return to Rome soon, and so he welcomed the chance to negotiate.

Mithridates had his own reason for negotiating besides his defeats in Boeotia: He was having a bad time of it with the Roman army already in Asia. Flaccus had long since reached the Propontis, between Bithynia and Thrace, and crossed over into the king's possessions.

The consul had been very unpopular with his soldiers because of his careless punishments and his greed, and soon fell out with Fimbria, who took his chance at command. When Flaccus sailed off to nearby Chalcedon, Fimbria riled the troops against him. Fimbria was already popular because he had allowed those troops under him to loot when he commanded them. Flaccus had left in command of the army a certain Thermus as propraetor. Fimbria had Thermus's *fasces* seized—the traditional symbol of authority, a bundle of wooden rods enclosing an axe—and himself took command of the army, claiming that the soldiers had chosen him commander.

Flaccus soon returned, angry of course, but Fimbria drove him off. Flaccus fled for his life, but Fimbria hounded him to Chalcedon and then to Nicomedia, where he was found and killed. It was an atrocious crime, like the murder of the consul Pompeius by Roman soldiers the year before. Why Fimbria did it is unclear. Appian says only that they fell out from an argument about an inn where they were staying. According to this doubtful story, Fimbria was angry with the quaestor, whom he believed to be responsible for whatever had upset him about the place, and Flaccus, in settling the matter, sided with the quaestor. This is hardly provocation for murder; the truth of the quarrel remains unknown.

Fimbria, in effect an outlaw, now led the army against Mithridates's son and won a string of victories. Any indulgence that his victories might have lent him was certainly lost, however, because he allowed his soldiers to loot the Greek cities in Asia, and when he came to Ilium[19] he besieged that city, which sent envoys to Sulla to ask for protection. Sulla agreed to rescue them and sent word to tell Fimbria that they had come under his protection. Fimbria, pointing out that they were already friends of Rome, ordered them to admit him, which they did. He proceeded to sack and burn the city and knock down its walls. The event is almost unfathomable because Ilium had already capitulated to Rome, as it were, by submitting to Sulla, and besides Roman myth stated that there was a distant relationship between the ancient Trojans and the ancestors of the Romans. To raze Ilium must have seemed to many almost a sacrilege.

Mithridates was probably less concerned with the propriety of Fimbria's campaign than with the likelihood that the renegade would run him to ground before he could get good terms from Sulla.

Sulla agreed to open negotiations with Archelaus, and the two met on the coast near Delium. Archelaus suggested that Sulla give up the war and offered to give him money, men and support for the upcoming war in Italy. Sulla, perhaps recalling his days of bargaining with King Bocchus for the betrayal of Jugurtha, countered that Archelaus ought to seize Mithridates's crown and become an ally of Rome. Archelaus declined such treachery, and after that the negotiations became more prosaic. Sulla had no supplies from Rome and was running short of money, and he needed to act quickly and return home to settle matters. Sulla dictated terms that were, on the whole, rather moderate. The main points were these: Mithridates was to return Roman prisoners and runaway slaves, send the people of Chios back to their homes and free any others he had taken to Pontus. He was to relinquish Asia and Paphlagonia, hand over Bithynia to Nicomedes and Cappadocia to Ariobarzanes, pay 2,000 talents and give Sulla seventy ships.

When Mithridates learned of the conditions he protested two of them: handing over the ships and giving up Paphlagonia. Sulla informed the ambassadors that he would not compromise on his demands and marched to Asia, sending Lucullus ahead. His legate had finally arrived with a cobbled navy of ships from various cities that he had used for coastal attacks and minor engagements with Mithridates's fleet.

Mithridates was in a poor position because Fimbria's military successes had forced him to flee to Pergamus, then to Pitane, and finally to Mitylene on the island of Lesbos. By the time he met Sulla at Dardanus in the Troad,[20] he was ready to accept the terms. The two men met in view of their two armies, each with a small force, and ended the First Mithridatic War.

CHAPTER 14

The Return

THE ROMAN ARMY WAS UNHAPPY WITH THE PEACE; THEY thought it too easy on the king, who had killed and provoked the murder of so many Italians, fought Rome for three years and made off with loot from the territories he had taken. Sulla took a simple position with them: He could not fight Fimbria and Mithridates at the same time.

Sulla maintained later that Flaccus had been sent east with an army to fight him—Plutarch, relying apparently on Sulla's memoirs, tells us this. It can hardly have been true, and Flaccus's march directly to Asia when he could have interfered with Sulla puts the lie to Sulla's assertion. Sulla's claim, however, puts a good face on his clear intention to clash with Fimbria. He rightly regarded Fimbria as a Marian and a representative of the government in Rome, and he knew that he could not leave Fimbria at his back while he prepared to return to Italy. Fimbria had not interfered with Sulla; each conducted his part of the war independently, but now that Asia was back in Roman hands and the Pontic holdings restored to their earlier status as client kingdoms, there was nothing to prevent Fimbria—in spite of his dubious status—from cooperating with Cinna and the government in Rome.

Sulla marched into Lycia to confront Fimbria, but there was no bloodshed: At Sulla's approach Fimbria's troops deserted to him, and Fimbria committed suicide.[1]

Apart from military matters, Sulla spent much time organizing the province of Asia and the neighboring territories. He quartered his soldiers in various cities during the winter of 85–84, and he rewarded and punished some of the towns according to whether they had actively supported Mithridates or not. He rescinded Mithridates's decrees freeing

slaves and ordered them to return to their masters. This was understandably unpopular with these men and quartering soldiers was a burden to
many others. Some cities revolted. These uprisings were put down,
towns were plundered and the citizens sold as slaves. Sulla was particularly harsh with Cappadocia.

He imposed a tax of five years upon Asia and levied it immediately,
and he charged the cities for the costs of the war as well. This must have
amounted to an immense sum with which he could liberally reward his
soldiers—he could be a patron to them indeed. He could now turn his at-
tentions to Italy.

*   *   *

At Rome things had continued apace. Sulla's intentions were never in
doubt, and they were all the more clear to everyone after he had arrogated Fimbria's army. With the death of Flaccus in 85, Cinna had taken
Gnaeus Papirius Carbo as his fellow consul and he either appointed
Carbo and himself to consulships for 84 and 83, or held pro forma elections with this inevitable result. Holding the reins of power for three
years, the consuls worked diligently raising armies with which to greet
Sulla's inevitable return.

The senate, by contrast, began to bruit about the idea of reconciliation
with the rogue general. Much of the aristocracy had been cowed by the
Marian violence, but though there had been quiet in Italy since the Marians had taken power, and though there had been the just social remedy
of enrolling the new citizens that conduced to a lasting peace between
Rome and her former allies, the patricians and nobles as a whole could
not have lent much real support to the new regime. The debt relief
pushed through by the consul Flaccus seems to have been regarded as
particularly pernicious, with Velleius Paterculus going so far as to call
Flaccus's death a just punishment for his action.

But most of all, there was probably a naked fear of what Sulla might
do to his opponents regardless of their station. Their true interests lay
with Sulla and the aristocrats who had fled to him during the purge. A
cleft opened between the consuls and the senate—or more properly the
cleft, already there, widened. Cinna wished to take hostages from among
the Italian cities to ensure their loyalty in the coming conflict; the senate
declined to allow it. The leader of the senate, Lucius Valerius Flaccus
(probably the father of the late consul who shared his name), spoke in the

senate and convinced the senators to send an embassy to Sulla with a view to making a peace.

Cinna mustered an army at Ancona and made ready to cross over to Illyria and advance against Sulla, a courageous act. He was willing to come to blows with the experienced general and his tried and proven army, but his men were less willing than he. A first crossing to Liburnia was made, but a storm interfered with the second crossing and those who made it back slipped off to their homes; the prospect of fighting Sulla was unappealing. When he tried to force more soldiers to make the crossing, they mutinied and stoned Cinna to death. Velleius Paterculus gives the senatorial view: "Before the arrival of Lucius Sulla, Cinna, the root of the insurrection, was killed by the army, a man who had more fittingly died by the judgment of the victors than by the anger of the soldiers."[2] After Cinna's death the nobility began to favor Sulla more openly.

Sulla told the senatorial envoys that he would be willing to put himself under the authority of the senate if those who had fled to him were returned to their positions at home. Carbo, the remaining consul, would not permit it. He rightfully feared Sulla; he must have doubted his chances of surviving the general's return and as a Marian he desired to protect his faction—both motives of self-interest, but beyond these considerations he was a Roman; he must have dreaded yet another march on his city, even though his faction had done the same. He might have justified Cinna's and Marius's seizure of the city as a legitimate response to the action of a tyrant—they had fought fire with fire. Sulla, on the other hand, had no compunction against applying the fire again. From a legal standpoint, of course, it is impossible to justify the actions of either: The constitution was in utter tatters. From a moral standpoint the Marians, in retrospect, had a better claim, if only because Sulla would prove himself many times more murderous than ever Marius or Cinna had been.

Carbo spent the interval before Sulla's arrival levying soldiers. He seems to have raised about 100,000 of them.[3] In the meanwhile Lucius Scipio and Gaius Norbanus were elected consuls and each given an army with which to meet Sulla.

Sulla advanced through Macedonia and Thessaly and into Greece, whence he sailed to Brundisium. Before embarcation the soldiers—unprompted it is said—took an oath to stay in Sulla's service and not to harm Italy. Further, we are told, they took up a collection among themselves for Sulla, who was short of money. This story comes from Plutarch, and therefore almost certainly from Sulla's own memoirs, which, we must imagine, did not fail to put his actions in the best light. With five years of Asian taxes in his pocket he could hardly have needed to take from his soldiers what he must have lavished on them for their loyalty; we can probably dismiss this part of the story as untrue, or greatly exaggerated. However, the point of it, and the point of the soldiers' oath, which we can pretty readily accept, was that this was Sulla's army, and no longer an army of the republic, which it had been during the Italian War. Sulla had treated his legions well during that war—he was said to have been lax about discipline. Because he could not have been careless about drill and yet so successful, this allegation must mean that he allowed a good deal of looting. Over time he had won them over to a de facto clientage, their march on Rome had amounted to a repudiation of any obligation to the state, and their adventures out east under their outlaw general had converted them into a private army such as even Marius could hardly have imagined.

Sulla marched from Brundisium with about thirty or forty thousand men toward Rome.[4] He met no opposition as he passed through Calabria and Apulia; he kept his army strictly in hand and did not trouble the countryside. As he progressed, much of the nobility and those who had been exiled by the Marians joined him: "Meanwhile, Sulla's army grew day by day through the influx to him of the best and most reasonable."[5] Among these best and most reasonable men was Metellus Pius, son of Numidicus, Marius's old patron, commander and political enemy. Here was a skilled commander; he had shown it during the Italian War and his loyalty was certain. He had been at Rome to oppose Marius and Cinna and had fled to Africa. He apparently commanded a number of troops, for he was still proconsul because he had never returned to Rome to surrender the office.

A more remarkable supporter was the twenty-three-year-old son of Pompeius Strabo, who had died defending the city from Marius and Cinna. This ambitious young man had gone to the family holdings around Picenum and raised three legions from his family's clients, many of them veterans from the army his father had commanded. He took the city of Asculum and then joined with Sulla.

This too was a private army, an army with no legal basis, for the senate would never have allowed a private citizen to raise such a force, still less would the senate, now bossed by the Marians, have allowed the recruitment of an army by a political opponent. Though seriously outnumbered, Sulla now had close to fifty thousand troops at his command, many of them quite experienced.

The consul Gaius Norbanus was the first to oppose Sulla. He and his colleague Scipio had been hesitant to do so with their newly raised troops and so this first engagement took place in Campania near Capua, only seventy miles south of Rome. Norbanus was soundly defeated and took refuge in Capua, having lost seven thousand men. Sulla claimed that it was this victory that caused his troops to adhere to him. In fact, their adherence seems never to have been in doubt, though the victory may have reinforced their determination to press on despite the size of the forces fielded against them.

Sulla's reputation alone was enough to undo Scipio. When the consul approached Sulla and Metellus with a dispirited army near Teanum, Sulla began to parley with him about making a peace. He spun the negotiations out, all the while encouraging his soldiers to fraternize with Scipio's, to bribe them and to wheedle with them. Scipio's men judged they would do better to serve under Sulla, and when he paraded near Scipio's men with twenty cohorts, Scipio's forty went over to him. The consul and his son sat in his tent, completely bereft of the army. Plutarch reports: "On this occasion, Carbo was heard to say that he had both a fox and a lion in the breast of Sulla to deal with, and was most troubled with the fox."[6] The event is altogether reminiscent of the Fimbria affair and shows not only the attraction Sulla held for soldiers, but also the lightness with which they regarded their duty to the state.

Sulla tried to win Scipio over to his side as well, but the consul refused and Sulla, though he had him in his power, let the consul and his son go.

Sulla then tried unsuccessfully to open negotiations with Norbanus at Capua; the consul had evidently learned from Scipio's example that it could be as dangerous to talk to Sulla as it was to fight him. Each man then led his army in wasting unfriendly territory.

On the political front, Carbo managed to have Metellus and those other senators who had allied with Sulla declared enemies of the state. About now the Capitol burned; no one knew how the fire started, and there were various theories propounded that reflect only the biases of the suspicious. Some blamed Carbo, others the consuls and yet others an agent of Sulla. It might more properly have been seen as an omen of what would come to the state.

During the winter of 83–82 Carbo raised more troops. The Samnites joined him; Sulla had not completely put them down and they had a score to settle. These tough men marched under Pontius Telesinus, their old general from the Italian War. Marius's son Gaius Marius the younger, only twenty-six or twenty-seven, was made consul, and this was particularly helpful to the defense of Italy for many of his father's veterans came to his standard. The Marian forces of 82 fielded a much better army than that of the year before.

Despite this improvement, however, Metellus and Sulla were able to win decisive battles against them in the spring of that year. Metellus first defeated a legate of Carbo named Carinas somewhere along the Aesis River. Carinas lost many soldiers and fled, and the countryside came over to Sulla. This was evidently in Picenum, where Pompeius's holdings were and where he had raised his army of clients; it may only have been uneasily under the control of the consuls to begin with.

In response to the defeat on the Aesis, Carbo came south against Metellus from Ariminum, but on learning of the younger Marius's defeat near Rome, he went back.

Sulla had engaged Marius's large army—eighty-five cohorts—near Praeneste. The battle was at first hard-fought, but Marius's left wing began to fail and at this point five infantry cohorts and a body of cavalry threw aside their standards and deserted to Sulla. Marius's shattered forces fled to Praeneste, which admitted many of them, but when Sulla came up in pursuit the gates were closed and many of the Marian forces were left outside the walls. Marius was taken up the city wall by ropes, but many of his men were captured, and Sulla massacred all of the Samnite prisoners. Plutarch says that Sulla lost twenty-three men, that the Marians lost twenty thousand killed and eight thousand captured. Though these exaggerated figures must be from Sulla's memoirs, they suggest the usual feature of ancient battle: few losses as the armies faced each other, and then a complete disparity in losses between the victors and vanquished as the defeated turned away and were slaughtered from behind.[7]

Marius, locked up in Praeneste, was unable to force his way out. Sulla now marched to Rome, but he was not able to prevent the killing, at the young Marius's request, of a number of Marian political opponents, most notably Mucius Scaevola, the popular former governor of Asia, now Pontifex Maximus.

Once in Rome, Sulla seized the property of his Marian opponents (they had fled) and put it up for sale. He then addressed the people in a popular assembly, regretted what he had to do under the press of circumstance, and told them that soon the government would be in order.

Further battles followed, but their results were always in Sulla's favor, with the exception of one near Clusium, where Carbo fought Sulla to a standstill. In the broad scheme of things this check was not important for things were going Sulla's way everywhere else, and particularly around Praeneste: Carbo attempted unsuccessfully to relieve Marius there. Metellus defeated Carbo at Faventia, and troops began to desert to the Sullan forces, a sure sign that the Marians were collapsing. The former consul Norbanus fled to Rhodes, while Carbo chose Africa, where he hoped to get support. The Marian forces near Clusium suffered a severe defeat, and the Marian army dissolved as men left for their homes.

A few remaining Marian cohorts joined Telesinus's Samnites and made a last effort to relieve Marius in Praeneste, but could not force a pass that Sulla was guarding. Turning away they advanced on Rome, which they hoped to take as it was not well defended; their strategy was to force Sulla to abandon the siege of Praeneste and thus free Marius and his troops there. The strategy failed: Sulla left his lieutenant Lucretius to continue the siege and sent his cavalry ahead to slow the Marians' advance. Notwithstanding this, Telesinus reached Rome and pitched his camp a little over a mile away.

Telesinus beat off a sally by the sons of the nobility, and then turned his attention to Sulla, who had by now reached Rome and encamped near the Colline Gate at the north of the city. Sulla, as usual, was victorious, though the battle was apparently close; the Samnites probably suspected the treatment they would receive if defeated, and they got it: Sulla killed some 8,000 prisoners because most of them were Samnites. Livy was appalled by this and by what was to come:

After he had recaptured the state he defiled a most glorious victory through cruelty such as there never was in any man. Eight thousand of those who had surrendered he cut down in the Villa Publica, he put up a list for proscriptions and he filled the city and also all Italy with murders, among which he ordered all the unarmed Praenestians killed.[8]

Telesinus died of wounds after the battle and the other Marian commanders Marcius and Carinas were caught the following day. They were beheaded and their heads sent to Lucretius, who displayed them to the defenders of Praeneste. The city surrendered to Lucretius; the young Marius committed suicide in a tunnel driven out from the city as a means of escape. Accounts of his death differ in detail, but he seems to have killed himself when he realized that he could not get away.

Sulla returned to Praeneste to clear up matters there to his liking, and he displayed further the cold cruelty that would become his hallmark. He divided the captives into Romans, Samnites and Praenestians. The Romans he spared, the Samnites and the adult male Praenestians he killed.

Sulla displayed the young Marius's head before the rostra in Rome.

A few towns held out and had to be reduced, but Sulla was now again master of the Roman state, and the last flickers of Marian power in the provinces were extinguished by 80 B.C.

After his victory Sulla addressed the senate in the Temple of Bellona, the goddess of war. It was an appropriate location, and as he spoke to the senators he had some six thousand Marian prisoners put to death in the Circus Maximus. The sounds attending this mass execution could be heard during the session, as they were meant to be, but Sulla told the terrified senators not to concern themselves with what was going on outside; instead they should listen to what he had to say. Undoubtedly they made their best effort in this regard.

But the killing had just begun. Sulla killed enemies in droves and let his lieutenants do the same. When Metellus Pius asked for less arbitrary killing, Sulla responded by setting up a "proscription list" in the forum: a list of men who might be killed—and those who did the murder were given a reward. He posted a second list, and then a third. Appian says that about forty senators and sixteen hundred knights were proscribed, and proscription took place, on a smaller scale, throughout Italy.

Sulla took the property of the proscribed: He needed money and land to fulfil his obligations to his soldiers, and quite naturally the rich suffered most often. Even the innocent might be proscribed as a way to get their property. Plutarch says:

> Quintus Aurelius, a quiet, peaceable man, and one who thought all his part in the common calamity consisted in condoling with the misfortunes of others, coming into the Forum to read the list, and finding himself among the proscribed, cried out, "Woe is me, my Alban farm has informed against me." He had not gone far before he was despatched by a ruffian, sent on that errand.[9]

The lucky were merely banished or despoiled of their property. Marius and Cinna had never approached what Sulla did: So many men died that he made a bodyguard of 10,000 from their slaves, whom he named the Cornelii for himself. He put the Samnites under heel while favoring his soldiers, and allowed them to pillage Samnium.

Sulla also settled a great number of soldiers, perhaps about 100,000, and put them in colonies throughout Italy. This helped him keep the country in hand, and because their tenure depended on the success of his government, they supported him utterly.

The senate, now completely in his power, gave the imprimatur to all the actions he had taken both as consul and afterward. His actions, however wrong, had been legalized, and now Sulla took another unprecedented action. There were no consuls: Marius's head had been displayed in the forum, and Pompeius had hunted Carbo down in Sicily and killed him. Sulla had worked successfully to legitimate his past actions, but his constitutional status was murky even though his power was evident.

Sulla instructed the senate to choose an *interrex*. This officer was responsible for holding the elections for consuls if, unhappily, there should be no consuls to do so. The senate picked Valerius Flaccus, the *princeps senatus*, and Sulla then addressed a letter to him in which he suggested that, given the disorder of the state, the senate would do well not to press forward with consular elections, but rather to appoint a dictator.

The office of dictator had been constitutional, but now it was archaic. Rome had not had a dictator since the war with Hannibal a hundred and twenty years before. What is more, Sulla suggested an innovation. While a dictator customarily served only in times of crisis and for a fixed term of six months, he suggested that the dictator stay in office until he had restored the state—in effect the new dictator would have no fixed term. Sulla wrote that he would be willing to undertake the office. He was of course raised to the dictatorship and he was to hold it as long as he liked.

Whenever he went out, he was preceded by twenty-four *lictors* with *fasces*, twice as many as a consul. To recall his good fortune he asked and was granted the surname "Felix." Although the republican forms remained, Lucius Cornelius Sulla Felix had become, in effect, the king of Rome.

EPILOGUE

In 78 B.C. Sulla died in bed at his country estate, a private citizen. He had ruled as dictator for three years, reforming the constitution and strengthening the position of the senate, and then he had retired. There had been no Roman before him so lawless and so bloody, and yet he was assiduous in mending the state he had rent apart.

He elevated hundreds of responsible knights to the senate to replace the losses of the civil wars—and of his proscriptions—and made it law that quaestors automatically became senators; in this way the senate could maintain itself. He made it law that no measure come before the people that had not been approved by the senate. He revived the law that mandated ten years between consulships and he regulated the *cursus honorum,* the fixed path through which men rose to power so that men might not reach high office too young. He reformed the courts and saw to it that only senators sat on the most important, and he sharply curbed the tribunes.

In a way the senate had found a friend—a cool one—but it had found a master as well. But work though he might to repair the state—and Sulla, for all his early disdain of the law, knew that there was no alternative—his constitutional reforms stood in the shadow of his actions. His constitution lasted only nine years: It was set aside by Gnaeus Pompeius, his protégé, and Marcus Lepidus as they carved up the state. After this came the rise of Julius Caesar, Marius's nephew, and in 49 B.C. another march on Rome. It was civil war again.

NOTES

Introduction

1. What the Romans called *mos maiorum*, "the ways of the ancestors."
2. Sallust, *Bellum Jugurthinum*, 41.2–5.
3. The Roman province of Africa corresponds roughly to modern Tunisia.

Chapter 1

1. Velleius Paterculus, *Historiae Romanae Ad M. Vinicium Cos.*, 2.2. Paris: Société D'Édition "Les Belles Lettres," 1982. All translations from the Latin in this book are those of the author.
2. A recorder of prodigies living in the first century A.D.
3. Julius Obsequens, *Ab Anno Urbis Conditae DV Prodigiorum*, 24, in *Works of Livy*, vol. IV, Loeb Classical Library Edition. Cambridge, Mass.: Harvard University Press, 1926, 1982.
4. Plutarch, *Life of Tiberius Gracchus*, in *Plutarch's Lives*, vol. IV, translated by John Dryden, revised by A. H. Clough. Boston: Little, Brown and Company, 1905.
5. Ibid.
6. Velleius Paterculus, op cit., 2.1.5.
7. Velleius Paterculus, op cit., 2.2.
8. And the patricians' later cousins the senatorial nobility. The latter were rich plebeians who had reached the senate and consulship and whose interests were substantially the same.
9. Géza Alföldy, *The Social History of Rome*, translated by D. Brand and F. Pollack. London and Sydney: Croom Helm, 1975, pp. 7, 8.
10. Ibid.
11. In Latin an old man is a *senex*.
12. Norbert Rouland, *Pouvoir Politique et Dépendance Personnelle dans L'Antiquité Romaine, Genèse et Rôle des Rapports de Clièntele*. Brussels: Latomus, Review D'Études Latines, 1979, p. 49.
13. Possibly a Latin and not an Etruscan; see M. Cary and H. H. Scullard, *A History of Rome Down to the Reign of Constantine*, 3rd ed. New York: St. Martin's Press, 1975, pp. 41–42.

14. Stirrups came into Europe nearly a thousand years later with the Avars, a nomadic people who moved onto the Hungarian plain from the steppe during the sixth century A.D.

15. Rouland, op. cit., p. 76.

16. Livy, *Ab Urbe Condita*, 2.23.11. Cambridge, Mass.: Harvard University Press, 1919.

Chapter 2

1. This figure is arrived at from an interpretation of Polybius's figures for the legion as a whole.

2. Jonathon P. Roth, *The Logistics of the Roman Army at War, 264 B.C.—A.D. 235.* Leiden: Brill, 1999, p. 20.

3. This figure seems to have declined in the next few decades. Rome bolstered her cavalry with hired horsemen from cooperative nations or tribes with a history of riding, such as Numidians, Thracians and Spaniards and, later, Gauls and Germans.

4. Lawrence Keppie, *The Making of the Roman Army.* London: B. T. Batsford, Ltd., 1984, p. 33.

5. These cohorts probably numbered about 450 to 600 men; this was the size of the cohort when the Roman legions were later divided into these units.

6. This may not have been uniformly the case. Auxiliary cavalry of the late republic and principate used oval or even long hexagonal shields, possibly because they were made up of barbarian troops. The Roman cavalry may have begun to take up such shields at this time.

7. Equipped in the Greek manner, as Polybius says.

8. Livy states that the light soldiers also carried a spear, but it must have been for other duties, such as guarding the camp. While skirmishing the light soldiers would have found it impractical to handle a spear with the shield arm while trying to cast javelins.

9. Per Delbrück, the lighter was for use in the field, the heavier to defend the camp. Hans Delbrück, *History of the Art of War, Volume I, Warfare in Antiquity,* translated by Walker J. Renfroe, Jr. Lincoln: University of Nebraska Press, 1975.

10. Polybius, *The Histories of Polybius*, Book 6, 23, translated by W. R. Paton, Loeb Classical Library Edition. Cambridge, Mass.: Harvard University Press, 1929.

11. See *lorica* in Charlton T. Lewis and Charles Short's *A New Latin Dictionary*, Harper & Brothers, 1879, p. 1078; also Hans Delbrück in his *Warfare in Antiquity, Volume I* of *History of the Art of War*. Delbrück came to this conclusion on the ground that the great mass of Roman infantry could not have gone to war with so little protection. See page 280.

12. Charles Jean Jacques Joseph du Picq, *Battle Studies, Ancient and Modern Battles,* translated by John N. Greely and Robert C. Cotton. New York: The Macmillian Company, 1921, p. 125. Du Picq, a nineteenth-century French colonel and

military theorist, had fought in the field at a time when soldiers still often faced each other at close distances. He was the first theorist to study the psychology of the combatant and write about the importance of morale.

13. See Delbrück, op. cit., p. 280, and Yvon Garlan, *La Guerre dans l'Antiquité*. Paris: Éditions Fernand Nathan, 1972, p. 99.

14. Sallust, *Bellum Jugurthinum*, 114.2.

15. Delbrück, op. cit., p. 273.

16. Livy, *Ab Urbe Condita*, 8.8.5, Loeb Classical Library Edition. Cambridge, Mass.: Harvard University Press, 1919. At the battle of Zama Scipio Africanus is said to have widened the spaces between the maniples so that the enemy's elephants could pass through them without disordering them. With a front of twenty men a maniple would have been about 60 feet wide. If he were concerned that elephants could not pass easily between his maniples, this also suggests that the spaces between the maniples were not 60 feet apart, thus as wide as the maniples themselves.

17. du Picq, supra, pp. 52–53.

18. du Picq, supra, p. 53.

19. Flavius Vegetius Renatus, *Epitoma Rei Militaris*, 1.21.

20. Polybius suggests that a Roman camp was square, but they seem to have been generally rectangular.

21. Polybius, op. cit., 6.37.5–6.

22. Ibid., 6.38.2–4.

Chapter 3

1. Velleius Paterculus also accuses Tiberius Gracchus of proposing Roman citizenship for all Italians. This may be a mistake: This issue was pressed years later by Tiberius's younger brother Gaius. See Velleius Paterculus, *Historiae Romanae Ad M. Vinicium Cos.*, 2.2. Paris: Société D'Édition "Les Belles Lettres," 1982.

2. H. H. Scullard, *From the Gracchi to Nero, a History of Rome from 133 B.C. to A.D. 68*. London: Methuen & Co., Ltd., 1959, p. 27; Peter Brunt, *Social Conflicts in the Roman Republic*. London: Chatto & Windus, 1971, p. 78.

3. Plutarch, *Life of Tiberius Gracchus*, in *Plutarch's Lives*, vol. IV, translated by John Dryden, revised by A. H. Clough. Boston: Little, Brown and Company, 1905.

4. Plutarch, op. cit.

5. A tribune only held office for a year. H. H. Scullard suggests that Tiberius Gracchus may have wanted to speed the land bill through the assembly without the delay of senatorial debate.

6. Scullard suggests that even the five hundred *jugera* that were to be conceded to those who held that much or more were to revert to the public, though it could be held without rent. Op. cit., p. 28.

7. This was a Hellenic kingdom in Asia Minor in part of what is now Turkey.

8. Velleius Paterculus, op. cit., 2.3.2.

9. Velleius Paterculus, op. cit., 2.3.3.

Chapter 4

1. In 131 the tribune Gaius Atinius tried to throw the censor Quintus Metellus Macedonicus from the Tarpeian Rock, a traditional punishment for traitors. He was restrained. M. Cary and H. H. Scullard, *A History of Rome Down to the Reign of Constantine,* 3rd ed. New York: St. Martin's Press, 1975.

2. Velleius Paterculus, *Historiae Romanae Ad M. Vinicium Cos.,* 2.4.4. Paris: Société D'Édition "Les Belles Lettres," 1982.

3. Plutarch, *Life of Caius Gracchus,* in *Plutarch's Lives,* vol. IV, translated by John Dryden, revised by A. H. Clough. Boston: Little, Brown and Company, 1905.

4. Now Marseilles.

5. Velleius Paterculus, op. cit., 2.6.1.

6. Plutarch, *Life of Tiberius Gracchus,* in *Plutarch's Lives,* vol. IV, translated by John Dryden, revised by A. H. Clough. Boston: Little, Brown and Company, 1905.

7. Ibid.

8. Peter Brunt, *Social Conflicts in the Roman Republic.* London: Chatto & Windus, 1971, p. 84.

9. During the Jugurthine War twenty-five years later a military legate of Quintus Caecilius Metellus was scourged before his execution. Sallust makes it clear he suffered this punishment because he was only a Latin citizen. *Bellum Jugurthinum,* 69.4.

10. Julius Obsequens, *Ab Anno Urbis Conditae DV Prodigiorum,* 33, in *Works of Livy,* vol. IV, Loeb Classical Library Edition. Cambridge, Mass.: Harvard University Press, 1926, 1982.

11. Cretan archers often served as mercenaries in the Roman army.

12. Plutarch, *Life of Caius Gracchus.*

13. Ibid.

14. Per Velleius Paterculus, Pomponius did this alone. *Historiae Romanae,* 2.6.6.

15. Plutarch, *Life of Caius Gracchus.*

16. Ibid.

17. Velleius Paterculus, op. cit., 2.6.5.

Chapter 5

1. Plutarch, *Life of Marius,* in *Plutarch's Lives,* vol. III, translated by John Dryden, revised by A. H. Clough. Boston: Little, Brown and Company, 1905.

2. Ibid.

3. T. F. Carney argues that this is a mere legend; as a patrician of the highest standing, Scipio would not have dined with a mere country knight. "The Changing Picture of Marius in Ancient Literature," in *The Proceedings of the African Classical Associations,* Leeds, vol. 10, 1967, pp. 5–22. He may well be right, and if so the story is really a later reflection of Marius's military successes.

4. Ibid.

5. Hispania Ulterior, roughly modern-day Andalusia.

6. Sallust, *Bellum Jugurthinum,* 114.2.

7. Julius Obsequens, *Ab Anno Urbis Conditae DV Prodigiorum*, 38, in *Works of Livy*, vol. IV, Loeb Classical Library Edition. Cambridge, Mass.: Harvard University Press, 1926, 1982.

8. Sallust calls him a "lictor," which, though a Roman term, implies that the fellow held some official capacity in Jugurtha's retinue. *Bellum Jugurthinum*, 12.3.

9. The territory around the ruins of Carthage, generally modern Tunisia.

10. Sallust, op. cit., 14.8. This speech, like almost all of those attributed to historical characters in ancient works, does not purport to be the speaker's actual words; it means only to express the speaker's sentiment.

11. Ibid.

12. Modern Morocco.

13. Sallust calls them, rather oddly, "adulescentes," perhaps meaning only that they were young men who had not yet entered the senate. These "young men" must surely have had sufficient social status to impress Jugurtha.

14. Sallust, op. cit., 25.3.

15. Near modern Ljubljana.

16. Julius Obsequens, op. cit., 39.

17. Sallust, op. cit., 31.9–10.

18. Sallust, op. cit., 31.18–19.

19. Albinus's colleague in the consulship for that year was Quintus Minucius Rufus, who had drawn Macedonia.

20. Sallust, op cit., 35.10.

21. Sallust states that this happened in January of 109, and later suggests that Aulus's defeat occurred before Metellus and Silanus, the designated consuls, had decided between themselves which provinces they would have.

22. Sallust, op. cit., 37.1.

23. Sallust, op. cit., 41.5.

Chapter 6

1. Sallust, *Bellum Jugurthinum*, 44.1.

2. Sallust, op. cit., 49.5.

3. Sallust says the Romans captured four and killed forty, surely an exaggeration.

4. Sallust, op. cit, 51.2.

5. Sallust, op. cit., 55.8.

6. Sallust, op. cit., 61.3.

7. Sallust, op. cit., 67.3.

8. Plutarch, *Life of Marius*, in *Plutarch's Lives*, vol. III, translated by John Dryden, revised by A. H. Clough. Boston: Little, Brown and Company, 1905.

9. Sallust, op. cit., 69.4.

10. Plutarch, op. cit.

11. Sallust, op. cit., 73.4.

12. Plutarch, op. cit.

13. He besieged Thala when he reached it. He must have had a good number of men.

14. Sallust, op. cit., 76.1.

Chapter 7

1. Plutarch, *Life of Marius*, in *Plutarch's Lives,* vol. III, translated by John Dryden, revised by A. H. Clough. Boston: Little, Brown and Company, 1905.

2. Sallust, *Bellum Jugurthinum,* 86.2.

3. The cost of these things was probably deducted from their pay as was done later, during the empire, but even so Marius had given them a start.

4. Velleius Paterculus, *Historiae Romanae Ad M. Vinicium Cos.,* 2.17.1. Paris: Société D'Édition "Les Belles Lettres," 1982.

5. Sallust, op. cit., 91.4.

6. Sallust, op. cit., 97.2.

7. These were near Cirta, as they had been when Metellus was in command.

8. Sallust, op. cit., 97.3.

9. Sallust, op. cit., 97.5.

Chapter 8

1. Apparently of southern Germany, or Switzerland. M. Cary and H. H. Scullard, *A History of Rome Down to the Reign of Constantine,* 3rd ed. New York: St. Martin's Press, 1975, p. 217.

2. Modern Toulouse.

3. The exact date is in dispute but must be within about three or four years of 390.

4. Brennus may be a title rather than a name.

5. Livy, *Summary* 67.

6. Cassius Dio Cocceianus, *Dio's Roman History,* 27.91.1, Loeb Classics. London: William Heinemann, 1914.

7. Modern Orange.

8. They were said to be as high as 80,000, a figure larger than the entire personnel of two consular armies.

9. Cary and Scullard, op. cit., p. 218. The battle of Cannae, in 216 B.C., was supposed have seen the death of 40,000 men.

10. Plutarch, *Life of Marius,* in *Plutarch's Lives,* vol. III, translated by John Dryden, revised by A. H. Clough. Boston: Little, Brown and Company, 1905.

11. Tacitus, *Germania,* 37. Cambridge, Mass.: Harvard University Press, 1914.

12. Flavius Vegetius, *Epitoma Rei Militaris,* 1.11, Lang's 2nd edition of 1885.

13. The Roman soldier's kit recalls a maxim of Napoléon: "There are five things a solider must never be without: his firelock, his ammunition, his knapsack, his provisions (for at least four days), and his entrenching tool. The knapsack may be reduced to the smallest size possible, but the soldier should always have it with him." *The Military Maxims of Napoleon,* translated by G. C. D'Aguilar,

introduction and commentary by D. G. Chandler. New York: Da Capo, 1995, maxim 59. Substitute "arms and armor" for "firelock and ammunition," and the lists are about the same.

14. Hans Delbrück, *History of the Art of War*, vol. I., translated by Walter J. Renfroe, Jr. Lincoln: University of Nebraska Press, 1990, p. 35.

15. F. E. Adcock, *The Roman Art of War Under the Republic*. Cambridge, Mass.: Harvard University Press, 1940, p. 20.

16. Tacitus, op. cit., 6.1.

17. For the figure 4,800 see Lawrence Keppie, *The Making of the Roman Army from Republic to Empire*. London: B. T. Batsford Limited, 1984, pp. 64–66. But see also Jonathan P. Roth, *The Logistics of the Roman Army at War, 264 B.C. to A.D. 235*. Boston: Columbia Studies in the Classical Tradition, 1999, pp. 19–20 and p. 20, note 89, for numbers up to 6,200.

18. Caesar, *Civil Wars*, 3.89, Loeb Classical Library Edition. Cambridge, Mass.: Harvard University Press, 1914.

Chapter 9

1. Hans Delbrück suggests caution when he observes that, in a general way, ancient accounts of the Cimbric war and the later Mithridatic war resemble each other. See *History of the Art of War*, translated by Walter J. Renfroe, Jr. Lincoln: University of Nebraska Press, 1975, p. 437.

2. L. Sprague de Camp, *The Ancient Engineers*. New York: Ballantine Books, 1974, p. 198.

3. Modern Arles.

4. The Teutones seem to have been reinforced by another tribe, the Ambrones.

5. Vegetius, *Epitoma de Rei Militari*, 3.3.

6. Archer Jones, *The Art of Warfare in the Western World*. New York: Oxford University Press, 1987, p. 47.

7. Ibid.

8. Livy, *Summaries*, 68.

9. Plutarch, *Life of Marius*, in *Plutarch's Lives*, vol. III, translated by John Dryden, revised by A. H. Clough. Boston: Little, Brown and Company, 1905.

10. Hans Delbrück, op. cit., p. 92.

11. Napoléon, maxim 1, *The Military Maxims of Napoleon*, translated by George C. D'Aguilar. New York: Da Capo, 1995, p. 55.

12. Livy, *Summaries*, 68.

13. Ibid.

14. Modern Aix-en-Provence.

15. Some modern authors speculate that Marius may have favored a two-line formation, the *acies duplex*, but I have been unable to find any ancient source that states this.

16. Plutarch, op. cit.

17. Caesar, *Bellum Civile*, 3.92.

18. Plutarch, op. cit.

19. Caesar criticizes Pompey's defensive tactic: "Indeed there seems no reason for this action by Pompey because there is a certain raising of the spirit and natural eagerness in everyone which is excited by battle, and generals should not repress this, but encourage it." *Bellum Civile*, 3.92. However, Caesar seems too hard on his opponent. In fact he was surprised by Pompey's tactic, but his men, experienced as they were, halted on the field of their own accord when they grasped what was happening. They rested, dressed their line, and then took up the advance once more. Caesar defeated Pompey by driving off a flank attack of Pompeian cavalry and then outflanking his infantry. It would seem that Pompey's defensive approach was not improper and had little to do with his defeat. We should probably see Pompey's tactic (and Marius's at Aquae Sextiae) as common where one side had the advantage of being attacked from low ground.

20. Plutarch says 100,000 were killed or taken prisoner. *Life of Caius Marius*. It seems unlikely that these Germans numbered half that, including their families. Livy gives even more amazing figures: 200,000 killed, 90,000 captured. *Summaries*, 68.

21. The Romans of this period did not consider the Italian peninsula north of the Po to be part of Italy.

22. Catulus is said to have commanded 20,300 and Marius 32,000. Plutarch, op. cit.

23. There is another Vercellae that should not be confused with it, lying north of the Po about thirty miles at the western edge of Gallia Cisalpina.

24. Plutarch, op. cit.

25. Ibid.

26. Ibid.

27. Vegetius, op. cit., 3.14, 15. He states that 1,666 men in a single line extended a Roman mile, which is slightly shorter than an English mile.

28. Vegetius, op. cit., 2.13.

29. As Caesar's men did at Pharsalus.

30. Du Picq, op. cit., p. 86.

31. Plutarch, op. cit.

32. Vegetius says: "But an open battle is defined by two or three hours of combat, after which the side which is overcome, casts away [*intercidunt*] all hope."

33. Plutarch, op. cit.

34. Both Livy and Plutarch agree on the prisoners: Plutarch gives 120,000 as killed, Livy 140,000. Plutarch, op. cit.; Livy, *Summaries*, 68.

Chapter 10

1. Appian and Livy, while they mention this murder, do not bring Marius into it. Plutarch probably used an anti-Marian source for the suggestion of Marius's complicity.

2. Plutarch, *Life of Marius,* in *Plutarch's Lives,* vol. III, translated by John Dryden, revised by A. H. Clough. Boston: Little, Brown and Company, 1905.

3. Velleius Paterculus, *Historiae Romanae Ad M. Vinicium Cos.,* 2.12.11. Paris: Société D'Édition "Les Belles Lettres," 1982. Author's translation. A slight exaggeration, but the sentiment is correct.

4. Appian, *The Civil Wars,* 1.4.29, translated by Horace White. Cambridge, Mass.: Harvard University Press, 1913.

5. Cary and Scullard suggest that this oath of obedience may not have been unusual, since a similar one was attached to another law of Saturninus's time. See M. Cary and H. H. Scullard, *A History of Rome Down to the Reign of Constantine,* 3rd ed. New York: St. Martin's Press, 1975, p. 614, n. 30.

6. Appian, op. cit., 1.4.29.

7. Appian, op. cit., 1.4.30.

8. Ibid.

9. Plutarch, op. cit.

10. Plutarch, op. cit.

11. Appian, op. cit., 1.4.30.

12. Appian, op. cit., 1.4.31.

13. Plutarch, op. cit.

14. Plutarch, op. cit.

15. Plutarch, op. cit.

16. Plutarch, op. cit.

17. Plutarch, *Life of Sylla,* in *Plutarch's Lives,* vol. III, translated by John Dryden, revised by A. H. Clough. Boston: Little, Brown and Company, 1905.

Chapter 11

1. Plutarch, *Life of Sylla,* in *Plutarch's Lives,* vol. III, translated by John Dryden, revised by A. H. Clough. Boston: Little, Brown and Company, 1905.

2. Ibid.

3. Velleius Paterculus, *Historiae Romanae Ad M. Vinicium Cos.,* 2.14.3. Paris: Société D'Édition "Les Belles Lettres," 1982.

4. Appian, *Civil Wars,* 1.5.36, Loeb Classical Library Edition. Cambridge, Mass.: Harvard University Press, 1913, 1979.

5. The Marsi were a people living some sixty miles east of Rome.

6. M. Cary and H. H. Scullard, *A History of Rome Down to the Reign of Constantine,* 3rd ed. New York: St. Martin's Press, 1977, p. 223, note 3.

7. Velleius Paterculus, op. cit., 2.14.2.

8. Appian, op. cit., 1.5.39.

9. Velleius Paterculus, op. cit., 2.16.4.

10. Velleius Paterculus, op. cit., 2.15.2.

11. For example, Rutilius had as another of his legates Gnaeus Pompeius, father of Pompey the Great.

12. Appian tells a fabulous tale in which Publius Pompaedius pretends to desert to Caepio and gives as hostages a pair of slave babies he claims are his own. To further his deception he hands over gold-plated lead. Having duped Caepio he then leads him into an ambush.

13. Plutarch, *Life of Marius*, in *Plutarch's Lives*, vol. III, translated by John Dryden, revised by A. H. Clough. Boston: Little, Brown and Company, 1905.

14. Plutarch, *Life of Sylla*.

15. Appian, op. cit., 1.6.52.

16. Appian, op. cit., 1.6.53.

Chapter 12

1. He may instead have been held prisoner and later freed by Pompeius. See Velleius Paterculus, *Historiae Romanae Ad M. Vinicium Cos.*, 2.18.3. Paris: Société D'Édition "Les Belles Lettres," 1982.

2. Velleius Paterculus, op. cit., 2.18.1.

3. Plutarch, *Life of Marius*, in *Plutarch's Lives*, vol. III, translated by John Dryden, revised by A. H. Clough. Boston: Little, Brown and Company, 1905.

4. Ibid.

5. Appian, *Civil Wars*, 1.7.56, translated by Horace White, Loeb Classical Library Edition. Cambridge, Mass.: Harvard University Press, 1913, 1979. Appian says here explicitly that Sulla was unaware of "the designs against himself." It seems quite unlikely, though, in view of subsequent events.

6. Ibid.

7. Both cities are near Naples, but in from the coast a short way.

8. Appian, op. cit., 1.7.58.

9. Plutarch, op. cit.

10. Plutarch, op. cit.

11. Plutarch, op. cit.

12. This would seem to imply that some of the Cimbri, at least, may have been serving as auxiliary cavalry to the Roman army at this time.

13. Velleius Paterculus, op. cit., 2.19.3.

14. Velleius Paterculus, op. cit.

15. Appian, op. cit., 1.7.52.

16. Velleius Paterculus, op. cit., 2.19.4.

17. Velleius Paterculus, ibid.

Chapter 13

1. A country of Greek cities along the southeast coast of Anatolia.

2. Appian, *The Mithridatic Wars*, 12.4.25, in *Appian's Roman History*. New York: The Macmillan Co., 1912.

3. Cassius Dio Cocceianus, *Roman History*, vol. II, 31.102, Loeb Classical Library Edition. New York: The Macmillan Co., 1914.

4. These men were certainly cousins of some degree; the *gens* or clan name of Pompeius shows this.

5. Plutarch says that Bruttius was instructed by Lucius Lucullus, Sulla's legate, to leave the war to Sulla, and that this was the reason for his withdrawal from Boeotia, though Appian's account seems, on the face of it, the more likely. See Plutarch, *Life of Sylla*, in *Plutarch's Lives*, vol. III, translated by John Dryden, revised by A. H. Clough. Boston: Little, Brown and Company, 1905.

6. *Diodorus of Sicily*, vol. XII, 38/39.7, translated by Francis R. Walton, Loeb Classical Library Edition. Cambridge, Mass.: Harvard University Press, 1967.

7. Appian, op. cit., 12.6.38.

8. Plutarch, op. cit.

9. Appian, op. cit., 12.6.39.

10. Appian's complete list includes Thracians, Pontics, Scythians, Cappadocians, Bithynians, Galatians and Phrygians, "and others from Mithridates' newly acquired territory" Appian, op. cit., 12.6.41.

11. Appian, op. cit., 12.6.41.

12. Ibid.

13. Plutarch, op. cit.

14. Appian, op. cit.

15. Plutarch, *Life of Marius*, in *Plutarch's Lives*, vol. III, translated by John Dryden, revised by A. H. Clough. Boston: Little, Brown and Company, 1905.

16. Velleius Paterculus, *Historiae Romanae Ad M. Vinicium Cos.*, 2.22.1–2. Paris: Société D'Édition "Les Belles Lettres," 1982.

17. Appian, op. cit., 12.7.49.

18. Appian, op. cit., 12.8.51.

19. The site of Troy

20. The area around Ilium, or Troy.

Chapter 14

1. There are several versions of the event, but in broad outline this is what happened.

2. Velleius Paterculus, *Historiae Romanae Ad M. Vinicium Cos.*, 2.24.5. Paris: Société D'Édition "Les Belles Lettres," 1982.

3. This is Cary and Scullard's figure. Velleius Paterculus says Sulla faced 200,000, but this huge figure must be too high. M. Cary and H. H. Scullard, *A History of Rome Down to the Reign of Constantine*, 3rd ed. New York: St. Martin's Press, 1975, p. 233. Velleius Paterculus, op. cit., 2.24.3.

4. Velleius Paterculus claims 30,000, Appian 40,000. Appian's figure might appear the more accurate as he is more specific: He says that Sulla brought over five legions, 6,000 horse and a number of Greek and Macedonian troops. However, after several years of war without reinforcement, the legions would have been

understrength. Paterculus may be closer to the mark. See Velleius Paterculus, op. cit., 2.24.3, and Appian, *Civil Wars,* 1.9.79.

5. Velleius Paterculus, op. cit., 2.25.2. Author's translation.

6. Plutarch, *Life of Sulla.*

7. This is an observation of du Picq, who, noting this sort of disparity, points out that there was in fact little fencing in ancient battles and says: "But very few fighters armed with cuirass and shield were killed in the front lines." Charles Jean Jacques Joseph du Picq, *Battle Studies, Ancient and Modern Battle,* translated by John N. Greely and Robert C. Cotton. New York: The Macmillan Company, 1921, p. 81, n. 1; p. 82.

8. Livy, *Summaries,* 88.

9. Plutarch, *Life of Sulla.*

BIBLIOGRAPHY

Ancient Authors

Appian. *Roman History,* vol. III, Loeb Classical Library Edition. Cambridge, Mass.: Harvard University Press, 1913, 1979.

Gaius Julius Caesar. *Civil Wars,* Loeb Classical Library Edition. Cambridge, Mass.: Harvard University Press, 1914, 1990.

Cassius Dio Cocceianus. *Dio's Roman History,* vol. II, Loeb Classical Library Edition. New York: The Macmillan Company, 1914.

Diodorus of Sicily, vol. XII, translated by Francis R. Walton, Loeb Classical Library Edition. Cambridge, Mass.: Harvard University Press, 1967.

Livy. *Ab Urbe Condita,* Loeb Classical Library Edition. Cambridge, Mass.: Harvard University Press, 1919.

_____. *Summaries,* Loeb Classical Library Edition. Cambridge, Mass.: Harvard University Press, 1959, 1987.

Julius Obsequens. *Ab Anno Urbis Conditae DV Prodigiorum,* in *Works of Livy,* vol. IV, Loeb Classical Library Edition. Cambridge, Mass.: Harvard University Press, 1926, 1982.

Velleius Paterculus. *Historiae Romanae Ad M. Vinicium Cos.,* edited and translated by Joseph Hellegouarch. Paris: Société D'Édition "Les Belles Lettres," 1982.

Plutarch. *Life of Tiberius Gracchus,* in *Plutarch's Lives,* vol. IV, translated by John Dryden, revised by A. H. Clough. Boston: Little, Brown and Company, 1905.

_____. *Life of Caius Gracchus,* in *Plutarch's Lives,* vol. IV, translated by John Dryden, revised by A. H. Clough. Boston: Little, Brown and Company, 1905.

_____. *Life of Marius,* in *Plutarch's Lives,* vol. III, translated by John Dryden, revised by A. H. Clough. Boston: Little, Brown and Company, 1905.

_____. *Life of Sylla,* in *Plutarch's Lives,* vol. III, translated by John Dryden, revised by A. H. Clough. Boston: Little, Brown and Company, 1905.

Polybius. *The Histories,* Loeb Classical Library Edition. Cambridge, Mass.: Harvard University Press, 1923, 1979.

Flavius Vegetius Renatus. *Epitoma Rei Militaris,* Lang's 2nd ed. 1885.
Gaius Sallustius Crispus. *Jugurthine War,* Loeb Classical Library Edition. Cambridge, Mass.: Harvard University Press, 1921, 1995.
Tacitus, *Germania.* Cambridge, Mass.: Harvard University Press, 1914.

Modern Authors

Adcock, F. E. *The Roman Art of War Under the Republic.* Cambridge, Mass.: Harvard University Press, 1940.
Alföldy, Géza. *The Social History of Rome,* translated by D. Brand and F. Pollack. London and Sydney: Croom Helm, 1975.
Bonaparte, Napoléon. *The Military Maxims of Napoleon,* translated by George C. D'Aguilar. New York: Da Capo, 1995.
Brunt, Peter. *Social Conflicts in the Roman Republic.* London: Chatto & Windus, 1971.
Carney, F. "The Changing Picture of Marius in Ancient Literature," in *The Proceedings of the African Classical Associations* (Leeds), vol. 10, 1967, pp. 5–22.
Cary, M., and H. H. Scullard. *A History of Rome Down to the Reign of Constantine,* 3rd ed. New York: St. Martin's Press, 1975.
Clausewitz, Carl von. *On War,* translated and edited by Michael Howard and Peter Paret. Princeton: Princeton University Press, 1976.
de Camp, L. Sprague. *The Ancient Engineers.* New York: Ballantine Books, 1974.
Delbrück, Hans. *Warfare in Antiquity,* volume I of *History of the Art of War,* translated by Walter J. Renfroe, Jr. Lincoln: University of Nebraska Press, 1975.
du Picq, Charles Jean Jacques Joseph. *Battle Studies, Ancient and Modern Battles,* translated by John N. Greely and Robert C. Cotton. New York: The Macmillan Company, 1921.
Earl, D. C. *Tiberius Gracchus, a Study in Politics.* Bruxelles-Berch: Collection Latomus, vol. LXVI, 1963.
Garlan, Yvon. *La Guerre dans l'Antiquité.* Paris: Éditions Fernand Nathan, 1972.
Grant, Michael. *The Army of the Caesars.* New York: Charles Scribner's Sons, 1974.
_____. *Greek and Roman Historians.* New York: Routledge, 1995.
Hammond, Nicholas G. L., ed. *Atlas of the Greek and Roman World of Antiquity.* Park Ridge, N.J.: Noyes Press, 1981.
Harmand, Jacques. *L'Armée et le Soldat à Rome.* Paris: Éditions A. et J. Picard et Cie., 1967.
Jones, Archer. *The Art of Warfare in the Western World.* New York: Oxford University Press, 1987.
Keegan, John. *A History of Warfare.* New York: Knopf, 1993.

_____. *The Face of Battle*. New York: Penguin Books, 1978.

Keppie, Lawrence. *The Making of the Roman Army*. London: B. T. Batsford, Ltd., 1984.

Lewis, Charlton T., and Charles Short. *A New Latin Dictionary*. New York: Harper & Brothers, 1879.

Parker, H. M. D. *The Roman Legions*. Oxford: Clarendon Press, 1928.

Roth, Jonathon P. *The Logistics of the Roman Army at War, 264 B.C.–A.D. 235*. Leiden: Brill, 1999.

Rouland, Norbert. *Pouvoir Politique et Dépendance Personnelle dans L'Antiquité Romaine, Genèse et Rôle des Rapports de Clièntele*. Brussels: Latomus, Revue D'Études Latines, 1979.

Scullard, H. H. *From the Gracchi to Nero, a History of Rome from 133 B.C. to A.D. 68*. London: Methuen & Co., Ltd., 1959.

Talbert, Richard J. A. *Barrington Atlas of the Greek and Roman World*. Princeton: Princeton University Press, 2000.

Taylor, Lily Ross. *Roman Voting Assemblies*. Ann Arbor: The University of Michigan Press, 1966.

Usher, Stephen. *The Historians of Greece and Rome*. London: Hamish Hamilton, 1969.

Webster, Graham. *The Roman Imperial Army of the First and Second Centuries A.D.*, 3rd ed. London: A & C Black, 1985.

INDEX